The Other Woman

The Other Woman

My Years with O. J. Simpson

A STORY OF LOVE, TRUST, AND BETRAYAL

Paula Barbieri

LITTLE, BROWN AND COMPANY

Boston   New York   Toronto   London

First Edition

Excerpt from "Why Can't a Woman Be More Like a Man" by Alan Jay
Lerner and Frederick Loewe, © 1956 (Renewed) by Alan Jay Lerner and
Frederick Loewe. Reprinted by permission of Chappell & Co. owner of
publication and allied rights / Warner Bros. Publications U.S. Inc.

Additional brief excerpts: "Completely" by Diane Warren, © 1993 Realsongs;
"Lean on Me" by Bill Withers, © 1972 Interior Music; "It's OK" by Keith
Thomas and BeBe Winans, © 1991 Sony / ATV Tunes LLC, Yellow
Elephant Music, Inc., EMI Blackwood Music and Benny's Music;
"Unforgettable" by Irving Gordon, © Bourne Co.; "High Flight" by John
Gillespie Magee, Jr., copyright © 1941.

ISBN 0-316-65113-3

LIBRARY OF CONGRESS CATALOG CARD NUMBER 97-73861

10 9 8 7 6 5 4 3 2 1

MV-NY

Published simultaneously in Canada
by Little, Brown & Company (Canada) Limited
Printed in the United States of America

To Mother,
A woman of unshakable strength:
The strength to raise us children during difficult times;
the strength to stand by me during difficult times.
You are my inspiration.

This is the story about — it sounds odd for me to say — my life. I prayed for guidance, through much heartache, keeping faith that all would work out according to God's plan. Most of the events related in this book occurred long before I became a Christian — before my church family became the most important thing in my life. It was painful to take a hard look at the person I was. But my hope is that these pages will bear witness to how I have changed. They can do so only if I am completely honest. Only the true story of my life can demonstrate how empty it would be without God.

If any of the contents of this book are offensive to you, please know that I believe in forgiveness. . . .

Psalm 23
Psalm 51

CONTENTS

The Other Woman

1

Over the Edge

On the morning of June 12, 1994, I nearly skipped into LAX for my flight to Las Vegas. I felt healthy and strong for the first time in months — I almost felt like myself again.

I was twenty-seven years old, but I bubbled like a teenager. Like a girl in a new dress, ready to be kissed for the first time.

As I waited at the gate to board my plane, I couldn't stop smiling and fidgeting. The man next to me, just a regular Joe, took one glance at me and said, "You look like you're happy to be going to Las Vegas."

"Oh, you just don't know," I replied with a grin. And then I told this total stranger, "I just broke up with my boyfriend, and I'm so proud of myself."

"Really," the guy said. "I guess things will be different now, huh?"

Different — that was a great word for me to hear.

I didn't mention my ex-boyfriend's name. I saw no need, though the stranger would surely have sat up and taken notice.

O.J. Simpson belonged to my past, and I was overdue for a burial.

O.J. and I had been together for the past two years. We'd had a love affair to pop a thermometer. I'd shared more of myself with O.J. than I ever thought I could share with anyone. I believed I knew him, body and soul, as well as a woman can know a man.

But O.J. had proven me wrong. He'd lied to me, more than once, till my trust had crumbled. Even as he swore that I was "the only one," I had a fair suspicion that he'd been with other women, including his ex-wife, Nicole.

We were fighting every other day. I couldn't eat or sleep. I lost my usual sparkle at my modeling jobs; you could see it in the photographs. O.J. was sapping my life away.

Until early that morning of June 12, when I left a fifteen-minute speech on O.J.'s voice mail — what the press would later call a "Dear John" message. I had to save myself, and I did it the only way I knew how. I couldn't afford to give O.J. a chance to beguile or seduce me yet again.

The year before, the first time we broke up, O.J. had walked away from me. Now it was my turn, and this time, I'd vowed, it would be for keeps. I made explicit what we'd both known for some time: We were through.

Now I was off to see someone new, a man I'd been thinking about for months: Michael Bolton. We'd met just once before, but I had that electric feeling about Michael.

Good-bye, Mr. Wrong, I thought, as we began our descent into Vegas. *And hello, Mr. Right.*

My friend and theatrical manager, Tom Hahn, had called me the previous winter with a possible job offer, a Michael Bolton music video, to be taped on February 14 in Los Angeles.

The notion of being the-girl-in-the-video hadn't appealed to me in the past; it didn't seem very challenging. But the idea of working with this particular artist intrigued me. You can't fool people for long in the music business; you can't have Michael's level of success without some real sensitivity.

I'd seen firsthand how Michael reached people. When my brother was laid up for weeks in the hospital, his leg snapped in a terrible fall, the one thing that kept him going was Michael's song "When I'm Back On My Feet Again."

The video had one more significant plus: It would keep me busy on my least favorite holiday. My last Valentine's Day had been an out-and-out disaster. It marked the first time I'd caught O.J. deceiving me, though hardly the last.

We eventually broke up in May of 1993. I hadn't dated since, not for nine long months. I hadn't wanted to be with anyone else while O.J. was still on my mind. I was still in a tailspin, mourning my lost love.

When I met the casting people for the video, they told me I'd have to be able to do three things: dance, cry, and show a range of emotions. I auditioned and got the job; I guess I was good enough at all three.

When I reached the set, Michael was playing softball with some children for a brief scene in the video. I smiled at his enthusiasm, how he'd lost himself in the game. He was really involved with those kids.

And, I must confess, he dazzled me. I'd never found long hair that attractive in a man, but Michael Bolton made it work. He was beautiful and smart and all man. I didn't know if he could cook or not, but he was awfully attractive.

Michael had his girlfriend on the set, and I have a strict rule against flirting with men who are taken. But I won't deny that Michael's presence improved my working conditions.

The video told the story of a man — Michael — who falls in love with a girl while watching her practice her ballet from his apartment across the street. The girl already has a boyfriend, who reminded me a lot of O.J. — he's very charismatic and lights up a room, but he isn't true.

When the boyfriend makes a pass at a waitress, the girl storms out of the restaurant — only to come face-to-face with Michael, who's been singing this soulful ballad, "Completely":

> *I wanna give my heart completely,*
> *To someone who'll completely give their heart to only me*

Those lyrics really got to me. I so much wanted to believe that there was someone out there for me, a man with the total devotion of Michael's character. I needed to trust again in real romance, and that I didn't have to settle for less.

"You're finally together," the director said simply as we moved into the closing scene, shot under a Hollywood rain. My eyes met Michael's and I felt mesmerized, swallowed up into my character. I looked at this gorgeous man and for that moment I believed that he *was* the one.

As I walked toward Michael, I spontaneously shed my raincoat; I had only some very scanty underwear on beneath it. That was how I embraced him — *completely,* with total abandon, with all of my need and desire.

My improvisation took everyone by surprise. Run the video on freeze-frame, and you'll see Michael's brief double-take. Professional that he is, he instantly recovered to meet me in a melting kiss. I threw my arms around his neck and drew one knee up against his hip. My eyes were closed to the rain and the moment. I lost track of time and place. I felt only the pressure of his lips, rippling through me. I wanted to hold that kiss forever.

I was known as a "One-Take Annie," and that scene worked so well that the director wrapped it right there. My physical contact with Michael was so fleeting, yet so intense, that I couldn't get it out of my head. When he called me months later and invited me to hear him debut "Completely" on his next tour, I didn't mind hearing that he no longer had a girlfriend.

The night before I left for Vegas, O.J. and I went out to a charity gala in Bel Air that we'd scheduled weeks before: our last date. I dressed in gold sequins, and O.J. wore a dashing tux. As we laughed and cuddled through the evening, we were to all appearances the perfect loving couple.

O.J. didn't know it, but I was already saying good-bye. That date was to be my final gift to him.

Shortly after O.J. dropped me off at home, Michael called to confirm our plans. I told him how excited I was about being a fly on the wall and seeing what his life was about.

An hour passed and neither of us wanted to hang up. We were tumbling into infatuation, when you want to learn all there is about the other person.

I went to sleep imagining our second kiss, with no director telling us to cut.

A limo was waiting at the airport in Las Vegas. I dropped my bags at the Mirage and went straight to the softball field where Michael's team was playing. I was dressed for the occasion — cute white dress, tennis shoes, my hair pulled back into a pony-tail — and settled into the dugout for a lazy afternoon.

Michael's team was in the field, and the first thing I noticed was how good he looked in his striped uniform. He's a powerful man who really fills out a jersey. He sent me a subtle welcoming look from the infield, then kissed me on the cheek when his team came in to bat. After introducing me around, we sat watching and holding hands. I know that my palms were sweating a little bit; I was pretty nervous out there.

When Michael went up to the plate and hit the ball hard, I whooped and cheered for him. It took me back to my adolescence in Panama City, Florida, when my girlfriends and I had crushes on the community college athletes in the dorms across from my house.

At the end of the game, Michael and I rode a golf cart back to the limo and returned to our hotel. I went up to my room to shower and change for the evening's big event: a birthday dinner at Spago for Louis Levin, Michael's manager. I put on a little

Chanel-style dress, black with a pleated skirt and a gold-link chain at the waist. My light auburn hair fell loosely below my shoulders. I felt very pretty that night; I wanted Michael to like what he saw.

On the way out to Caesars Palace, I was walking along with Mickey Sherman, Michael's close friend, when we got slightly delayed by a craps table. I was rubbing Mickey's shoulder, playing the Lucky Lady. I usually had good luck at casinos — I once parlayed two quarters into $7,200 — and before long my partner was way ahead.

By the time Mickey and I got to Spago, they'd already sprung the surprise on Louis. Michael took one look at me, and I could tell he wasn't mad that I was late. "You look beautiful," he said.

Dinner was lively. All of Michael's music people were there as well as the softball players, and the champagne flowed.

Michael and I held hands under the table. We played kneesies and traded shy glances that no one else could see. I felt special to be there. Los Angeles and O.J. seemed a million miles away, a thousand years ago.

Dinner was followed by blackjack. It was past midnight when a few of us retired to Michael's huge suite back at the Mirage. I gabbed along with Louis and Mickey and Michael's bodyguard. Everyone was jovial and relaxed.

At one point I excused myself to check for phone messages at my condominium in Los Angeles. There were a number of disconnects, one or two calls from my mother — and three messages from O.J. Simpson. I'd been expecting and half-dreading O.J.'s calls. He was a man who thought he could charm his way past anyone, and usually he was right.

"Girl, what is it now?" went the first message in O.J.'s normal voice, loud and playful. "I thought we were going to fill the house with babies."

It sounded like he'd gotten my "Dear John" call, and that he wasn't taking it all that seriously.

"I know you're there," the second message began in much the

same tone. "Pick up the phone, Paula, pick up the phone." When we were having hard times, O.J. knew I'd often let the phone ring. I'd been deliberately vague with him the night before about my immediate plans. It was no longer O.J.'s business to know where I would be.

Much later, O.J. would testify that he'd hoped I could take him to the airport for a late flight to Chicago. Thank heaven I wasn't around — had I given O.J. that ride, I would have landed in some very hot legal water.

The third call was different. "I understand what you mean," O.J. said. His tone was darker, softer — resigned? The message unnerved me. Had O.J. accepted our breakup, or was this just another ploy to put me off my guard? What would his next move be?

During O.J.'s civil trial, the plaintiffs would place into evidence a phone log. It suggested that he'd left the third message at 10:03 P.M., roughly half an hour before two people died at 875 South Bundy Drive.

Later on I'd have plenty of time to mull over that last message and shake it for hidden meanings. I never reached any firm conclusion. Like so many details that would come to light over the next two and a half years, the message might have meant a lot.

Or it might have meant nothing at all.

By 2 A.M. everyone had left the suite except Michael and me. We talked for a while, had one last glass of champagne. Then it was really good night, as Michael had to get up early the next day to work with his celebrated songwriter, Diane Warren.

We had a long good-night kiss, and I felt the same wild energy between us that I'd experienced on the set four months before. The same sweetness and mystery and raw attraction — all were present and accounted for.

Except this time it was better. This time neither of us was acting.

It was the perfect ending to a spectacular day. I went up to my room and fell into bed, sleepy and giggling, eager for the next day's adventures.

I woke up early, put on my sunshine-yellow bikini, and joined Michael by the pool. To break the Nevada heat, we found a cabana with a cold-water misting device and set up camp. Michael began oiling my back. When he caught his bodyguard ogling me in my bikini, he joked with the guy, "Because it's you, I'll let you get away with looking at her like that."

Here we go, I thought. I'd reached the phase with Michael where you know you really like a man, but he keeps surprising you. Michael's looks, his manner, his little turns of speech — everything was fresh and appealing.

It was a wonderful feeling, one I hadn't had for so long.

After sharing some fruit for breakfast, Michael went off to work and I went in for a manicure. At the beauty shop, small world, I ran into my friend Suzanne. We'd met years ago at modeling school in Pensacola and later at the Elite agency in New York. Suzanne was dating Mark Packer, a good friend of O.J.'s, and I felt a little awkward telling her that O.J. wasn't there with me.

We were walking back toward the pool when my cell phone rang. It was Tom, my theatrical manager. As soon as I heard his voice — strained, nearly breaking — I got scared.

"Something terrible has happened to Nicole!" Tom said.

"What do you mean?"

"Go back to your room — I'll call you there."

With Suzanne at my side, I made tracks to my room, with one stop along the way, at the gift shop for a pack of Marlboro Lights. I smoke only when my nerves are shot; I had a feeling this would be one of those times.

As it turned out, that first pack would last me barely two hours.

The phone was ringing as we passed through the door. "Turn on the television," Tom said. Now he sounded even worse.

Within ten seconds I'd heard the nation's top news story:

Nicole Brown Simpson and Ronald Goldman had been found murdered near the front steps of Nicole's condo.

I felt like I'd been hit in the head with a brick. I sank crying to my knees, and as pictures of the murder scene flashed over the TV, I prayed hysterically:

"Please please please forgive me, please please please forgive me, please please please . . ."

I was pleading with a woman I'd barely known when she was alive.

I was asking forgiveness from the person I'd despised in my most anguished hours. I had been full of resentment because she'd beaten me and taken my man away.

How many times had I wished — my awful private secret, breathed aloud to no one — that Nicole would just vanish from the face of this earth?

You must be careful of what you wish for . . .

I was sickened with guilt. As I knelt before the television, nearly out of my head, I was sure of one thing: Something had been taken from me that morning, and I'd never get it back.

"Please please please forgive me, please please *please* forgive me . . ."

With robot fingers I dialed into my answering service. There were a dozen or more messages: from Cathy Randa, O.J.'s longtime secretary; from his friends on both coasts.

And there were several messages from O.J. himself, all pretty much the same: "I need to talk to you right away, please call me." He didn't sound good.

My mom called the room. A little high-strung in the best of times, she was ready to break. "Whatever you do, *promise* me that you won't go back to Los Angeles," she cried.

I was trying to deal with all of this like a rational person, but I felt very spacey. The sounds in the room seemed far away, like they do before you faint.

Suzanne had left and come back with Mark Packer. They hovered in disbelief around the television.

Mickey Sherman called, just to see what I was doing. No one in Michael's party was aware of my involvement with O.J. Michael knew that I'd broken up with someone like the cad in our music video, but he'd been too much of a gentleman to pry.

Now the secret was out. Mickey was at my door in seconds, armed with his laptop, and took charge. "Now calm down," he said. "Everything's going to be all right." He started tapping at his computer to get more information.

I can't be sure of what happened next. I was so fogged in that I lost my sense of sequence. But it might have been around then that I watched O.J. return to his Brentwood home — he was back from Chicago.

Then I watched him get handcuffed by the police, who were taking him to Parker Center for questioning. It was true: O.J. was a suspect.

That's impossible, I thought. I couldn't imagine how O.J. could cope with what was happening; it must be tearing him apart. And what about Sydney and Justin, his young children — were they okay?

Sitting there in my bed, I felt paralyzed. It was just too much to absorb. I cried and drifted and smoked till my head swam. "What should I do?" I said, half-aloud.

"To begin with, you shouldn't call O.J. back," Mickey said in his criminal attorney's voice. "He might say something incriminating to you over the phone, and if he does, that would be the worst thing for you to have to handle.

"Now let me ask you this," he went on. "Did O.J. ever hit you?"

"No, he didn't," I said. As volatile as our relationship had been, as obsessively jealous as O.J. could be, I didn't consider him a violent man. His rage had scared me once or twice, and I'd seen him go berserk in a hotel room, but that was as far as it had gone. I'd told Mickey the truth, and yet I couldn't believe I was having this conversation.

Mickey left to talk to Michael. I knew I should break the news first and rang Michael's suite. I took a breath and said, "I have something that's really hard to tell you. I don't know exactly how to say it."

Go ahead, Michael said.

"Remember I told you about my ex-boyfriend?" I took another deep breath. "Well, it's O.J."

"You know, I kind of figured that," Michael said gently. He tried to soothe me, and we agreed to get together later.

Mark Packer took me by the hand and said, "Look, you've got to get out of this room and eat something."

It was hard for me to move, but I knew he was right — the room was closing in like a tomb. Mark and Suzanne and I went back to the cabana, which had a phone. Despite Mickey's warning, I thought about calling O.J. back. He had no idea where I was, and he needed to talk to me.

"Paula, you've *got* to call him," Mark said. "You've got to be there for him, you've got to support him — you're the one that he's going to turn to."

You're the one, you're the one . . . The words echoed in my head. Where was all this heading? Where would it take me?

Mark punched in O.J.'s cell-phone number. He reached him, I believe, as O.J. was coming home from Parker Center after his interrogation. "I have someone here to talk to you," Mark said, and then he passed the phone to me.

"How are you doing?" I said, straining to sound normal.

"I need you," O.J. said. His voice was flat and dull, like a bad imitation of himself.

Then he asked me a question: "What happened to the messages I left you last night?"

"I erased them," I said. Having no reason to vary it, I'd just followed my routine.

"Good," he said. "I don't need them to start picking on that, too."

That sounded reasonable to me. If the police were looking to stick these crimes on O.J., it was a terrible mistake. I wouldn't want his messages confusing things even more. I was glad that I'd erased them.

"I need you," O.J. said again.

"Look, I can't talk any more right now — I just can't," I said. I felt myself losing control, and I didn't want to bring O.J. down with me.

"Okay," he said.

"I just can't make sense right now."

"That's all right," he said. He was strangely calm, and it worried me. He sounded like a man resigned to the worst.

After so much chaos in so little time, I felt unsure of my next move. I thought Mark was probably right: I *was* the one. No one else knew O.J. as I did. And he had sounded so pathetic, like a little boy lost, that I wished I were with him that moment.

But I stopped at the lip of the waterspout. One more step, and I'd be funneled into a place with terrifying question marks.

I thought I'd left O.J. in my past. Now he might devour my future.

So I hedged my bet. I didn't tell O.J. where I was staying or give him my room number. But I promised I'd call him back.

The suction pulled stronger by the minute.

After an early dinner with Mark and Suzanne, I kept my promise. O.J.'s sister Shirley answered the phone at his house in Brentwood. O.J. was very bad off, she said. He was already in bed and had asked not to be disturbed. Unless I called, that is, and then they were to put me through right away.

"How are you?" I said after O.J. picked up.

"Every time Shirley goes out of the room I pick up the gun," he told me. "If she wasn't here, I would have done it."

I didn't know which was more alarming, the words I was hearing or O.J.'s deadly, somber tone.

"You can't do that," I begged him. "People who commit suicide don't go to heaven."

"You've got to come back," O.J. said. "I need you."

For me it was a pivotal point. Once I heard O.J.'s pain, my decision was made. I might have broken up with the man, but that didn't change my human obligation to him. If I didn't go back, O.J. would die. It was, I thought, that simple.

Besides, I was responsible here. Hadn't I wished the fatal wish?

"I'll be there for you," I told O.J. "If you need me, I'll be there."

"We're going to change houses tomorrow," O.J. said. "Cathy will arrange your flight and where to take you from the airport."

When I heard O.J. making plans — actually thinking about the next day — I knew I was doing the right thing. Other people weren't so sure. My mother had been pushing Tom Hahn to do something, anything — lock me up in a cabin in Montana if he had to. When she heard what I'd decided, she was beside herself.

"He's going to kill you both," she sobbed.

Even as I tried to calm her, I thought to myself, *That would be all right, too.* I knew exactly what O.J. was going through. I was feeling so much hurt myself that I just wanted it to stop. I gave no thought to my own welfare. I would do what had to be done, and whatever happened would be okay.

Michael came to my room, concern furrowed into his face. "You don't realize the magnitude this is going to take on," he said. "You can't even imagine how it's going to change your life."

No one could move me, not even the most beautiful man in the world. "I can handle this," I told him. "Everything's going to be okay."

Michael softly touched my face. He would miss me. "I won't be able to be there for you," he said. "It's just too huge."

Good-bye, Mr. Right.

Cathy Randa had advised me to stay put until Wednesday, June 15, when O.J. would be settled in at a friend's house, outside the city and the media glare.

Stay put is what I did. I spent the next thirty-six hours in limbo, the place next door to hell. I walked around like a zombie, bumping into furniture. Or I sat, catatonic. I picked at my room-service tray. I gazed at the television, trying to grasp the unfathomable: that O.J. was suspected of committing this gruesome crime.

That people believed he could have killed the mother of his children, while those children slept just yards away.

That's absurd, I kept thinking. Or maybe I was talking aloud, to the walls. *Something is terribly wrong — can't they see?*

My new friends feared for me to be alone. As Michael got ready to perform Tuesday night, Mickey brought me into a backstage dressing room. I sat there, staring off into space.

Later I went out front to hear Michael sing "Completely." He squeezed the last ounce of feeling out of it, till I broke from my trance and flashed back to our first kiss. Now the memory felt bittersweet, a souvenir from a place I'd never see again.

But it was another ballad that really moved me that night. If I still had any doubts about the course I'd chosen, Michael erased them as he sang:

> *Lean on me, when you're not strong*
> *And I'll be your friend, I'll help you carry on*

I had to go back. There was too much guilt and pain to resist. Too much history with a man I thought I'd left behind me.

For the past ten years, ever since I'd started modeling, I'd kept a calendar book for jobs and social engagements. I was detailed and dutiful, and nearly every page was full.

But the last six months of my 1994 book would stay blank. Not one single entry after the day of Michael's concert.

Once you're inside the waterspout, you see, you tend to lose track of time.

2

On the Run

I said good-bye to Michael after his concert. He gave me a hug of reassurance, nothing like our good-night kiss two nights before.

It wrenched me to break that hug and let him go, but what else could we do? There was no room for us in the nightmare world I'd entered; I couldn't even regret our bad timing. I was so zoomed in on O.J., and on what he needed, that I couldn't begin to focus on anyone else.

On Wednesday, using an assumed name, I caught a 7 A.M. flight to LAX, where Cathy Randa had arranged for a limo. The driver, Allan Park, told me that he'd picked up O.J. for the red-eye to Chicago Sunday night.

Allan volunteered no more than that. I didn't press him for details, nor did I tell him how I fit into the picture. I was happy to keep it light. I think Allan was nearly as confused and shaken up as I was, grateful for small talk about the weather. We pretended that this was just another ride to just another place on just another ordinary day.

We headed north, into the San Fernando Valley suburbs. After half an hour we passed through a wooded area and pulled up to a large, modern, cream-colored house in an isolated part of Encino — the home of Robert Kardashian, a close friend of O.J.'s. Cathy Randa met me in the marble entryway and walked me into the sunken living room. By that time both of us were crying.

"Okay, let's calm down," Cathy said. She knew we had a long haul ahead of us. We were both closet smokers — I'd never lit up in front of O.J., who disapproved — and we went out back by the pool to indulge. The lighter shook in my hands. I smoked the cigarette halfway down, felt lightheaded, and stubbed it out.

I took my bag upstairs. To the left was an office, to the right a small den. Between them I found a simply furnished guest bedroom with a queen-size bed and boxes of stored clothes. O.J.'s Louis Vuitton brown leather traveling bag sat on the floor. It was weirdly comforting to see it there; I'd been on a lot of trips with that bag.

And now I was back at O.J.'s side. Back where I belonged.

O.J. was out, visiting the funeral home that was handling Nicole's funeral arrangements. I kept dwelling on the guns locked up in his office at home, the revolver he kept in his car. I considered hunting through his bags but shrank back. I didn't want to add to the invasion of his life. O.J.'s sister and brother-in-law would have packed O.J. for the trip. Surely, I thought, they wouldn't have let a weapon get through.

As much as the guns worried me, I thought they could work in O.J.'s favor. Even if O.J. was capable of killing someone, a claim I would not accept, why use a knife when he had a gun?

Clothes arrived from O.J.'s house for the next day's funeral. I hung a suit and a pair of dress shirts in the bedroom closet, checking first to see if anything needed pressing. I left a box of underwear and socks on the couch in the den.

Whenever I walked down to the living room and peeked at the big-screen television, I was assaulted by scenes of pandemonium around O.J.'s house. There were cameras everywhere; the media seemed totally over the top.

It wasn't much better in Panama City. The press had put two

and two together about the mystery girl O.J. had been seen with the night before the murders at the high-profile fundraiser. They were bombarding my mother with phone calls, turning up the heat.

The press offensive made me wonder anew: What had I gotten myself into?

Mom wasn't taking it well. By the time I called her from Encino, she was a basket case. Once again she begged me to come home. "He's going to kill himself and kill you too," she kept repeating. I tried to settle her down, but it didn't help that my own voice was quavering.

Panic is contagious. After we hung up, my mother's fear ran riot through my head. *He's going to kill himself and . . .* I tried to blot the words out, but they kept coming back, like a song you hate but can't forget.

That afternoon I heard some noise at the front door and rushed to the entryway. It was O.J., shell-shocked. He seemed so sad and beaten. His face was drawn, his brawny shoulders hunched down. He looked somehow *smaller* than the cheerful, confident man I'd left four days before. Seeing Nicole in her casket must have destroyed him.

If the notion that O.J. might commit suicide ever seemed abstract to me, it didn't anymore.

O.J. looked relieved when he saw me, though he couldn't muster a smile. "I'm glad you're here," he said. He hugged me with more need than strength, like a man clinging to a life raft in the middle of the ocean. I watched his every expression and movement. I expected him to collapse, right there.

I took O.J. up to his room. Helped him undress to his briefs. Watched him crumple into bed. That was a knife to my heart, to see the most exuberant person in the world look so helpless and vulnerable.

Back downstairs, Cathy called me to the kitchen. I met Dr. Saul Faerstein, a psychiatrist enlisted by O.J.'s attorney, who handed me a vial of sedatives. I was to give O.J. one pill in the morning and another one at night.

The doctor looked at me closely and said, "Let's just keep these pills from all being taken at once."

I got the message: O.J. was hanging by a string.

Then I met the owner of the house, Robert Kardashian, who'd been out with O.J. that afternoon. He was short and intense, friendly but contained, like a character out of *The Godfather* with some big secrets to protect.

Kardashian said that they'd been staying with O.J. every minute. The only time O.J. had been on his own was in the bathroom.

Now it would be my turn.

As O.J. slept, I searched the bedroom and adjoining bath for razor blades, finding none.

At dinner I got O.J. to eat some lasagna. Then I went back to my vigil — with O.J. so stoned out on the sedatives, we had few options. I gave him his evening pill and unplugged the phone, and soon he was deep in slumber.

I sat on the bed all night and watched O.J. sleep. The night was still, but my mind skittered through a jumble of anxious thoughts. I brooded about O.J. and what would happen to his children if he wasn't around. How they'd hear ugly whispers for the rest of their lives.

I mentally played back the "Dear John" message I'd left for O.J. Sunday morning — had I said the wrong thing? Had I somehow set off this terrible chain of events?

Yet I wasn't thinking that O.J. might be guilty. It was more that *I* had done it, by wishing Nicole away.

You could say that I wasn't a model of clear thinking that night.

Most of all, I prayed. Not for a happy ending, nor to see our lives go back to normal. That seemed too much to ask.

I just prayed for the strength to make it to the next day.

The next morning O.J. woke up groggy and full of dark thoughts. "You realize," he said, "you're the last woman I'll ever make love to."

Hearing that, I knew I could take no chances. When O.J. went to the bathroom to shower, I followed and perched on the toilet until he was through. Though I'd found no sharp objects there, I was afraid there might be something I'd missed.

Then we got O.J. dressed. I laid his shirt and funeral suit out for him — he was so changed, so needy. I did all I could, but how do you help a man who seems dead inside? How do you give him his life back?

After O.J. left for the service, I cleaned the room and made the bed with new sheets. I felt better as long as I stayed busy, and no task was too small.

Downstairs the television played on. I heard snatches of commentary as I walked through the living room, about trails of blood and suspicious gloves and the rest. I shut my ears to all of it. It was as if the reporters were speaking some strange, ancient language where the words were familiar but the meaning lost to me.

"Get out of there, Paula," my mother persisted. It was her fifth call of the day. "You don't belong there."

"I'm fine, Mom," I said. "Everything's okay, and I'll be home soon."

She wasn't convinced. "I'm a little older than you are," she said, "and I know that we all have a breaking point. These people were divorced, and they couldn't leave each other alone — Paula, if he did it, people would understand. Everybody has that breaking point —"

The floor heaved under my feet. "He didn't do it — he *didn't!*" I snapped. "Don't talk like that!" Mom's doubt set me off; I'd been working overtime to dodge my own.

My mother never questioned O.J.'s innocence again.

When O.J. came back, I noticed that he'd changed into a suit that was too big for him. After the funeral, he and the bulky Al Cowlings — "A.C.," as we knew him — had traded clothes and cars to decoy the media. Now, on TV, we saw A.C. covering his head and running into O.J.'s house.

"This is absolutely amazing," said Bobby Chandler, another of O.J.'s former teammates and closest friends. "He looks so much like O.J."

O.J. enjoyed the ruse — he was always the practical joker — but I could tell he was fading fast. He said he'd fallen asleep in the car during the funeral procession. Now he just wasn't with us. "Who would do this to Nicole?" he'd moan, out of nowhere.

When O.J. was coming down off the sedatives, he seemed to get even more depressed. I worried that the prescribed dose might be too heavy. O.J. didn't seem more stable than the day before. I thought he could try to end it at any time.

"Just keep watching," Dr. Faerstein told me over the phone.

Our second night mimicked our first, except that I might have dozed fitfully for an hour or two. As the Turner Classic Movie channel droned on in the dark, I put my arm around O.J.'s bare shoulder. I felt protective, almost maternal.

When I'd been trying to leave O.J., I couldn't stand to be near him. His voice made me wince; his touch made me feel dirty. But that seemed like a lifetime ago. Those feelings belonged to a different person. I looked down at poor O.J., his face gray and drawn in the TV's flicker.

I touched his hand and softly said the words we both needed to hear:

"I'm there for you, darling."

Friday, June 17, began much as the day before: O.J. groggily surfacing from sleep, staring vacantly at another old movie. At eight-thirty I asked him if he'd try to eat and went downstairs in my pajamas to find some cantaloupe.

In the kitchen I found Bob Shapiro, O.J.'s newly appointed attorney, freshly creased as always. Right away I felt the difference in the house. A sure, steady hand was in control.

I'd met Bob when I was eighteen years old and my agent took me to a screening at the producer Bob Evans's house. He later helped me with a relative's legal problem. He'd always been good to me.

But even Bob Shapiro, I quickly saw, could do little against the snowball rolling down upon O.J. "Wait a few minutes before you go back up with breakfast," he told me. "I have to go up and tell O.J. something."

As Bob headed upstairs with Robert Kardashian, a tight silence hung in the kitchen. Then someone — I can't recall who — filled me in.

Bob was there to escort O.J. down to Parker Center, where O.J. would turn himself in on two charges of murder. He had to be there by eleven o'clock.

I burst into tears, truly stunned. Neither O.J. nor I had discussed the likelihood of his arrest. All my will had gone into keeping him afloat one more day, one more hour.

I tried to muffle my crying to keep O.J. from hearing me. "I don't understand," I kept repeating. The world seemed upside down. Nicole Pulvers, a young lawyer who worked for Kardashian, did her best to console me. I gathered what composure I had left. I had to be strong, for *him*.

O.J. had pulled on some pants to meet with Bob in the upstairs office. Fifteen minutes later, I found him alone in his room, seated in bed, blank shock on his face.

The bad dream was real. They were arresting him.

I had to snap him out of it. Tears and sympathy weren't going to get it done. "Okay, there's really no time to be upset about this," I said briskly. "You've got to get this legal stuff taken care of so you can be there to raise your kids."

At the mention of O.J.'s children, I saw a glimmer of response. I kept going: "You have to be there, because Sydney has to go to Vassar — she has so much potential."

"Sydney is a very smart girl," O.J. said.

"And Justin will do great things in his life."

"There's nothing better," said O.J., lost in space, "than one of Justin's hugs."

This wasn't going so well, I thought. O.J. sounded like someone remembering the wonderful things in his life one last time.

He sounded like someone saying good-bye.

"There's just no time to think like this," I said, my voice rising in pitch. "If you're not there to tell the kids the truth about your life, they'll hear lies from someone else, and that will be so awful for them. You have to be strong for them."

No response — he was slipping away from me.

"You've got Bob Shapiro taking care of this," I said. "It's going to be all right — you just have to get over this hurdle."

O.J. stayed vacant.

"You're innocent — you can *beat* this. Bob told me that he has the best doctors in the country coming to examine you." In truth, I thought O.J.'s body might be his best defense. I hadn't seen a scratch or bruise on him.

O.J. kept staring straight ahead, and I thought: *This is the last time I'll ever see him.* I was certain he would kill himself; the only question was where. He cared about Kardashian too much to do it in the house.

But I also knew that O.J. Simpson was a very resourceful man.

Time was up for pep talks; O.J. had to get ready for the doctors who'd been hired by the defense to gather any physical evidence that might help his case. He took a shower and I waited in the bathroom, as before. He put on some jeans and a golf shirt, and then he went into the den to talk to A.C. I gave them a few minutes' privacy. I knew that nothing bad would happen while A.C. was with him.

When I entered the den, I found O.J. on the phone with Louis Marks, a friend and financial adviser. What I heard chilled me to the quick: O.J. was discussing his will and asking Louis to make sure that his children were taken care of.

O.J. put down the phone and looked at A.C., who said, "It's going to be okay, man." I sat there like a stone. If anyone could rescue O.J. from his pain, it would be Al Cowlings. The two of them had looked after each other since third grade. They'd stayed together through college, all the way to the Buffalo Bills. Once, on a drive with O.J. and his kids, I heard him point toward A.C.'s house and say, "Your uncle lives over there."

Now the two football players were crying together, and I made it a threesome. After a while, I went downstairs for a glass of water. When I got back, O.J. was writing on a sheet of unlined paper. He looked up at me and said pensively, "I can't forget my Peola."

That was O.J.'s nickname for me, a simple play on my first name that he used when he felt sexy or affectionate or playful.

Now he was using it in a totally different tone of voice.

I didn't know it yet, but now he was writing his good-byes.

I smiled at O.J. and kissed him lightly on the cheek, and then I gave him back his quiet with A.C.

When I went back to check on them later, I found them down the hall, at a small conference table in Kardashian's book-lined office. O.J. had stripped down to his briefs again, ready for the doctors' inspection. As I took up my vigil on a couch by the door, A.C. said sadly, "I thought we were going to grow old together, man."

That shook me. If even A.C. feared that O.J. might kill himself, I knew the threat was real.

A.C. kept talking as though he was afraid to stop. About how much O.J. had to live for. About how much their friendship meant to him.

"I love you," A.C. said.

O.J. just sat there with his shoulders slumped. Every now and then he'd look over to me with a ghost of a smile, as if to contain my worry. Those looks demolished me. The lump in my throat grew till it hurt.

The medical people swarmed in with a flurry of activity. O.J. sat on the table and submitted to rounds of blood samples and photographs. There were four doctors working at once, along with several nurses. I was especially impressed by Dr. Henry Lee, the famous Connecticut criminologist. He had such an aura of confidence; he seemed to soak in everything around him.

As people buzzed about us, I stayed in my private bubble with O.J., speaking with my eyes: *Don't worry. I'm here.* Every now and then I'd reach over and touch his hand. Or I'd use my acting training to find an optimistic voice and say, "Everything's going to be all right." Then I'd feel the tears welling up and I'd turn my head to fight them down so I could look back over at him.

When it got to be too much to bear, I ducked out of the room and reeled blindly through the house. Whenever my path crossed Cathy Randa's, I hugged her close but tried not to look at her face — that would set me off all over again.

At some point Bob Shapiro came upstairs with an announcement: "Look, we're not going to make it. They're on their way here." O.J. had missed his eleven o'clock deadline, and the police had lost patience. They were coming to pick him up.

It was around then that O.J. seemed to straighten up. Something clicked inside. He looked at me and said, "Paula, I don't want you here with all the photographers coming. You should be with your family — please pack your things and go."

I was moved by his effort to protect me, to gain some control over the tumult around him. But I wanted to see him get in that police car. Then I'd know he was okay, at least for the time being. "I'll wait till you leave and then I'll go," I said.

"Don't argue with me," he said, more pleading than impatient. "Just get your stuff together and have Tom come get you."

I knew O.J. well enough to know he wouldn't budge. I went back to the bedroom, called my theatrical manager, threw my things in my bag. There was nothing else to do. I had played out my string, passed the baton to A.C. And now O.J. was pushing me away — but not, I was convinced, for the reason he'd stated.

He needs me gone so he can end it. . . .

The doctors were done. I met O.J. at the staircase, my bag in hand. That's when I lost it, as we walked down those stairs with his arm around my shoulder. Death was in the air, choking me — I couldn't catch my breath between sobs. I begged O.J. again to let me stay, but he wouldn't hear of it.

"Then promise me," I said desperately, "that I'll see you again. Please, *please* don't hurt yourself. Promise me that you'll see this through."

And finally: *"Promise me that you won't do it."*

It, I said. I couldn't speak the actual words, because then they would be real. Then they would translate into action.

Noon approached. We went out the back door and saw Tom

waiting by the pool, flushed in the heat of the day. We circled back toward the front drive, and O.J. said, "I've got to talk to Tom for a minute. A.C.'s got something for you."

As O.J. and Tom huddled on the front steps, A.C. handed me a wad of hundred-dollar bills, around $2,000. "O.J. wanted me to give you this so you can get on a plane and go home," he said.

A.C. took my bag as O.J. caught up with us and walked me out to Tom's Jeep. "I love you, I love you, I'll be there for you," I kept repeating.

O.J. opened the Jeep's passenger door — a gentleman to the end, I thought grimly — and closed it after me. I held my hand up to the window, and O.J. put his long fingers up to mine. Such a sad sensation, I thought, to be so close to someone and yet feel only glass.

Then O.J. said good-bye to me in a way I'd never want to hear again. He reminded me of a boy I'd known back in high school, the class valedictorian and a rock-solid Christian. Whenever O.J. claimed that all men cheated, I'd point to that young man as proof that he was wrong.

"Now you promise me something," O.J. said through the closed window. "You promise me that you'll get out of California and go back to Panama City and marry that guy back home."

I sat there, in a puddle of tears. I knew that boy was long gone; he'd moved on to West Point and an Army commission. My life had been a roller coaster, crammed with people and activity, yet I felt so alone.

And now I'd no longer have O.J. Because I knew that was the last thing that I'd ever hear him say.

As Tom pulled away from the house, I looked back at O.J., standing there so defeated. There must have been other people milling around — A.C. and Kardashian and a number of secretaries — but I saw only O.J.

Our eyes remained locked for as long as he stayed in view. When he disappeared, my imagination took over. I saw him going down the hill, walking into the woods . . .

Three years later, it is hard to explain how my mind had worked in that house in Encino. I was so caught up in fighting for O.J. It felt like us against the world, and I knew the world was wrong. I didn't question the emotional logic of O.J.'s ending his life. The loss of Nicole, the brutality of the crime, the humiliation of being a prime suspect — wouldn't I want to end it had I been in his place?

And yet . . . as Tom and I drove away, I got all twisted. I got lost in the place, deep down inside, where our scariest thoughts live without words.

An innocent man going down without a fight? A man like O.J., so strong and with so much to live for —

"He killed them, didn't he!" I burst out to Tom. Now my conflict was an open wound. I started babbling like a madwoman, straining to make some sense of things, going back and forth and back — "No, he couldn't do it!" "Yeah, he did!"

We were climbing Mulholland Drive, into the canyons; Tom lived on top of a mountain. With a hysterical woman beside him, he had all he could handle to keep the Jeep on the winding road.

I felt dizzy and blown apart, even after we finally stopped.

I tried to sit still in Tom's tasteful living room: wood floors, stone fireplace, Santa Fe decor. No good. I went outside to pace and smoke on his porch, then came back and sat some more. Here was pure torment — to think about everything O.J. might be doing without any idea of what was going on.

I listened for the phone, hoping Cathy might call. But my first information came over Tom's television instead, in a live news conference at around 2 P.M. Police Commander David Gascon took the podium — and I gasped as I heard him declare O.J. a fugitive.

"He is a wanted murder suspect," Gascon said, "and we will go find him."

I immediately feared the worst: The police would never find O.J. alive. That's when I lost my last shred of self-control. "He's killing himself while we're here talking!" I cried over the phone to my mother.

It was probably too late already, I thought. I could barely speak, but I forced myself to call O.J.'s house in Brentwood. Jason, O.J.'s grown son from his first marriage, would be there. I didn't know Jason all that well, but I loved him through his father. I wanted to tell him I'd be there if he needed anything.

"Dad's gone — nobody can find him," Jason said, cutting me off. "You've got to tell me where he is."

"I can't," I said. "I don't know."

"Come *on*, this is really important." Jason sounded scared to death. "If you don't tell me, something bad is going to happen."

"I know that," I said. That's why I was calling, to console a boy about to lose his father.

"Look," Jason said, "the police are here — they want to talk to you."

I slammed down the phone, my heart pounding. Two seconds later, it rang. The police were moving fast. "We need to speak with you," the officer said.

"I don't know anything," I said. "I just left the house a little while ago, and I really don't know where —"

"Just stay where you are — we're on our way."

Not ten minutes later we heard a loud, chopping whir. Tom and I hustled outside and saw three helicopters overhead. We ran around to the garage, looked down the road. A string of black-and-white LAPD squad cars was crawling up our way.

Tom was terrified. "Paula, there's a path down the side of the mountain," he said. "You can make it out the back way."

I could feel my blood pulsing; I was afraid, too. But I wasn't going to run; I could just see myself getting tackled and arrested. "I didn't do anything wrong, and I'm staying right here," I told Tom. "I'll just tell them the truth." I was starting to get my dander up. They could ask me all the questions they wanted, but that wasn't going to help O.J.

It didn't take those police officers long to realize I knew less than they did. They were aggressive and mechanical, and I could see how they'd scared the pants off Jason. When I warned them to get the guns out of O.J.'s house, they didn't seem to listen. They were too busy searching Tom's garage, and then they were gone.

The waiting game resumed. I was just about cried out by five o'clock, when a CNN bulletin introduced two people I'd left just hours before: Bob Shapiro and Robert Kardashian, who proceeded to read the letter I'd seen O.J. write that morning.

The letter destroyed me. From the first sentence, long before we heard about O.J.'s "last wish" (for the media to leave his children in peace), I knew just what it was: a suicide note.

As he'd promised, O.J. didn't forget his "Peola." I broke down as Kardashian read:

"Paula, what can I say, you are special. I'm sorry we're not going to have our chance. God brought you to me. I now see, as I leave, you'll be in my thoughts."

Most poignant of all was when O.J. wrote how he'd done *"most of the right things. So why do I end up like this? I can't go on, no matter what the outcome, people will look and point."*

Ever since his college days, O.J. had fed off the public's love for him. I didn't think that the prospect of jail, or even the electric chair, would drive him to suicide. But to lose people's respect and affection, to be shunned for the rest of his life? That, I believed, was something he could not bear.

"I've had a good life. I'm proud of how I lived, my mamma taught me to do unto others. . . ." I thought of how many times I'd heard O.J. say that to me. I thought about how much the words in that letter must have meant to him, how he'd pushed through his wall of pain to speak to the ones he loved.

When the letter talked about Nicole, it really hurt me to hear the obvious — that O.J. still loved her, and that he'd hoped they'd have a future. But I couldn't think about that, not now.

When you're in denial, you have to be there all the way.

An hour later, CNN broke into *Larry King* with a shot of the San Diego Freeway, northbound. I gaped at the sight of A.C.'s white Bronco rolling down the middle of the road, with a dozen or more squad cars in slow pursuit.

O.J. was in the backseat, the newsman said — *he was alive!* Ecstatic at that simple fact, I began to piece together what might have happened. Though the district attorney would try to suggest otherwise, there had been no conspiracy at Kardashian's house. Given the sedatives he was taking and the despair that had swamped him, O.J. lacked the heart or mind for any escape.

But when he and A.C. saw how easy it was for Tom and me to drive off, it probably occurred to them that they could do the same. After all these years, they were still guys from the streets.

O.J. had fled not to run, I knew in my gut, but to die. By riding off with A.C., he'd seized his last chance to go out on his terms.

As I watched the screen, barely blinking, my elation faded. Now there were two ways that O.J. could end his life: by his own hand (my instinct told me he had a gun with him) or by one itchy policeman's.

I was desperate for the Bronco to pull over, for O.J. to step out. I think I shared everyone's thoughts: *Just let this not be a catastrophe.*

I checked for messages at my home phone. With one eye on the television, I heard several disconnects, then a dazed but familiar voice: "Paula, are you there?" Of all the unreal moments I'd experienced, that one might have been the most bizarre — to hear O.J.'s disembodied voice as I watched his voiceless presence on TV, passing waves of cheering onlookers.

I wanted more than anything to call O.J. back, but I lacked A.C.'s cellular-phone number. Cathy Randa might have had it, but she was stuck at Kardashian's house with the rest, being questioned by police. The truth was, O.J. was calling from his own cell phone, but that possibility never dawned on me. I could do only what millions of others were doing: watch and pray.

As the Bronco swung west on the 91 freeway then north on the 405, I found myself melting into the truck's backseat. I felt O.J.'s fear and confusion, his sense of being hunted. I had to hold on to every bit of my focus. If I faltered for even a second, I was sure O.J. would die.

And so I shushed all my questions aside. I locked my forbidden doubts away, triple-bolted the safe. I had lain next to this man in our most private hours. I'd shared my secrets and my life. I had never stopped loving him, in good times or hard.

How could I have loved a murderer? I couldn't conceive of it. Not if I was to give O.J. the absolute loyalty he needed.

Not if I was to stay sane.

From that point on, through all that was to follow over the next sixteen months, I never doubted O.J. again.

Countless half-cigarettes later, as the shadows lengthened on Tom's mountain, A.C.'s Bronco left the freeway at Sunset Boulevard and turned toward O.J.'s home. I'd been feeling a little better since hearing that O.J. wanted to talk to his mom. He worshipped his mother. Once he reached her, I thought, there was no way he could do *it*.

I suffered through the final hour's standoff at the house. And I can hardly describe my relief when O.J. was finally coaxed out of the truck and into custody. The tension propping me up was cut, like the strings to a discarded marionette — I felt like sinking to the floor. I wept with relief and thanked God.

O.J. would see another day.

Only months later, after a private talk with O.J. in jail, would I learn just how dangerous his journey had been. Well before the police picked up his trail, he'd asked A.C. to take him to Nicole's grave in Orange County. That was where O.J. planned to use the revolver he was holding in his lap, wrapped in a towel.

When they found that the police had the cemetery covered, they pulled off into an orange grove instead. A.C. got out of the truck — perhaps O.J. had asked for a few moments alone.

According to O.J.'s testimony at his civil trial, he then took his gun out, but A.C. came back before he could use it.

The full story is even more chilling. "I took the gun and

I put it in my mouth," O.J. told me. "I pulled the trigger — and the towel jammed the trigger."

As soon as I knew O.J. was safe, my exhaustion took over. I'd been running on adrenaline the last five days, and now I needed a haven. I couldn't go to Mom and Panama City, where the media would have me cornered. And as much as I wanted to stick by O.J. in Los Angeles, I knew I couldn't weather the insanity there on my own.

I needed time to regroup, space to breathe.

I had dear friends in rural Tennessee, the Whitehurst family. I knew them from Florida and had never been to their home, but it sounded like the safest, quietest place I could imagine. I knew that I'd feel better there.

I called and asked, "Can I come?" By that point they'd already answered my question; their invitation lay waiting on my answering machine.

I arranged to take the red-eye that night to Memphis, a good time to go to LAX, when fewer people would be there.

As I left the lights of Los Angeles below me, I had no idea what the future held — when I'd return or what would happen when I did.

But one thing seemed certain: Michael Bolton had been right. My life was changing in ways I couldn't have dreamed of.

It wasn't over for O.J. or me. Not by a long shot.

3

Heisman Who?

Tragedies don't start out all dark and fateful, like the backdrop to some Dracula movie. They begin with quirks and accidents, just the stuff of normal life.

At least that's the way it began for me, back in 1992.

I came into that year with a feeling I'd never had before: a sense of failure.

Don't get me wrong — I'd known my share of rejection. You can't be a model or an actress and not lose out on countless jobs. But I'd never taken those as failures. As long as I picked myself up and tried a little harder, I thought, success would eventually come my way.

For the most part, it had. I'd been fortunate enough to work for some of the greatest fashion photographers in the world. At the age of twenty-five, I owned a house in my hometown in Florida and a condominium in Los Angeles. I was making more money than I once could have imagined.

But my brother Michael, hooked on cocaine, had touched off another family crisis, and somehow I was to blame. Fresh out of my first family Al-A-Non program, I had learned about Tough Love — which, if you've experienced it, is like detaching a part of your body. I had always been the person who took care of everyone else in the family, or else I heard about it nonstop. My family, to put it mildly, wasn't real happy with my new philosophy of how to take care of my brother.

My father wasn't in any better shape than my brother. I had asked Mom to let him move into a town house she owned — a huge thing to request on behalf of a man who had walked out years before — but it was either that or pay rent for Dad to live somewhere else.

My father continued to nosedive, just locking himself in to drink. "You need to look for another place to live," I told him. "You've got to get out and do something." He plunged even deeper into depression. He had his beloved cat put to sleep. He sat at the kitchen table making a hangman's noose: more guilt for his guilt-ridden daughter.

"Let me take care of it all, let me take care of you." That's what Dean Hamilton, a fella I'd met at the gym, said to me as I sat sobbing in my living room. It was our second date, and it had been wrecked by a series of wrenching phone calls from my family. My guardian angel! I thought. A couple of weeks (at the most) later, I ran off to Las Vegas and married him. I may have botched romance before, but this was a fiasco from the start. It was annulled. That was hard for me to swallow — now there was a failure in black and white, a part of the public record. I could never blot that one away.

Work became my refuge, more than ever. Whenever there was a modeling job, I was ready to go; no one had to ask me twice. Off I went to Miami or St. Martin, wherever the booking took me. For months, I barely paused to catch my breath. If I slowed down, I knew I'd have to face my loneliness. Or, scarier still, get involved with another man.

On one of my rare afternoons off, I was catching up on my errands, tooling around the freeways in my Toyota 4Runner. It was a spectacular day in May in southern California — high sky, flowers blooming like they'd been colored with Crayolas — and I was neck-deep in the dumps. I wanted nothing more than to get home, lock my door, order Chinese food for delivery, and curl up with a Katharine Hepburn movie.

As I turned off busy Wilshire Boulevard in Westwood and into my valet-parking stand, a black Mercedes pulled in behind me. A handsome, bullnecked man jumped out and greeted me — Marcus Allen, the NFL running back, whom I'd met years before. We'd never dated, but Marcus was one of those upbeat people who'd always had a smile for me. We exchanged phone numbers and said good-bye, and I thought no more of it.

Not an hour later, as I relaxed in my apartment, Marcus called. He was with a friend who was in the middle of a rough divorce, he said. Did I know someone who might want to go out with him?

As Marcus filled me in, I thought instantly of a woman named Pam: a Zoli model, blond, mother of a little girl. Marcus's buddy apparently liked blondes and had two young children of his own.

This could be great, I thought.

"Why don't you come out here, and we can talk about it?" Marcus proposed. He named a good address in Brentwood, his friend's house, and I was on my way. It would be exciting to be around some new people, maybe even make a match. If nothing else, it would distract me from my own troubles.

En route I tried to place Marcus's friend. I'd heard the name O.J. Simpson before, but I honestly had no idea who he was. I paid no attention to football. I rarely watched the kind of TV shows that aired O.J.'s famous Hertz commercials. As far as I was concerned, O.J. Simpson was just a lonely friend of Marcus Allen's.

Not that I was in the hunt for someone new. Sure, all my life I'd dreamt of having a perfect, all-American family, but you can't wish a dream true — as my nonmarriage had taught me. I knew I needed more time to heal. I'd been out of circulation for months and planned to stay that way.

It took about ten minutes to get from my place to the hilly streets of Brentwood. I thought it was the nicest neighborhood in L.A., with larger lots and more privacy than in Beverly Hills or Bel Air. I rolled up to the corner lot at 360 North Rockingham, a sprawling, ivied, Tudor-style mansion.

I checked in at the gate, drove up the cobbled drive, rang the bell. It was a lovely house, with orange trees dotting the gracious grounds, but I wasn't awed or intimidated. In my work and play around the globe, I'd seen palaces; I'd gotten to know some of the most successful people in the world.

The housekeeper steered me to Marcus, in the kitchen. We were chatting at the table when I heard someone tromping heavily down the back staircase. Then a loud voice, a bellow, really: "What's going on —"

The voice froze as the man had, three steps from the bottom, the moment he saw me.

I stood up and extended my hand and said, "Hi, I'm Paula. Nice to meet you. I'm going to introduce you to my friend, Pam."

What was my first impression? With his big head and long fingers and skinny body, O.J. Simpson reminded me of E.T., the extraterrestrial. I'm not saying he wasn't handsome; he would have been one of the more attractive aliens on a *Star Wars* set.

That's all right, I said to myself. *Pam likes unusual-looking men.*

I liked O.J.'s smile, which was loose and goofy and infectious. I felt his physical presence. He seemed larger-than-life — you might call it star quality, I guess, or the air of a man used to being the center of attention. But mostly I felt sympathetic and sorry for him. Beneath O.J.'s bravado I sensed a person in pain.

I was about to tell him about Pam's wonderful qualities, but O.J. fixed me with a funny look and said, "What's wrong with *you?*"

"*Everything* is wrong with me," I said sarcastically. From that moment — and for much of the next two years — the conversation flowed. My friends will tell you that I am rarely at a loss for words. In O.J. I had met my match.

He wasn't bothered a bit that I didn't know who he was. Later on, when we went out together, I'd find that he was easy with his fame. He wasn't like a lot of well-known people in Hollywood who wore dark glasses into movie theaters, to radiate mystery and beg to be noticed.

Looking back, O.J. might have appreciated the opportunity to start from scratch, to get to know a person without the baggage of his name and reputation.

It turned out that we were both fans of the bestseller *Men Are from Mars, Women Are from Venus*. Like me, O.J. had even been to a John Gray seminar. Soon we were discussing the verbal gender gap, how men tend to leap in with both feet and *solve the problem,* when women merely want a sympathetic hearing.

How the opposite sex, in short, could be so confounding.

At one point, after Marcus had quietly vanished, I winced from some shoulder pain. When I've been under stress, it seems to collect right there. "Hold on," O.J. said, "let me get you some Mineral Ice. This stuff works great for my knees."

I met him back in his living room, passing a trophy case with O.J.'s Heisman trophy. It barely registered. (Who was Heisman, anyway?) I was more intrigued by the art on the walls, especially a print of a Paris street scene, full of the color and high style I loved in that city.

Oh great, I thought, as O.J. prepared to rub the salve in under my sleeveless silk shirt. *Now he's going to try to get fresh.* I made no move to stop him. Maybe I was subconsciously testing the waters to see what would happen — to see if I'd have to dust off my right hook.

But O.J. was a perfect gentleman. He kept massaging that one spot on my shoulder. As he talked about how alone he was, I felt comfortable and connected to him. But not so connected that I could accept his invitation to Hawaii — the next *day* — for a week's holiday with Marcus and Cathryn, Marcus's fiancée.

O.J. just wasn't my type, I'd decided. For starters, there was our age difference. I was helpless at guessing someone's age, but I knew O.J. was joking when he said he was thirty-nine. In fact, he was forty-four, or nineteen years older than me. And while O.J. seemed like a nice enough sort, he was also boisterous and kind of arrogant. I usually went for the quiet and sensitive guys. I wasn't quite sure that I trusted this one.

My suspicions were confirmed by a softer tread down the stairway. Then I saw what O.J. had forgotten about for the last hour or so. She had long, straight brown hair and more curves than a mountain pass. Her name was Robin, and she put her hand on O.J.'s chest with pride of ownership. She draped herself all over him as she purred, "Honey, why didn't you come back upstairs?"

So much for our lonely guy.

I guess I should have known there and then that I was getting in over my head.

I didn't plan to date him; I was still fending off my ex-husband. I was trying to simplify my life and figure out where I'd messed up.

But O.J. was persistent. He called me two nights later from Hawaii, obviously tipsy, giggly and relaxed and terribly appealing. "I was on the beach having margaritas with Marcus and Cathryn, just sitting there in paradise, and now I'm locked in my hotel room on the phone with you for two and a half hours — do you realize that?

"You should *be* here — I don't understand why you're not here. I just can't get you out of my mind."

"Yeah, *sure* you can't," I said, rewinding my image of Robin at Rockingham.

I was flattered but very hesitant. I'd done a little security check on O.J., enough to know that he was one of the most eligible and flirtatious men on the West Coast. How could I possibly take him seriously?

But as he kept calling me for hours at a stretch from Hawaii, I found myself flirting back. I'd wonder what O.J. was doing . . . and then the phone would ring again, and it would be him.

For the next two weeks or so — I still refused to go out with O.J., even after he came back — we spoke every day, often two or three times. I found O.J. to be a book of facts: curious, funny, never boring. He'd traveled all over the world and hungered for more, nearly as much as I did. Where I liked psychology books, O.J. read all the latest novels and quoted easily from Shakespeare. And not just two or three lines, like a lot of people, but three or four minutes at a stretch from *Macbeth* or *King Lear*.

Later on, many people would poke fun at O.J. as dim and uneducated. But the man I came to know in 1992 was a very smart guy. He had tremendous experience in human behavior; he'd seen a lot and remembered it all. O.J. was a terrible speller, for sure. He was more at home talking than writing. But I've never met anyone more eager to soak up information.

There were no dry spells in those phone calls, and we talked about absolutely everything. About *Men Are from Mars* . . . ("Is that *you?*" one of us would say, cracking up, as we reread a favorite page). About our similar backgrounds, as poor kids who'd found paths to wealth but remained wide-eyed in our journey. About our career successes — and our family crises. Both O.J. and I had a brother with problems, a father who'd abandoned us when we were small, and a mother who'd kept the family going. We even missed the same foods from back home, like collard greens and black-eyed peas.

Most of all, we were fellow searchers. In O.J. I heard my own need to be safe, my grief for a failed marriage. As broken as I felt, I knew that O.J.'s situation had to be much worse. He'd been with Nicole for seventeen years, and he desperately missed living with his children.

Why had his marriage soured? O.J. was more sorrowful than accusing. He said he'd worked hard to give his family material comforts. But within their affluent lifestyle, he and Nicole were moving on two separate tracks.

It was as if, O.J. said, he'd kept trying to buy his wife's love and approval. Not just with gifts and vacations, but by supporting her entire family. He'd bought and bought until their romance had turned into a transaction. Until their marriage was a commodity, an empty shell.

As the days passed, our mutual crush became a full-fledged infatuation, thanks to Ma Bell. O.J. and I actually got to know each other, to really *like* each other, over the phone. There was sexual tension crackling over those wires, but it had a light quality. Physicality wasn't possible, and for me that was a great relief.

I'd never communicated like this with a man before. O.J. held nothing back. He seemed a man who had nothing to hide. How could I help trusting him?

It was only much later that I'd find a hidden side to the man, like the dark side of the moon — or the bottom of a rock.

At last I gave in. I agreed to come out to Brentwood and take a walk: my first date with O.J. I went casually dressed — a summer sweater, black jeans, cowboy boots — but I couldn't check the eagerness I felt.

I wasn't yet sure where O.J. and I were going, but I couldn't wait to get there.

The day was cool and sunny. The air smelled clean. O.J. and I held hands and talked about movie musicals. When O.J. found out that I'd never seen *My Fair Lady,* he got all enthusiastic; we'd have to rent it and watch it later on.

"You know," he said, "I'd like you to be *my* fair lady." We turned and looked at each other; his eyes were large and soft, with long, curly lashes. He tilted his head toward mine, and we had a light, sweet kiss. I remember thinking that it was the first time I'd kissed someone with lips as large as mine — they were like big, soft pillows, and I kind of bounced off them.

It was a fabulous kiss, for what it was and what it promised.

That evening we were back on the couch that divided O.J.'s living room from the dining room, facing his big-screen television. There were two smaller TVs, on either side, to show various football or basketball games at the same time. The cabinet was set in a wall of Tudor windows, so you could see out to the flowers and the swimming pool beyond. It was an informal house, a place to put your feet up.

Watching *My Fair Lady* with O.J. was a multimedia experience. He knew most of the dialogue by heart and all of the songs, and he sang along with each one of them. He wasn't the greatest singer in the world — he'd hit about two notes out of three — but he loved to sing and never got embarrassed.

"Wouldn't it be fun," he said, "if we could go through life singing everything that we thought?"

Not for me — I wouldn't even sing in the shower. When I was a little girl, someone told me never to sing in front of a man I loved, because he would surely run away. I'd felt inhibited ever since and envied O.J.'s lack of self-consciousness.

We'd started the movie sitting up on the couch and soon were leaning on one another. By the intermission we were lying down, cuddled together. I noticed that O.J.'s eyes kept flitting from the screen. Whenever he talked to me, they were fixed on my summer sweater.

To be precise, he was talking to my breasts.

"I'm up here, I'm up here," I said, laughing . . . and then he was up there, too, for another kiss, this one more searching. I hadn't been with a man since my marriage had ended, five months earlier, and I was thirsting for physical affection.

My Fair Lady is a very long movie. You can really get to know someone before Eliza gets to the dress ball. By that point we were kissing even through the songs, and I can't swear I heard every chorus.

It took most of my self-control to get through that movie with my sweater in place. It took the rest of it to leave O.J. after our good-night kiss, so deep and hard and long that my knees about buckled. Months later, when O.J. fully understood how a kiss can set me off, he'd tease me without mercy about that night. "Boy," he'd say, "you must have been going *crazy*."

He was right: I was.

Once we started going out, O.J. gave me a videotape of his greatest athletic hits. I was moved to see him carry the torch at the 1968

Olympics and bowled over by his football highlights. It was just amazing to me how he could twist up like a pretzel and change direction. Though I knew nothing about the game, I could see that he'd been a spectacular runner.

He'd also paid the price. O.J.'s knees were shot. The cartilage was completely gone; his joints were bone on bone. His doctor in New York kept telling him that he needed his knees replaced, and O.J. kept putting it off. It was so, so sad to watch him creak up the stairs or have to lean on me when we went out — he could remind me of his arthritic chow, Chachi. O.J. was a Hall of Fame running back, one of the most gifted athletes ever, and now he couldn't chase down his four-year-old son.

But O.J.'s knees were the only old part of him. In spirit, he was more youthful than men I knew in their twenties. O.J. was still learning, still growing. For me, that mattered more than any number.

I knew he had his flaws. Sometimes I'd step back and look at him and think, *What a peacock.* When O.J. invited me down to San Diego for a golf lesson with Marcus and Cathryn, I jumped at the opportunity. I imagined O.J.'s arms entwined around me, guiding my swing, as if he were teaching me a new dance . . . But when we got to the course, O.J. dashed my fantasy. He found a partner and jumped on a cart, leaving the three beginners with our teacher. He just couldn't be bored to stick around.

I got over that small disappointment, only to be confronted with a bigger one. O.J. came out to my condo late one Sunday, and I could tell something was wrong by how subdued he was. "You know, I really like you, and I need to tell you this," he said. "I lied to you when I said I was playing golf today. I was at Disneyland with Nicole and the kids."

Seeing me knocked off-balance, O.J. earnestly went on, "I want our relationship to be honest, and you need to know this had nothing to do with Nicole. It was just a day for the children."

I might have taken the news as a yellow flag. But I didn't *want* to see it that way. I'd taken heart when O.J. told me that Nicole had met someone in Mexico just days before my first trip to

Rockingham. I'd cheered to myself when Nicole started asking O.J.'s advice on what to do with this man — it turned out that an ex-girlfriend remained in the picture. It sounded like O.J. and Nicole were both moving on.

I was betting my heart on it. I was falling in love, plunging headfirst.

Everything about O.J. now had a rosy glow about it. I loved the way that he talked with his hands, how those long E.T. fingers would reach out for me. Even O.J.'s strutting became a sweet thing. I was charmed by how he walked into his barber shop and bantered with the lady who'd cut his hair for years. He carried himself with so much self-confidence; he just loved being who he was, and it showed.

More and more, we felt like a perfect match. At six-two to my five-nine, O.J. was just the right height for me, with a shoulder I could literally lean on. When we walked side by side, he seemed a tower of strength.

And, oh, the way he smelled — vanilla with citrus when he used the Fahrenheit I got for him, pure vanilla when he didn't wear cologne. Even when O.J. had played golf and perspired, he smelled of that same sweet scent. I could never be too close. I could never get enough.

O.J. and I just clicked from the start. In those first few weeks of dating, I could sense what he was thinking or feeling. Which wasn't always so difficult, admittedly, since a good deal of the time it centered on sex.

Often we'd say the same thing at once, or he'd grin when I stole the words from his mouth. There were times when I felt enchanted, bewitched — and more and more ready to be seduced.

Shortly after O.J.'s arrest, in my first appearance with Diane Sawyer, I described O.J.'s allure this way: "I think the connection we have is spiritual. It was always from the beginning . . . a thing of communication — what we're feeling, what we believe, aren't we lucky in life?"

As any red-blooded girl will tell you, however, you can't split the spirit from the body. O.J. never let me forget I was a woman, *his* woman. His masculine style was one part chivalry (O.J. was strictly from the old school when it came to chairs and doors), one part verbal seduction (his "Good *morning*, Peola" could set me off), and about five parts sheer animal magnetism.

To feel O.J.'s hand on my arm, at my waist — his lightest touch would give me gooseflesh. His briefest kiss would make me lose my place; I'd actually forget where I was. Then O.J. would whisper something romantic in my ear, and I'd feel my toes tingle. . . .

We were so in tune that we'd get giddy, so in tune that I couldn't imagine dating anyone else. No two people could possibly share so much unless their wavelength was exclusive. O.J. and I had our own private channel.

And yet . . . a tiny voice deep inside me kept crying for attention. It warned that our timing was rotten — that O.J. had yet to absorb his separation, while I had scarcely bid good-bye to my short-lived groom. It was an old story for me: to exchange Band-Aids with a man before we'd cleaned out our wounds.

I closed my ears to that small voice. I would hear no evil, even after the warning came true and my whole world tumbled down.

Years later, I would wonder what might have happened if I'd stayed true to my purpose and set O.J. up with Pam. I do believe that we could have been friends. Where would he and I be today? There is no way of telling and no use in guessing, but it tempts me to wonder just the same.

Early in our courship, O.J. called me and said, "You know my beach house in Laguna that I told you about?"

"Yeah?"

"Why don't we drive down on Friday — we'll have a great weekend."

I didn't know what to say. To go away with him was a huge step — was I ready? Sensing my reluctance, O.J. added, "Don't take this the wrong way — you can have your own room, and Marcus and Cathryn will meet us down there."

I told him yes, and then I was *really* nervous. Laguna was what I'd call a road trip, some fifty miles down the coast. By the time that weekend was over, we'd have spent enough time together to know if our relationship was as wonderful as it seemed.

Or, on the other hand, if we would drive each other crazy.

Come Friday, we set off in O.J.'s black Bentley, a plush boat of a car that floated over the road. It was something like a Rolls-Royce, all leather and polished wood inside. We played the CDs we both liked best — Aaron Neville, the Winans — and talked and talked the whole way.

We were a few miles from Laguna when O.J.'s cell phone rang. He clicked on the speaker; it was Cathryn. "Hey, what are you guys doing?" she said brightly.

O.J. immediately clicked off the speaker and picked up the phone to talk. But it was too late. "What is — what was — what does she mean?" I stuttered. O.J. sighed and put the speaker phone back on, and I said to Cathryn, "What do you mean, what are we doing? Aren't you on your way down to Laguna?"

"I don't think so," Cathryn said, sounding puzzled. "Marcus is watching some game or something, and he's looking pretty comfortable."

With that, O.J. and I burst out laughing. His game was up. "Well, I knew you wouldn't go unless I told you they'd be there," he said, trying to sound apologetic but knowing I wasn't really angry. In truth, I appreciated O.J.'s craftiness.

And anyway, I'd still have my own bedroom.

The old-fashioned beach house was secluded and all that I'd imagined, with driftwood and shells scattered about. We did meet one of O.J.'s friends there: Dino Buccola, who used to live with Denise Brown, Nicole's sister.

The three of us drove out to a Japanese restaurant. We ate sushi and drank more than a few cups of sake, setting the pattern for many a romantic time to follow.

Then we went to play pool. I don't play very well, but I could tell that O.J. admired my game, especially when I bent over to hit the cue ball and I felt his eyes on my bottom.

"She's awful cute in those black jeans," O.J. said, nudging Dino. Still bent over, I turned my head to look back over my shoulder and smile. Some heavy-duty flirting, and I was relishing every minute of it. There's nothing like five months of celibacy to heighten a girl's sexual tension.

Dino drove the Bentley home, with O.J. in the front seat next to him and me in the back. "Hey, I feel like the chauffeur anyway," Dino said. "Why aren't you sitting in the back with Paula?"

"Yeah, why aren't you?" I chimed in.

Say no more. The gimpy-kneed O.J. Simpson climbed over the seat to join me, as nimble as the man for Hertz. He put his arm around me in that cushioned backseat and gave me a kiss that laid me out, right there. It was a kiss that said, *This girl likes me — I'm in.*

Back at the house we said good night to Dino, who was clever enough to go straight upstairs. Then we found a soft loveseat on the deck and sat barefoot and talked. And talked. And drank lots of champagne. The moon shone silver on the water. The surf met the shore just yards from the deck.

Some girls get excited by flowers or candy, others by champagne or soft jazz. I'd enjoyed all of the above from time to time, but for me one aphrodisiac beat all the rest: intimate conversation.

As I've already said, no man had ever talked to me like O.J. That night he was on his best form. We talked about family and friends, our careers and our dreams.

Most of all, we talked about our feelings for each other. It seemed a miracle: One afternoon Marcus Allen happened to spot my Toyota, and that fluke had changed everything. It was phenomenal to feel so connected, to find someone who really *understood.* "That's what I love about you," I told O.J. "You really listen to what I'm feeling."

"I was just waiting," he said. "And the first time I saw you, I fell in love with you — I just *knew* you were the one, girl, as soon as I saw that smile. . . ."

I tugged at O.J.'s wrist and asked him to take me to the beach. As we stepped down the stairs, O.J.'s arm around my waist, he never stopped talking. When O.J. got romantic, his patter went on automatic, like a melody he knew by heart: *"Girl, I want you; girl, you're the one for me; girl, I want to make you happy —"*

On paper, that might look like just another line from a guy in the heat of desire. But float those words in the sea breeze, dip them in bubbly, and lock them in with a football player's tight hold — how could any girl resist?

O.J. was still crooning when he kissed me and ran his fingers through my hair. My skin tingled from the salt air and Dom Pérignon, and now from his touch. He stroked my cheek, my neck, his hand at once tender and strong. I pulled his face to mine, and we kissed deeply. The night had been warm to begin with, and now it felt positively tropical.

Then I broke the clinch. O.J. looked surprised. He looked more surprised when I shed my blouse, my jeans, and then my very lacy La Perla panties, which I flung into the Pacific surf. I ran from him to the cold water, with a little scream as I met a wave. I felt so free, so in love.

I'd assumed that O.J. would follow. Here I was, naked and hot in the ocean. I might as well have held up a neon sign: *Take me here, take me now*. But O.J. just stood there, and laughed, and watched. I didn't know then how uncomfortable he was around the water. He was a guy with a beach house; I figured the beach was an extension of his bed.

"Come on, come on out," he waved. I ran to him and grabbed his hand, tried to pull him into the water. He wouldn't budge. Instead, he pulled me to him. Naked and shivering, I found him warm to the touch. His hug was a haven amid the crashing waves, a still retreat from the whirl of the world. I felt a sense of safety in that embrace, a feeling long lost to me. *I would follow this man anywhere,* I thought.

Just then, O.J. wanted me to follow him to the stairs leading back to the deck. I stopped to kiss him, to nibble on his neck. I was envisioning that steamy love scene in *From Here to Eternity,* when

Burt Lancaster and Deborah Kerr fling themselves upon the sand.

But O.J. pulled on. "I hate sand," he whispered apologetically.

We stopped at the top of the stairs to gaze at the ocean. What a sight we must have been — O.J. fully dressed and drenched from my hugs, me butt naked and quivering in his arms.

I ran into his room and hopped onto the four-poster bed. O.J. followed. "Aren't you going to your room?" He smiled, like a little boy who'd just found a hidden treasure.

I shook my head. I wanted him so much.

As O.J. methodically undressed, I marveled at his body. I'd never seen such a sculpted torso. His abdominal muscles looked carved from granite; his bottom was high and round. But those skinny legs seemed so out of place. I couldn't help thinking of E.T. again.

I sat up on the bed and kissed O.J.'s rib cage. As my lips moved down his side, O.J. gently cupped my head and told me to stop. As the director of this scene, he wanted to stay in control.

He lay down beside me, and our pillow lips touched. Yes, it was electric. But I noticed something then that I'd see over and over in months to come: As soon as O.J. felt impassioned, he'd close his eyes. I wished that he'd open them. I wanted him to look at me, look *into* me. But I said not a word.

O.J.'s hands roved down my body. He started talking to my breasts as if they were two other girls. "You are beautiful," he said to the right one. Then he kissed the left one and said, "I'm not ignoring you."

Our foreplay was brief, which was fine by me, since I was working on endless anticipation. O.J. pinned me to the bed and took control of me, practically smothering me with the mass of his body.

We're finally making love. The thought exhilarated me — more so than the act itself, I'm afraid. Was it the alcohol? Too much buildup in my imagination? In any case, our fantasy ended too quickly for me. Yet I wasn't disappointed. It's hard to explain, but the simple fact of our intimacy had fulfilled me, though the lovemaking itself had been less than satisfying.

O.J. was done, and there would be no more conversation that night, not with my breasts and not with me. He quickly fell asleep. Still giddy with my thoughts, I left him on the bed and resumed my skinny dip. The beach felt like it belonged to me; the ocean was my private pool. I was alone and free, or so I thought.

Only later would I realize that my freedom was an illusion. That my happiness hinged on a man who slept on, oblivious, as I swam naked through the sea.

If parting made the heart grow fonder, no one could be more in love than O.J. and I. Between my photo shoots and his appearances for Hertz and other sponsors, at least one of us was constantly leaving. Every minute together was precious. We'd juggle our flight schedules to meet at the airport in Atlanta or Chicago and have a cup of coffee — or, more than once, just a kiss on the run.

With Dolph Lundgren, the Swedish actor who was my first love, I'd learned what it meant to date a well-known face. I hadn't altogether liked it. Once I was seeing Dolph off to Dallas, and at the last minute he begged me to come with him. I hated leaving him; I got on the plane.

After landing we went straight to a mall for a video signing. As the line snaked up to Dolph for autographs, I spied a chesty young woman who had *trouble* written all over her. Sure enough, when she got to the front she stuck her hand in Dolph's pocket and actually grabbed his crotch. She looked right at me and said, "Is that your girlfriend?" With cameras all around, I knew I couldn't react. It was such a terrible, trapped feeling.

But nothing like that ever happened when I was with O.J. It wasn't that he avoided the public. Where Dolph was self-contained and protective, O.J. was accessible to everyone. He'd joke with people about their accents, ask where they were from. He'd strike up conversations with fellow customers at a clothing store or with some kid who pumped his gas. We were both that way; we liked to find out what made people tick.

I never saw O.J. brush anyone off, even when he was in a hurry. Once we were late for a flight when a guy came up alongside and asked O.J. for his autograph.

"Sure, man, if you can keep up with us, gimme your pen," O.J. said. The guy grabbed O.J.'s bag, and O.J. took his pen, and they were running down the concourse with O.J. signing at the same time.

That summer we established our relationship of good-byes. Though we'd rarely go more than two or three days apart, I hated those leave-takings. I wasn't any good at them. I'd say "See ya" instead. That didn't sound so sad and final.

I'd miss O.J. terribly. Then, when I was about to see him again, I'd get as nervous as a teenager, even if I'd left him but the night before. I'd change my clothes four or five times, until I looked just right.

It meant everything to make O.J. smile and look at me in that smoldering way of his. After our night by the beach together, it was as if the dam had burst. I wanted O.J. all the time. I think he knew full well the hold he had over me, and he slyly pushed his power to the limit.

At restaurants or dinner parties, where we'd sit side by side, I'd feel O.J.'s knee pressing into mine before the first glass of wine was poured. By the time the entrees came, those long fingers would be roaming under the tablecloth . . . caressing my thighs . . . until I'd lose track of what the people across from us were saying and just nod and smile and glassily repeat, "That's great."

Which could be embarrassing if the topic was a friend's recent appendectomy.

These little games of his were torture, and so delicious. In bed, however, O.J. was hardly the sexual Superman that the world may have assumed. He never went down, as they say in football — his lips worked best in telling me how much he loved me, not in exploring my body. For myself, that was more than a fair trade.

Just as he'd always played running back in football, O.J. liked the familiarity of one basic position when loving me. He always wanted to be on top — not just to control the situation, but to keep my appetite in check and preserve his strength for the next morning's golf game.

But to O.J.'s credit, he had the gift of finding my most sensitive spots without my having to guide him: the delicate skin above my collarbone, the tips of my earlobes, the outline of my breasts. He loved my long legs. "They just go on forever, don't they?" he'd say, as he caressed them up and down. He'd brag about my body to our friends: "She may not look it, but she has really nice breasts." A true gentleman.

I didn't mind his coarser moments; I was flattered by his attention, his admiration. My biggest thrills with O.J. came outside the bedroom. I'd had a much better lover in Dolph — more creative, more energetic. But what O.J. lacked in stamina or imagination he made up in humor and romance. "With love, all things are possible / If we just believe . . . ," he would sing at the top of his lungs, with a big, big smile. Our duet may not have sounded precisely like BeBe and CeCe Winans', but the intensity of the words swept us away. O.J. made me feel like he needed me. He made me feel like the center of his universe. As I listened to him, I believed.

The first week of July was abuzz with plans for O.J.'s forty-fifth birthday party, an outdoor blast for more than a hundred people at Rockingham. O.J. took me to Azzadene Alia's designer shop on Rodeo Drive to buy a dress for the occasion. He was very patient, told me what he thought looked pretty. I settled on a black lace evening dress, cut just above the knee.

Cathy Randa, O.J.'s secretary, handled most of the organizing. I had little to do but hope that it wouldn't rain, which of course it did: a classic L.A. downpour, with those big, fat drops that soak you to the skin. The dance floor got so slippery that one guest fell down, but we all partied on just the same.

Midway through, O.J. stopped the music and signaled for attention. The two of us stood close under an umbrella as he raised a toast "to the girl who has changed my life." As the crowd let out one of those corny groans and O.J. kissed me, I positively shone. I felt so loved and appreciated, so right with this wonderful man.

Five minutes later I turned around to catch O.J. reaching over to kiss a petite blonde who'd arrived with an NBC executive. This wasn't a social peck on the cheek. O.J.'s tongue was down her throat.

O.J. flirted every day of his life: a look here, a smile there. Mostly I ignored it, because I knew it wasn't serious, just a game some men play. But that kiss was disrespectful, and I asked some friends to drive me home.

"Look, I'm really sorry, I was an idiot," O.J. said when he rang me the next morning. "I had too much to drink — it wasn't like it seemed."

"That's so typical," I shot back. "You can't blame it on the alcohol."

"You *have* to forgive me," O.J. said. "Please, please, *please* let me take you somewhere to talk."

I listened to him and agreed to make up. The next day O.J. took me to a jeweler's and gave me a gold friendship ring he'd had prepared there. Given his timing, I think it was O.J.'s way of saying, *I take you seriously — you matter to me.*

The ring was made in the deco style I adore, with a cluster of small diamonds and rubies. As O.J. placed it on the fourth finger of my right hand, he told me how much he loved me, and we kissed.

That night our loving had a ferocious urgency — I wanted to lose myself in our tangle of limbs. I needed to erase the tension and distance between us, to exorcise the abandonment I felt. And it worked, of course, at least for those fifteen minutes.

Our little crisis was officially over.

But I stayed mad for some time. I couldn't just put that party kiss away. It brought me back to the first day we'd met, when Robin came down the stairs and all my better judgment told me not to take this man seriously.

Better step lightly here, girl, I told myself.

Men were one of life's great mysteries. The more I thought I knew them, the more I found I didn't know at all.

Later that month we went back to Laguna for my third time. This time Marcus and Cathryn did come along, and the four of us went out to the pool hall after dinner.

For privacy we played at a table that was railed off from the rest. I noticed a man standing just outside our area, watching us play. It's possible I smiled at him; I'd had my quota of sake that night and was feeling very relaxed.

In the middle of our game the man asked me some harmless question. It wasn't a come-on, and I answered without thinking twice. But O.J. had noticed my open body language — I was leaning against the rail, with one arm over my head — and assumed the worst. He put down his cue and walked out. I knew he was furious.

By the time Marcus and Cathryn and I got outside, the Bronco was running. We were barely out of the parking lot before O.J. jumped on my "flirting." I denied it but he wouldn't let it drop, and soon we were shouting at each other.

I don't put up with verbal attacks; my first instinct is to leave. "Look," I told O.J., "I'm just going to go home." I picked up the Bronco's cell phone and started to dial a car service — and O.J. grabbed the phone and knocked it out of my hand, hurting me.

Our friends looked nervous in the backseat; they knew that this quarrel wasn't over. As soon as we got to the beach house, I jumped out of the car and ran into the downstairs master bedroom. I locked the door and threw my things into a bag.

By that time O.J. was knocking at the door, full-fisted, demanding to be let in. I yelled at him to go away. I was angry and frightened, and I didn't want to deal with him.

"Open this door," O.J. barked, "or I'm going to kick it down." As he kept banging, I got more and more frantic. I packed my things and called a car service, then burst into tears and hung up after getting put on hold.

"Open the *door!*" O.J. hollered. The banging got louder. I curled up in a ball in the farthest corner of the room. What could I do? How would I get out of this? Finally, after what felt like an eternity, I decided to leave and find a taxi.

Feeling defeated, I opened the door and walked by O.J. to get past him. But he grabbed my bag, and as we stood nose to nose in the doorway I could see how ashamed he was.

"I'm so sorry," he said softly. "I love you — I *never* want to hurt you."

As you might have guessed, I wound up staying. I went out for another night swim, and O.J. watched me again from the beach. He never went in the water — not in the ocean, not in the pool in his own backyard. I figured it was some phobia he had. Or maybe the memory of Aaren, his little daughter from his first marriage, who'd drowned in the Rockingham pool in 1979.

When I got out he toweled me off and we sat there watching the waves, not speaking for several minutes. Finally O.J. said, "You know, I never want to be in that kind of relationship — I *hate* that."

Then he told me about the now-famous incident in 1989, after he and Nicole came home from a New Year's Eve party. They got into a huge argument, O.J. said, and Nicole started screaming and breaking their Tiffany lamps.

"I was trying to push her out of the bedroom, and she fell down," O.J. explained. The police came, he added, and he eventually pleaded no contest to a misdemeanor.

"Right then and there," O.J. said emphatically, "I swore that I'd never lay hands on another woman like that."

I wasn't sure how to react. My mother was a battered woman, and O.J.'s story took me back to some scary days and nights. But though I'd be horribly embarrassed to face Marcus and Cathryn the next morning, I felt good about O.J.'s candor with me. I could tell that he'd waged a big struggle with himself to control his temper. I wanted to believe that the fight with Nicole was an isolated incident.

He didn't really hurt me, I thought. *He didn't really hit me.*

It might sound naive, but I'd promised myself years before

that no man would lay his hands on me without feeling *really* sorry.

Dolph Lundgren could testify to that.

A third-degree black belt, Dolph had taught me a fair amount of karate. One night, at a VIP party after the Tyson-Spinks fight in Atlantic City, I got up to dance with a bunch of girls. When Refrigerator Perry, the jumbo-size football player, joined our group, Dolph got mad. He grabbed my upper arm to pull me away, at which point Mr. Perry's massive friends circled Dolph and removed his hands from me.

"Quit manhandling the girl," one of them said in a tone that brooked no argument.

Drunk and frustrated, Dolph stewed in the limo all the way back to New York. When we got to our hotel suite, he erupted. I ran into the shower to get as far away as I could. After Dolph invaded the bathroom, I shuffled by and picked up my bags. Dolph tried to yank them away from me, and then he threatened, "If you leave, I'm gonna jump" — as in out the window.

I didn't want to hear it and kept moving toward the door. Enraged, Dolph grabbed me around the shoulders, hard.

Big mistake.

I flattened the back of my hand and hit Dolph square in the nose, just like he'd taught me. He went down like a tree, holding his nose — the only thing missing was someone shouting, "Timber!" I ran from the suite, not wanting a rematch.

Like Dolph, O.J. Simpson wasn't a passive personality. Loud and animated when trying to make a point, he'd get louder still when on the defensive. But that moment in the Bronco was the only time he'd ever touch me in anger.

In the months and years that followed, he never struck me.

At least not in the ways that show bruises.

The truth is, I felt closer than ever to O.J. after our fight in Laguna. When he held me that night, he was so patient, so sweetly attentive, as if to show both of us that he wasn't some fearsome beast. When it was over, *I* was the teary one. I was touched by O.J.'s shame and by his eagerness to be better.

Everything's fine, I thought as I lovingly held his head to my breast till I knew he was asleep. *Everything's fine.*

In early August I flew out to join O.J. at the Barcelona Olympics, where he was covering track and field for NBC: my first opportunity to watch him on the job.

As someone who had trouble getting her hair dryer to work in foreign countries, I was fascinated by the track and field studio. There was so much going on in such a small space, and somehow it all fit together.

O.J. was conscientious about his assignments. He'd prepare for an event days ahead. He'd get all the background he could about each athlete, studying the stats till he could rattle them off.

But O.J.'s strongest suit was his intuition. From his own athletic experience, he knew that motivation outweighed statistics. After interviewing the top contenders in a race, he'd have a pretty strong feeling as to who would win. I remember how impressed he was with Gail Devers going into the women's 100-meter hurdles, even before she picked herself up from a fall and persevered to place.

One evening, when O.J. was off, we had tickets to a Dream Team basketball game. I was taken by how the American players could pass the ball without looking at one another. They were obviously far and above their competition.

A day or two later, a walk through the Olympic Village put that game in perspective. It was startling to see such contrasts of wealth and poverty in such close quarters. I'll never forget a group of Kenyan long-distance runners who'd run barefoot all their lives lining up to get free shoes from Reebok.

For passionate travelers like O.J. and myself, Barcelona was a nonstop adventure. We went to the Picasso Museum, where I discovered how much I liked the artist's early work. We found a delightful restaurant down a narrow, cobblestoned street, and I had my first paella.

Much of the time we played tourist, buying T-shirts and souvenirs. Despite the crowds, no one ever bothered O.J. Even Magic Johnson and his lanky teammates strolled about without getting hounded for autographs. They could just be normal people for a change.

In addition to our hotel in town, the network had booked cabins for its people on a cruise ship docked nearby. We had a tiny one right next to the engine room, which boomed all night long — and we didn't mind a bit. We were like kids in a candy store. Our lovemaking was full of silliness and play (O.J. could be a relentless tickler). And O.J. put on a one-man show, marching around the tiny stateroom in his knobby-kneed altogether. Henry Higgins and Colonel Pickering would have been . . . proud? appalled? Me, I thought he was cute — a peacock, yes, but a charming peacock.

> *Why can't a woman be more like a man? . . .*
> *Men are so pleasant, so easy to please.*
> *Whenever you're with them, you're always at ease.*
>
> *Would you be slighted if I didn't speak for hours?*
> *Would you be livid if I had a drink or two?*
> *Would you be wounded if I never sent you flowers?*
> *Well, why can't a woman be like you?*

"Good thing I'm not!" I laughed, tauntingly.

> *One man in a million may shout a bit.*
> *Now and then there's one with slight defects.*
> *One perhaps whose truthfulness you doubt a bit . . . but . . .*
> *By and large we are a marvelous sex!*

One of our fellow passengers was an eight-year-old child who'd been sponsored by the Make-a-Wish Foundation. The boy had lost his hair from chemotherapy, but he seemed happy and unafraid, and O.J. sort of adopted him. He made that boy laugh and laugh, just by cracking his corny jokes. Just by treating him like anyone else.

I could see how much it meant to the boy, who looked at O.J. as if he were a superhero.

That was the man I loved. There were no cameras on that ship, nothing to gain by catering to a sick child.

It was a side to O.J. that few would ever see.

I think I started taking our relationship seriously on August 13, 1992, the night before Magic Johnson's birthday party at Magic Mountain.

My day had gotten off to a rough start. Early that afternoon I was minding my own business in the bathtub, my place to be lazy and relax. I'd light a candle, put on my music, and let Calgon do its soothing work. If I could fit them in, I'd take two baths a day.

I was rousted by a surprise visitor: Dean Hamilton, my ex-husband. He came with his standard tale of woe: He was about to lose his house in Malibu, he lamented. His father would be out on the street.

Dean was doing his best to charm me, but I knew he was after a loan. I also knew that O.J. would be picking me up any minute, and that life would get lots more complicated if Dean wasn't out of there first.

My phone rang: O.J. from his car, about to pull in to my building. "See you soon," I said to O.J.

"I can't talk right now," I said sharply to Dean. "You've got to go."

Figuring he had some leverage, Dean said, "Aren't you going to kiss me good-bye first?"

I didn't want to kiss him, but this was an emergency. I shut my eyes and kissed Dean on the lips and wondered: *How could I ever have married this man?*

Just seconds after Dean made his smug little way out the door, the phone rang again. It was Paul, my concierge: "O.J. Simpson is here; should I send him up?"

At that very moment Dean passed O.J. in the lobby, looking like the cat who'd swallowed the canary. O.J. apparently recognized him from a photo in my living room. "I guess I came at the wrong time," O.J. said, loud enough that I could hear him through Paul's phone.

Damn, I thought. *What am I going to do?* I had one foot in the future, the other stuck in the past; I felt like I was being split in half. I can't even date two men at the same time, much less have them pass each other in my lobby. For lack of a better idea, I told Paul, "Send him up."

I took stock. It did not look good. I was in my bathrobe. My hair was disheveled. A pile of laundry sat in my living room; Dean's visit had left me behind schedule.

My heart was pounding. My lips still burned from my guilty kiss with Dean. What would O.J. think? What could I possibly tell him?

I frantically picked up the clothes and threw them into the laundry room. Then I opened the door and faced the music.

"I guess I came at the wrong time," O.J. repeated with that funny smile of his. As he followed me into the living room, I nearly screamed. My cream-colored La Perla panties were lying in the middle of the floor — I'd apparently dropped them in my hurry. I stopped dead and tried to cover them with my feet.

"You know, I can't talk right now," I said. I knew I was blushing. I felt like Lucy Ricardo after Ricky caught her in some outrageous predicament.

O.J. ignored me. He was staring straight at my feet, at the cream silk peeking out from between my toes. "Let me guess," he said, drawing it out for effect. "You saw him, and your underwear just dropped off your body."

It was time to forget about the evening, if not the relationship. Time to go back to the tub for a good soak — say, about three days' worth. "This is difficult for me, so let's make it easy, okay?"

I said, fighting to keep my voice steady. "Why don't you just leave now."

And that is when O.J. began to truly win me. "No, I want to stay," he said. "I like you, I really like you, and I want to find out what's going on here."

We sat down. I was right about one thing: There was no simple way to explain. When I insisted that Dean meant nothing to me, O.J. said that made no sense. If it was over between us, why had Dean been here?

John Gray could have had a field day with the two of us.

O.J. stayed at my apartment, held me in his arms till morning. That was special for me — he'd gone the extra mile to understand. He could have been solemn and accusing about Dean and our little French farce. Instead he was supportive and loving.

When we touched that night — and I needed so much to touch O.J., to feel that he was really *there* — it was a little different from before. Our passion still burned, but it was laced with a caring and gentleness that made it even more powerful. And, I thought, more significant.

At the start of our romance, O.J. had declared, "As far as I'm concerned, you were a virgin until the day we met." Now I saw he was as good as his word.

As I snuggled up against him, I admitted that I still felt responsible for Dean. O.J. cut to the heart of it: "Why do you need to take care of everyone — you mother, your father, your brothers, even this guy who takes advantage of you?"

I thought of what my older brother Vinnie once told me: "Do you realize that you've been giving me advice ever since you were eighteen, and I'm the big brother?"

O.J. could identify — he played the same role in his own family. After he told me he'd helped one relative buy a home, O.J. found out the man's master plan: to move in with a friend and keep a second home while O.J. footed the bill.

In most of my relationships, I was the responsible one, the person in control. But O.J. was different. However strong and independent I might be, he was still a man to be leaned on. One who'd never let me fall.

We took each other as equal partners, the way I'd always wanted it to be.

Heading out for Magic Johnson's birthday party the following evening, I dressed a lot more casually than I felt: white jeans, white tank top, cowboy boots. I put on my usual minimal makeup: some light spice lipstick, my nude color.

As soon as O.J. and I emerged from the Bentley to enter Magic Mountain, I got my second big shock in two days. I'd known this would be a big party. But I hadn't counted on the flock of photographers flitting about the admission gate. Flashes were popping like the Fourth of July.

I panicked. It was the first time for O.J. and me as a public item, and the potential for backlash suddenly hit me.

My mother already knew about us. Though concerned about our age difference, she hadn't been fazed by my dating a black man. But Dad would be different. I'd been deathly afraid to tell him about O.J.; I knew too well his strong and hostile views about interracial relationships. I can't tell you why I had to please my father. He'd deserted our family and had never been around when I needed him. I knew he was wrong about race, among many other things.

But I was still his daughter; I still yearned for his acceptance. I would break the news about my famous boyfriend in time. For now, though, the last thing I wanted was for Dad to pick up his morning paper and see his daughter on the arm of O.J. Simpson.

There is a poignant photograph of our entrance into Magic Mountain. It shows me putting as much distance as I can between me and O.J., the guilt and turmoil plain on my face. And there's O.J., looking back for me, picking up on my withdrawal, but all the while keeping his meet-the-public, "got-to-get-it-together" smile.

Once the paparazzi gauntlet was behind us, we had a good time that night. O.J. didn't like roller coasters, but he won me a stuffed bear in a fishbowl game. En Vogue sang an incredible "Happy Birthday" to Magic. And I had my first Shaquille O'Neal sighting. "Oh, my goodness," I said, when I saw how tiny O.J. looked next to him.

(When his grown daughter, Arnelle, started dating Shaquille, O.J. would voice some fatherly concern. "Do you think that he's ruining my daughter?" he asked me in jest.)

During the trial, one of the tabloids would claim that O.J. was so upset with me at Magic's party that he punched me in the stomach. It was a total fabrication, but we *did* have some physical contact that night. We ducked behind a row of bushes to neck, long enough to make the friends we were with come hunting for us.

When I was in O.J.'s arms and felt his lips on mine, the rest of the world didn't matter so much.

4

No Complaints

I felt most content at Rocking-
ham outside the house, in the garden, where roses and jasmine
sweetened the air. I'd grown up by the water, and my favorite
days were passed in O.J.'s swimming pool, with its slide and water-
fall, or in the adjacent Jacuzzi. A bridge between the two led to a
gazebo, thoughtfully equipped with a telephone, with the tennis
court beyond.

It was intoxicating to swim among the flowers; I felt like I'd
stumbled upon the Garden of Eden. The water gave me peace,
suspended any stress.

The house itself was more than comfortable, though its off-
white color scheme was too subdued to fit O.J.'s personality. There
was a baby grand piano that O.J. didn't play and some lovely stone
fireplaces that were rarely lit.

O.J. had paid Nicole to decorate their home when they were
married. But I felt little of her presence there, though I did ask
O.J. to remove a set of photos, lining the stairway, of Nicole holding their children as infants. They were beautiful pictures, but it

was hard to feel romantic when I passed them going up to his bedroom.

O.J. liked staying at my place, and I preferred it, too. It made me feel safe to have my own identity, something apart from any man. That apartment was perfect for me. It felt modern, yet soft and sensual at the same time: lots of glass and wood, with dried-flower arrangements everywhere.

The color scheme ran mainly to emerald and white. A marble entryway led to a kitchen with white countertops and black appliances. In the living room I had an L-shaped couch, cream-colored with a white silk print. I'd painted the walls blue-gray, the color of the sky back home in Florida when a storm was brewing.

A certified neat freak, I kept the place uncluttered. I'd collected a few special objects: a statue of a mother and child, draped in cloth; a painting of angel-winged clowns climbing a ladder into the clouds; a ceramic, life-size Doberman pinscher that never failed to scare the UPS man.

O.J. liked the lighting from my crystal chandeliers, which we'd soften to match our mood, and the way my stereo piped the Four Tops into my bedroom. On rainy afternoons we spent many an hour there, lazing in our cave under the blankets.

For dinner I might cook some stuffed peppers or my renowned chili — my chili got marriage proposals. I remember planning one meal around artichokes, only to find out at the last minute that O.J. didn't like them. Without a moment's thought, I started a new meal from scratch.

I was crazy in love; I wanted everything to be special for my man.

In the evening we'd click on one of the old-movie channels and settle in on the couch. O.J. liked almost anything in black and white, especially with Cary Grant or Jimmy Stewart. A good tear-jerker, like *It's a Wonderful Life,* would get him every time. He'd cry more than me, which was saying something.

As much as we liked staying in, a fine sushi restaurant like Matsuhisa was always in order. O.J. liked to drive, but for relaxation, not speed. He rarely took out his red Ferrari, the one with JUICE on the license plates. He preferred to stretch out in the Bentley, turn up the music, cruise down the freeways.

I drove the Bentley just once — I don't think O.J.'s insurance covered me — and it felt like an eighteen-wheeler. I thanked heaven that I didn't have to parallel park.

By the time we met, nightlife held little appeal for O.J. Unless there was some special occasion, he'd want to get home and to bed by 9:30. I'd be a happy camper with my book in my lap and a movie on in the background; O.J. couldn't sleep without the TV on all night. And he needed his rest to be able to rise before dawn and pursue his one great passion in life: his golf game.

Golf was O.J.'s release. At home he'd play nearly every day at the Riviera Country Club. A good day was eighteen holes, a great day was thirty-six. At night he'd be thinking about the game to come. He'd putt in the living room, giving me pointers the whole time. "It's like a handshake," he'd say, and I'd nod politely.

I wanted to share his enthusiasm, but I just didn't get it. It seemed cruel and unusual to get up in the dark for the privilege of chasing a little white ball.

My view changed after O.J. bought me a set of clubs for my birthday and got me some lessons. Then I understood — golf was fabulous therapy. For however many hours, all you worried about was how to avoid the next sand trap. Soon I was putting on the rugs myself at night, and O.J. was so thrilled that I was trying.

"The best thing in the whole wide world," he said, "would be if I could get old playing golf with the person I love."

I might have gotten hooked on the sport, but my jobs kept me hopping around too much to play consistently. I didn't have the patience to check any bags, and I wasn't up to lugging my clubs through an airport. So I didn't mind when O.J. went back to playing those morning rounds without me. It gave me quiet time to myself, not to mention the extra sleep.

⋆ ⋆ ⋆

O.J. rarely went back to San Francisco. I thought that strange — if I lived an hour away from home, I'd be there every weekend. Boys were different, I supposed.

He did talk every week to his mother on the phone, and Mrs. Simpson and her daughters came down to visit a couple of times a year. They were gracious to me, and accepting, but I also picked up on their protectiveness toward O.J.

I remember Shirley, O.J.'s sister, relating something she'd once told Nicole about O.J.'s first wife: that she'd seen Marguerite come and seen Marguerite go, but that Shirley was still there. She told me the story more than once. I took it as a hint not to push O.J.'s family away, that they'd be there after *I* was gone as well.

I felt no hostility from anyone about my being white. O.J. and I moved in a mixed crowd, where race wasn't an issue. I never sensed anything like the time I walked into a soul-food restaurant in Los Angeles with Randy and Jackie Jackson, Michael's brothers. I was the only white girl in there, and several women were pointedly less than pleased to see me with the Jacksons.

For that brief moment, I felt what it meant to be on the receiving end of racial hostility.

O.J. had a lot of friends, but none closer than his old Buffalo teammates. Wherever they gathered, they'd retell their old war stories, embellishing as they went. They even had their own bizarre lingo. I felt like I was back in my early modeling days in Rome before I learned Italian.

I always enjoyed the story about the stuttering lineman who'd freeze up when he came into the huddle to give the next play. One time it got so bad that the Bills were verging on a penalty for delay of game.

Then O.J. got an idea. "Sing it, man!" he said.

Once he put the play to music, the lineman sang it out without a hitch.

Al Cowlings, Bobby Chandler, Reggie McKenzie, Sherman White — they were all hopeless practical jokers. The first time we all got together, in Tahoe, O.J. went on the offensive.

Sherman was about the sweetest soul in the whole world, and very married, though his wife wasn't with him that trip. The night we got to the hotel, before anyone had met me, I knocked on Sherman's door. O.J. was hiding around the corner, two doors down.

"Excuse me, Sherman White?" I drawled in an accent as thick as Louisiana gumbo.

"Yes?" said Sherman, always helpful.

"My name is Mary Jean — your friend Bobby sent me to come by and say hello."

I could see I'd thrown Sherman off, and I pushed right past him and inside. "Oh, this is a pretty room," I said. "Are you going to be here long? I sure hope so, 'cause I just *love* it here in Tahoe."

I flopped down on the couch, and Sherman's mouth dropped to his knees. "Boy, you're tall, aren't you?" I said, and then: "My *goodness,* you've got the biggest hands — let me *see* them."

At that point I noticed that the door had closed behind me. "Ah-ah-ah-would you like something to drink?" he said.

"Oh, I'd *love* a glass of wine."

As Sherman wrestled with the corkscrew, I heard a light knocking at the door. O.J. was ready to end the joke and have a laugh.

"Let me get the door," Sherman said, looking a little relieved.

"Oh, don't bother about that," I said. "Let's just sit here for a while — I want to learn more about you." I turned my head away and bit my lip to keep from howling.

I jabbered on for a good two or three minutes to keep the conversation going. The banging outside got faster and faster, louder and louder. Sherman broke into a grin; he'd finally caught on. He got up, opened the door, saw O.J., and said, "Oh, no, man, come back later."

"That's my girl!" O.J. said, laughing.

I got him good that time, and with his own medicine, too.

But there was another, softer side to O.J.'s friendships. After one of his old pals, a man named Billy, had gotten out of jail, we celebrated by taking him to a movie. Billy had been away so long that he'd never heard Surround Sound. The first time it came on, full blast, he ducked and looked around, obviously startled.

After we dropped Billy off, I could see how sad O.J. felt. He realized how much had changed around his friend, and how hard it would be for Billy to rebuild his life. O.J. felt guilty, too, because he'd never visited Billy in jail.

It was a lapse he'd have time to ponder in days to come.

On October 15, 1992, O.J. went to court and came back smiling. His divorce from Nicole was final. There wasn't any anger in the courtroom, he said. After all those years, all their ups and downs, it felt more like business than anything else.

Rather than pay out monthly alimony, O.J. gave Nicole a lump sum — I believe it was $750,000. He said he wanted to close the book as quickly as possible. That sounded good to me. O.J. never grilled me about Dean or any other men I'd known, and I'd tried to return the favor. It was easy because we were two lonely souls trying to comfort each other.

Now, with the divorce settled, O.J. and I could start fresh.

Looking back, it still rocks me to think how naive I was.

While Nicole and I barely knew each other, I can't say our encounters had been pleasant. One morning at Rockingham, O.J. and I were lingering in bed together, hanging on to a few more delicious minutes before starting our day.

Then I heard footsteps coming up the stairs toward us, and I sat up with a start. A woman's voice rang out: "Anybody home?"

"Damn!" O.J. said. It was Nicole. The front door had been open and she'd strolled right in. Still in my sheer nightgown, I didn't know where to go, what to do. I felt out of place, like *I* was the intruder.

O.J. ran downstairs in his briefs to intercept Nicole. I could hear him grumble, "You know, you can't just walk in here like that." Nicole quickly left, and it took me about five minutes to follow suit. It was time to go to work, anyway, and I didn't feel comfortable hanging around.

We actually met some weeks later, when Nicole came by O.J.'s house to pick up the children. I was struck by how much she looked like Cathryn, Marcus's fiancée: blond and athletic and beautiful.

I went up to Nicole and smiled and stuck out my hand: "Hi, I'm Paula, nice to meet you." I was so happy then, so much into my own world, that I assumed we'd get along. Nicole was seeing someone else, after all, and why not be civilized about it?

Nicole nodded her hello and walked past me. She looked pre-occupied, or in a hurry to get the kids out of there. I was left with my hand out, feeling foolish.

I'd run into her one other time, when I went to pick up Justin at his karate school. Once again, a short hello. By then I wasn't expecting much.

Come autumn and the football season, O.J. moved his base to New York. In a typical week, he'd fly out Wednesday or Thursday to some NFL city to tape a halftime interview for the big game that week. Then he'd edit the interview at his NBC studio in New York. On Sundays, he'd either do commentary from the studio or fly out again to work from the sidelines.

I'd be hopping out to Miami or Los Angeles, meanwhile, on occasion to London or Paris. I still enjoyed modeling, and it was very lucrative; I'd get up to $5,000 a day for my regular catalogue clients, $10,000 a day for a TV commercial. I salted away a little cash into a money market fund, but I wasn't much of a saver. I was living high, and two mortgages were a lot to keep up with.

Then, too, I wasn't pushing quite as hard as I used to in my career. I'd become more selective, less frenetic. I'd learned there was more to life than work.

In particular, there was O.J. New York was like fresh soil for us, and our love grew by the day. We spent nearly all our time together yet couldn't spend enough. I took more red-eyes home than I could count, just to get back to O.J.'s apartment on East 65th Street and see him that much sooner.

When we were both on the road, we still rendezvoused to grab those fleeting kisses. Once O.J. had to choose between jumping on a plane — without his luggage — to have dinner with me at the next airport or waiting for his scheduled connecting flight. When he left the luggage behind, I knew we still had a hot romance. As O.J. never tired of telling me, "The first day I met you is the day that I fell in love with you."

We talked like lovers, and we didn't care if someone overheard. O.J. liked to call me "sweetheart" or "Peola," his special name for me. He still charmed me relentlessly. He still opened every phone call with, "Hey, good-lookin', what's cookin'?"

"*You* are," I'd answer back. It was corny, but I ate it up.

I didn't call him "Juice," which seemed more of a guy thing. But I loved using his full name, Orenthal James, so long and so pretty.

When we stayed with our friends on Long Island, Bobby and Robin Bender, I'd refer to O.J. as "Old Nasty." The owner of a prosperous textiles business, Bobby was a big guy with slicked-back hair, à la Pat Riley. He could match O.J. dig for dig, needle for needle, and I suppose I was trying to keep up with their sarcastic humor. But no one could mistake the affection in my voice for O.J., no matter what I called him.

Los Angeles can get exhausting. I find people there consumed with how they look and what they own and who they know. New York is more exciting to me, because you can be yourself and no one cares. Even celebrities can be anonymous.

And New York is never dull, even when you're doing absolutely nothing — there's so much happening around you. When we stayed in Manhattan, no one hassled us when we were out walking or interrupted us at dinner. In big cities, I've found, it's uncool to act impressed. In New York I was just a girl with her fella, and I loved how normal it seemed.

"Look at that," I'd say lightly when he left me to catch his Wednesday flight. "A guy with a job, going out the door."

Most mornings we'd start our day at a little coffee shop on the corner: bagel and lox for me, a roll and juice for O.J. For dinner we might stroll to Ferrier, a cozy bistro down the block, where we both enjoyed the pasta with lots of fresh garlic.

O.J. liked to eat about as much as he liked to talk; I was lucky to have a metabolism that allowed me to keep up. He'd run through three or four courses, rarely skipping dessert. If he thought he was gaining too much weight, he'd go on a watermelon diet for a few days. It worked every time.

The one thing O.J. passed on was coffee. He just didn't need caffeine. Get him his seven hours of sleep, and he'd be bright and bouncy all the next day.

Aside from meals or some light window shopping or an occasional foray to a club, we didn't go out much in New York. We never quite made it to the theater, though O.J. loved show music. He could sing from *Cats* all day, especially the song that went, "If you touch me, you'll know what happiness is . . ."

(During the trial, when reporters overheard O.J. whistling that tune on his way to the courtroom, a big commotion ensued. People analyzed the lyrics and the hidden meanings they might hold. The reality was more boring: O.J. just happened to like the song, and it lifted his spirits.)

I didn't miss going out. At work, we were professional. Our public faces were glued on — O.J.'s for his sponsors, mine for my clients. When we had the chance to be homebodies, we jumped at it. We were relaxed, frivolous.

His apartment was your basic bachelor two-bedroom, simply furnished, with a great view of Manhattan. It might have been stark, except for a set of bright scarves that O.J. had bought on the street, then had stretched and framed for his walls.

I added a few small homey touches, like some silver decanters for cotton balls in O.J.'s spectacular bathroom. It had an extra-long vanity and the biggest marble bathtub I'd ever seen.

A housekeeper came weekly to clean and stock the refrigerator with milk and juice and diet colas, but otherwise the cupboards were pretty bare. Except for one time when I came back in town to find the fridge loaded with my favorite things: Brie cheese and caviar, peach pie and cheesecake. O.J. had gone shopping, and he was so proud of himself. It was quite a romantic gesture on his part, and we feasted that night.

But the fact is, we didn't need much. Some pretzels or one of O.J.'s beloved cantaloupes to get through an old movie, and we were set. After the movie was over we'd make our own entertainment — we'd talk and make love, then go to sleep early.

I'm not a person who lets anything fester in a relationship. If there's a problem, I like to get it all out there. When I thought that O.J. was in a receptive frame of mind, I'd say, "You know what really bothers me?"

Early on, he'd be excited to work things out: "Yeah, let's sit down and talk about this." By the fall, he knew me well enough to roll his eyes and laugh and say, "What now?"

O.J. would be open to hearing me out, though I sometimes lost him with my psychological analysis. "I know just what you mean!" he'd say with mock enthusiasm. "That's just like the bullfrog who went hopping through the snow till he crossed the pond and fell into the water!"

While we never got tired of saying how much we cared for one another, we also addressed the bigger world out there. When we read the *New York Times,* O.J. grabbed the sports section first, like most men I know, before tackling the front page.

In the presidential campaign that year, both of us liked Perot. O.J. wound up feeling silly when Perot pulled out of the race the same day O.J. publicly came out for him.

Like most successful businessmen, O.J. was politically conservative. But unlike some of them, he had a heart. I'd get appalled by one opinionated friend of mine who wanted to "reform" welfare by cutting everyone off. I'd think about my mom, who never took welfare, but worked so hard to raise three kids without help, and I'd argue back for better education and child care.

O.J., whose own mom had worked the night shift at San Francisco General Hospital, shared my sympathies. He knew there were no easy answers.

One night we were at a dinner when I noticed O.J. had stopped talking; he was just watching me converse with another guest. Later that evening, back at his apartment, he took my hand and said, "When I was with Nicole, I had to work so hard all the time to keep the conversation going. But with you, I can sit there and listen to you all night, and I've got to tell you I love it."

O.J. never put me down or corrected me in public, never made me feel young or dumb. At his side I felt self-assured, free to be myself. During the trial, I'd get puzzled when the papers said that O.J. didn't accept women as real friends. I saw the strong friendship he had with his assistant, Cathy Randa. Then there was Tawny Kitaen, an actress and former Elite model with whom O.J. once had an affair during a rough time with Nicole.

Tawny was an extremely bright girl with a great sense of humor — certainly nobody's bimbo. She and O.J. stayed friends, even after she moved in with Chuck Finley, the California Angels pitcher.

Most of all, I saw how seriously O.J. took me. He didn't need me as a trophy. There were plenty of pretty girls in Los Angeles who'd have demanded less commitment than I did.

After two traditional marriages, O.J. took special delight when I showed how I could take care of myself — like booking my own way to Barcelona out of a phone booth and getting there quicker and cheaper than his office had estimated. I'd hear him praising me over the phone, telling his friends about "this wonderful girl — she works, she's self-sufficient, she's strong, she's secure."

It's a great feeling to be loved for who you are, rather than for some ideal a man wants you to be. I don't wear makeup, for example, even at formal occasions. I got my fill of it on the job, and I'd come around to the French point of view: that women often used makeup as a way to hide.

Dolph Lundgren had loved bright red lipstick, and to please him I'd worn it, against my better judgment. My oversized lips — "sultry," if you wanted to be kind — would arrive three days before the rest of me. The red lipstick made me look like Batman's Joker.

But O.J. was happy with me in my Carmex lip gloss, unadorned. It wouldn't occur to him to tell me what to wear, any more than to order for me at a restaurant. He thought I had natural style, which was liberating for a woman who liked to get dressed and out in ten minutes flat.

For himself, O.J. had his share of male vanity. Juanita, his hairdresser, would carefully snip out each gray hair. But he wasn't obsessed with how he looked. I've known men who had to be fought for the mirror, who took inventory of every calorie they ate. But O.J. wasn't uptight or self-absorbed that way.

In his dress he liked classic styles, clean lines, and natural fabrics: silk, linen, cashmere. Though I eventually turned him on to Donna Karan, O.J. wasn't fixed on any particular designers. He was actually rather frugal and liked to buy on sale. When someone gave him a Versace leopard-print silk shirt and O.J. found out it cost $2,700, he was almost too embarrassed to wear it. (I was happy to borrow it and belt it over my jeans, and O.J. professed amazement about how good I'd made the shirt look.)

I think O.J. had reached that point where he needed no one's stamp of approval. He knew who he was and who he wasn't, and he was satisfied with that. His life seemed completely in order.

Or at least so I thought.

It was a special treat to join O.J. on one of his out-of-town assignments. Once we took the train to Philadelphia, where O.J. interviewed Reggie White, the great lineman who is also a Christian minister.

During a break, Reggie sat alone with me and asked if I'd been saved. We spoke for twenty minutes, no more, but I was enormously impressed by him. Of all the football players I met through O.J., he was my favorite.

As I confessed to Reggie, religion wasn't a big part of my life then. When O.J. and I were in New York on a Sunday, we'd stop at St. Patrick's, light a candle, and say a brief prayer: "Thank you for having this person next to me"; "Thank you for all our blessings." Just standing in that towering cathedral made us feel closer to the Lord, as though we'd fulfilled our obligation by walking in.

Looking back, I had a shallow faith. I didn't give much of myself, didn't go out of my way. It would be a long time after I met Reggie before I found a new relationship with God. But that talk of ours set me to thinking about what I might be missing.

Another time we went out to a game in Buffalo, a homecoming for O.J. The murmur began as soon as we walked into the stadium: "Juice, Juice, Juice . . ." As we made our way down the aisle more and more people picked it up, like they were doing the wave, until you felt thousands of people loving him for the way he once had run.

O.J. was lit up that day. He had great stamina for his fans, engaging each one who came up to him, all afternoon long. I felt so happy that he could have this sweet echo of his athlete's prime.

After the game was done and O.J. had finished his interviews, it was cold and dark. I could tell he was tired. We were scheduled to head straight back to New York, but O.J. insisted that I see Niagara Falls.

We made a forty-five-minute detour to reach the falls, only to find that they'd turned off the lights: Tourist time was over. There we were, freezing our gigglewaters off, by this awesome power of nature that we could hear but barely see. I stood shivering between kisses, clutching O.J. close for the warmth of his body.

It was one of the most romantic times of my life.

New York had one big drawback: its distance from Sydney, who was six, and Justin, then four. Though he considered Nicole an excellent mother, O.J. felt perpetually guilty that he didn't see his kids enough.

Whenever we were back in Los Angeles, our schedules revolved around the children. O.J. would pick them up from school when he was able and keep them at Rockingham for the weekends. A nanny watched the kids during O.J.'s morning golf games, but for the rest of the day he was theirs.

I looked forward to those times; they were all about fun. I'd do splits and cartwheels with Sydney in the yard or join a family game of "horse" on the basketball court. Sometimes we'd rent movies or truck out to a theater in Santa Monica. I felt like I was living my childhood again.

When I had a shoot out at Joshua Tree, in the desert, O.J. brought the kids along to observe and climb rocks. And when O.J. played in the Bob Hope Classic, we all went to Palm Springs. We got adjoining rooms, and the kids and I played in the pool or shopped while their father flailed away on the course. We ate at Mikado, the Japanese restaurant, and I remember how grown-up Sydney seemed with her cherry Coke.

I thought they were wonderful children: curious, unspoiled, loving. Going to Sydney's dance class, buying Justin a pair of tennis shoes — those were absolute dreams to me. I couldn't play enough games, couldn't hug them enough. At age twenty-five, I guess I wanted babies of my own. I was geared to love any kids within range.

O.J. was such an affectionate, doting father that I often wondered what it would be like to have our own family. If I found any fault in his parenting style, it was that he lacked any concept of discipline. Once he took the kids to my apartment while I was out of town. We were talking on the phone when O.J. said, "Oh, no."

While running around with his sister, Justin had toppled my cherished ceramic Doberman, which now had one ear. O.J. could tell I was upset, but he didn't so much as reprimand the children or ask them to stop roughhousing. "That's kids for you," he said philosophically. "They'll play hard."

The occasional accident aside, I never felt at odds with Sydney and Justin. I was careful not to act as if I was trying to replace their mother. I wanted to be their friend, and I think that I was.

The highlight of our Christmas season in New York was a black-tie party thrown by Liza Minnelli. I bought a red party dress by Giorgio Santangelo: a long-sleeved wool sweater cut to the middle of my hips, with a number of long, layered red scarves beneath it, sort of like Tinkerbell's getup in *Peter Pan*. It was an amazing dress, and it conformed to my number-one rule: It didn't droop or pull anywhere it shouldn't.

On the big night, I put on a little bit of matte lipstick and a touch of matte powder. I donned my three-inch heels; I wore heels so much at work that they felt more comfortable to me than Reeboks.

I started feeling nervous. I always get butterflies before public occasions, no matter who's on the guest list. Dino Buccola, our Laguna "chauffeur," was going with us, and spirits were high in O.J.'s condo. We had music on, and whenever I passed Dino or O.J. we broke out into spontaneous dancing.

When it came time to leave, I wrapped myself in one of O.J.'s oversized cashmere coats. It fit me like a blanket, but it kept me warm. (With no idea of how to dress for New York winters, I got colds there all the time.)

Liza Minnelli's apartment was like a gallery: large rooms with lots of windows, dramatic lighting, fabulous art on the walls. My butterflies vanished as soon as we got there, and I knew I wouldn't want to leave.

Lauren Bacall was holding court in a black pantsuit. I was fascinated just standing near her, listening to that deep, sexy voice I'd heard so often on the screen. Brooke Shields looked stunning in a floor-length red velvet dress.

O.J. casually mentioned that he'd once dated Brooke, and I guess it says something that I felt not a pang of jealousy. I knew that I couldn't compete with Brooke Shields, and I knew I didn't have to. O.J. made me feel like I was the only woman in the room who mattered. "You're my girl," he told me. I'd heard those words before, but O.J. had a knack for saying them at just the right time.

Liza was incredibly gracious. We'd run into her a few days before, at Bloomingdale's, and I'd been impressed by how warm and unpretentious she seemed. As the evening wore on, she wound up sitting at the piano and singing with a couple dozen guests. O.J. sang along, of course, belting out each line, a man at home with himself wherever he went.

A few weeks earlier, Sydney and Justin had been set to join us in New York for Thanksgiving, a workday in the NFL. But Nicole had canceled at the last minute, to O.J.'s deep disappointment. He really missed his kids on the holidays. "If that's the way it's going to be," he said then, "we're going to go back to the court rules and do this every-other-holiday thing the way we're supposed to."

That meant it would be O.J.'s turn for Christmas. I wouldn't be with them on Christmas Day — I'd spend it with my family, in Florida — but I was glad to help get the apartment ready. I bought the biggest, fattest tree I could find on the street. Then I went to Bloomingdale's and spent a thousand dollars on ornaments: glass hearts and balls, all red and gold, plus crystal icicles and the ultimate angel. I found some gorgeous teddy bears for the kids' beds. I wanted everything to be perfect when they arrived.

O.J. appreciated the trouble I'd gone to and couldn't stop flattering my choices. After some sad good-byes, I took off for home. I started missing O.J. as soon as I stepped on the plane. I jumped at the phone when he called on Christmas Day, and instantly I knew something was wrong.

"I can't *believe* she's here," O.J. said, and his voice sounded funny — angry, but also defensive. Nicole had come along to New York with Sydney and Justin and taken a room in a nearby hotel.

I was sympathetic, and a little miffed myself. That took a lot of nerve, I thought, for Nicole to just show up like that.

Some days later, when O.J. and I had a chance to talk about what had happened, he'd cooled down. He really didn't have a problem with Nicole being around for the holidays. Sydney and Justin were her children, too, he reasoned, and it was natural for her to want to be with them. But I continued to be troubled by Nicole's presumption. I kept thinking about the next Christmas, and the Christmas after that. Would we be setting a place for O.J.'s ex-wife at the table?

It was the first real inkling I had that Nicole would be a part of our future, as well as O.J.'s past.

That I had entered a relationship not of two people, but of three.

My birthday falls on New Year's Eve, and O.J. and I were going to south Florida to celebrate. He surprised me by stopping over in Panama City en route to meet my family and friends: another big step.

My anxiety was blown away as soon as O.J. stepped through our door with that goofy grin of his. Mom was wary at first — she didn't want to see me go rushing off to the altar again, and she thought he was too old for me. (O.J. didn't. He could be the most infuriating chauvinist. The great thing about being with me, he'd say, was he'd never be around to see me get old and fat. When it came out at the trial that he had called Nicole horrible names when she was pregnant, I wasn't surprised.) But protective as my mom can be, she didn't stand a chance against O.J.'s charisma. Given enough time, I suspect, O.J. would have won over the whole Florida Panhandle and most of southern Alabama.

That night we had a little party for him, and O.J. fit right in. He couldn't sit down without a bunch of children climbing all over him. Mother tried to pull them off, but O.J. was in his element, laughing louder than any kid. We cooked up a banquet of southern food — fried chicken and catfish and collard greens. The following evening, after a long day on the local golf course, O.J. joined Mom and me for dinner at Captain Anderson's, one of

Panama City's best restaurants. At the end of the meal, as O.J. laid down his napkin, a line formed at our table for autographs. It was all the young kitchen help, the dishwashers and busboys.

O.J. was tired that night, but he signed every napkin, every last scrap of paper. Not only that, but he took the time to talk with each one of those young people. He asked how they were doing in school or about their play on the high school football team. He soaked up their appreciation and sent it right back at them.

I watched the slow procession and marveled at this man I loved. I have never known anyone who enjoyed people so much; I doubt I ever will.

We celebrated my birthday at Turnberry Isle, a spectacular resort with a rather exclusive clientele. (With O.J. I met Adnan Kashoggi and his wife, whose arm was encircled from wrist to elbow with diamond bangle bracelets.) O.J. presented me with a small box, and I nearly fell over when I opened it. Three or four months earlier, while strolling in Manhattan, we'd stepped into a little antique store down in the twenties. "Isn't that interesting," I said. A ring, dated 1910, had caught my eye. There were little ruby chips set in a figure eight, with diamond chips inside and around them.

Now I discovered that O.J. had gone back to buy the ring for me. I knew it wasn't all that expensive, but his effort touched me deeply.

Generally speaking, O.J. was more thoughtful than extravagant. He didn't shower me with lavish gifts, and I didn't need or expect them. (Contrary to widespread reports, O.J. didn't buy me the Ford Bronco I still own today; I have the payment book to prove it.) The exception was a full-length mink coat that O.J. surprised me with after the Liza Minnelli party. I was overwhelmed; I'm afraid I didn't handle it very well. A few weeks later, at a café in Los Angeles with some friends, I got flustered when Cathryn asked me what O.J. had given me for Christmas. Not knowing what Marcus had given her, and not wanting to sound like a braggart, I tried to play it down.

"He got me a fur coat," I said. "I'm an animal lover, and I don't know how I'm going to wear it."

I saw O.J. scowl and realized I'd wounded him. He'd been so proud of that gift — he'd noticed how cold I was in New York — and now I'd belittled it. When we were alone, I got the silent treatment. Ouch.

O.J. didn't give to get a hold over people or to advertise himself. He took care of his mother and his brother and sisters without expecting anything back. He never talked about all the sports equipment he donated to kids in Potrero Hill, his old neighborhood in San Francisco. When people like Jim Brown attacked O.J. for not "giving back" to the black community, I saw that they didn't know this man at all.

The Super Bowl was in California in January 1993 — a hard grind for O.J. At our hotel he barely acknowledged me. I was still in the doghouse over the mink-coat episode, and O.J. kept his nose buried in his NBC briefing book.

"Paula," said Robin Bender, who'd come out with O.J.'s friend Bobby just for fun, "you have *got* to do something to lighten O.J. up."

"You're right," I said. "It's time to take his mind off the game."

I devised the perfect plan. After changing out of my clothes in the Benders' room, I put on the mink over La Perla's finest: a black lace bodysuit, with a strip of faux fur atop the heart-shaped bodice. I had nothing else on, just a pair of high heels to complete the package.

Hiding a bottle of champagne under my coat — the glass was ice against my skin — I sashayed down to the lobby, stalking the wild TV commentator. O.J was so engrossed in his work that he didn't notice when I stole up behind the man he was talking to.

All work and no play, I thought. *Here goes . . .*

Keeping his colleague's back in front of me, I flashed the coat open for a good second or two. There was no way O.J. could have missed the display, but *still* he kept on talking about screen passes and nickel defenses. Talk about blows to a girl's ego . . .

Bobby and Robin were watching at a discreet distance, but not discreet enough — I could hear them laughing hysterically.

I lost patience. I whipped out the bottle of champagne, which had always seemed to work before. I thought my message was pretty clear: *Take me to bed or lose me forever!*

But O.J. never took my hint. He went by his own agenda, and this night I wasn't on it.

Where had our spontaneity gone? Some might say we were getting stale, but I sloughed it off; I was an expert at sloughing.

New York Giant star Lawrence Taylor hosted the big Super Bowl party that year in a converted airplane hangar. I wore a white Alia sweater dress that was unusually revealing for me, clinging to every dip and curve.

O.J. and I danced for a while — when his knees allowed it, he was a very good, expressive dancer. During a break, when O.J.'s back was turned, a young football player made a series of unmistakable hand gestures. Given O.J.'s proximity, I thought that was very brave. I hadn't seen anything so blatant, in fact, since I'd lived in Italy.

Sorry, my eyes answered, *I'm a taken girl.*

O.J. had noticed what was going on, but he took it in stride. He was proud of me and how I looked; he didn't mind when other men stared. "Yes, she *is* really beautiful," he might say, catching them short.

The main point was that O.J. trusted me. Which made me all the more inclined to trust him in turn.

Our romance was only eight months old, but I had a hard time remembering my life without O.J. One thing was certain: I had come a long way from my southern upbringing in Panama City. Ten years before, I couldn't have imagined loving a black man. Now it seemed natural, unremarkable. He was simply a man — my man.

My new outlook hadn't flowered overnight. On a trip to Palm Springs, shortly after O.J. and I started dating, he and Marcus Allen went off to Frank Sinatra's golf tournament. Cathryn and I headed to the hotel gym to work out. As we pedaled away, I noticed she was reading *Ebony* and I kidded her, "A little confused, aren't we?"

Cathryn looked at me, the hurt plain on her face, and I realized what a stupid comment that had been. Why *shouldn't* a white person read *Ebony?* But even then, I considered myself more ignorant than racist. I knew I had a lot to learn about people, about how little we are different and how much we are the same.

At the Super Bowl party, a girl came up and took our picture with O.J.'s arm around me. When I saw the print, I thought we looked beautiful together. O.J. was dressed in black and I was all in white, but it wasn't the contrast that struck me.

I saw the love in our eyes, and how much we belonged together, and that race didn't matter at all.

I saw that love every morning, whenever we awoke together. O.J. and I had a little ritual. I'd look at him and say, "Do you have anything to complain about today?"

O.J. would smile and say, "No, Peola, I don't have anything to complain about."

And it was true, he really didn't. He loved his job and his golf. He owned homes in two of the most thrilling cities in the world. He had two healthy children who were well taken care of, yet he also had the freedom to do what he wanted.

And, oh yes, he had a girlfriend who unconditionally adored him.

What's more, that girlfriend wasn't exactly pushing him toward the altar. Since my annulment, I'd tried not to think about marriage. At the moment, it didn't compute. I felt like I could be with O.J. forever, but I also wanted to have children. How could a veteran of two families share my excitement for a new baby?

That wasn't a problem, O.J. argued: "When Justin was born, I was just as excited as I was for Arnelle and Jason. Each kid has his own personality, and you look at each one in a whole different way."

I listened, but I wasn't convinced.

On the other hand, if O.J. had asked me then and there to elope with him that night and get a head start on our first five babies together, I can't swear that I would have said no.

When I was an adolescent and ripe with curiosity about boys, my mother had a saying: "Sex is the frosting on the cake."

I always trusted she was right, that love and caring came first, and then sex naturally followed.

But in practice, I seemed to be getting things backward. I was bingeing on the frosting, even when the cake was stale.

By the time I broke off with Dolph Lundgren, my boyfriend in the late eighties, I was an emotional mess. I'd had little experience with men before Dolph. He was the only one I'd ever lived with, the first I'd gotten so attached to — and the first to tear me into bleeding pieces. How could I have chosen so badly?

After months of therapy with a woman named Margaret Paul, I began to get a handle on my problem: I was using intimacy in an unhealthy way. I wasn't promiscuous; I've always been a one-man woman. But in my urgency to connect with Dolph, I rushed into sex too early in our relationship.

As a result, I had no chance to get to *know* Dolph, to communicate on other levels. Most important, I hadn't taken the time to find out if he was right for me. Passion was clouding my vision, sinking me into wrong relationships for the wrong reasons.

Dolph and I were nearly always great as lovers. The bells rang, the earth moved — all those clichés. There'd be times I wanted to belt out the Swedish national anthem just by way of thanks. I behaved like a lot of men; I assumed that as long as we were making love everything else was okay. I was enthusiastic about everything Dolph taught me. I welcomed his every whim (even if that meant relinquishing control of the TV clicker in bed; now that's *really* a man's fondest fantasy!). I transformed myself into the epitome of that old saying: I was a lady in public, a chef in the kitchen — and pleasing in bed. (Well, hey, that's how *I* say it.)

In the process, I blinded myself to how Dolph was cheating on me right and left.

Margaret Paul prescribed abstinence. I would defer having sex for at least my first six months with a man.

It was around that time that I started dating George Hamilton. He was about the sweetest, most charming gentleman I'd ever met, the kind of man who'd walk in and hand you a single rose, perfectly pruned.

George and I were kissing one night when hands began to stray. I broke the clinch, took a deep breath, and told him, "Look, my therapist said I can't do that. I'm sorry."

George was a great sport. He even went to see Margaret with me several times. We talked about what we were after in life — how I wanted children, how George was past that stage. The three of us concluded that George wasn't the right guy for me, and I wasn't the right girl for him — here was a new kick on dating, right? A whole new kind of triangle: boy, girl, psychotherapist.

Looking back, I might have done well to bring O.J. to Margaret Paul before that fateful first night in Laguna. But I'd never been so sure that a man was right for me. I'd never doubted it through our first eight glorious months. All the time we spent together, those marathon talks we had — they made me feel incredibly connected.

Where other men might shrink back into silence, where I couldn't reach them, O.J. was always *with* me. There were no rules for us, except we were monogamous. We said what we felt, and no feeling was out of bounds.

You could even say that O.J. regularly talked me into sex, not by coaxing or pressure, but simply by *talking*. The seduction was in the conversation itself. Our pillow talk didn't have to be mushy. We'd spend hours in bed considering family or friends, or some trip we'd planned, or some photographer I'd recently worked with. But no matter the subject, it would feel romantic every time, because we'd be sharing our hearts.

When you are so deeply in sync with a man, the act of love consumes you. You feel totally uninhibited. It's like that song "All of Me" — you don't want to hold anything back. Just as O.J. never tired of talking, I was insatiable in our lovemaking. "I don't know what I'm going to do," he'd joke with Bobby Bender in mock desperation.

O.J. was more or less happy to cooperate, but he was also pushing fifty, and golf would be beckoning just hours away. He couldn't possibly keep up with me. Many times he'd lie there with his eyes closed, and I'd say, "I know you're awake . . ."

More often than not he kept the charade going and refused to stir. Over time, I would come to accept O.J.'s lack of stamina; I'd no longer take it so personally. My need was for simple closeness, first and last, and a reasonable amount of passion to make me feel wanted. In a sense, O.J. was not so different. He feared abandonment as much as I did, and making love reliably drove that fear away.

By early 1993, we had mastered our roles in bed together. O.J. liked to stay in control, of both himself and his girl; I was driven to let my man have his way, regardless of my own desires. If I was "selfish" in sex, I feared that O.J. would feel inadequate, and then I would lose him. There weren't enough orgasms in the world to risk that.

When our bond was tightest, intimacy affirmed it, no matter how humdrum the actual act of passion. If O.J. and I differed about something and couldn't talk it out, making love was a neat way around it. And if we had a knock-down, drag-out argument — as we would soon enough — passion would bring us together, however briefly, and let me forget my pain.

5

Mixed Signals

Though I didn't know it at the time, the trouble started back in December 1992, at the Christmas party put on by Elite, my New York agency. I'd flown in for the event from a shoot; I remember wearing a long red Donna Karan dress that was especially flattering.

O.J. was busy with an interview that day and would be coming late. I passed some time with John Casablancas, Elite's chairman, whom I'd dated earlier in my modeling career.

Enter Donald Trump.

Donald came up to me in that self-important way of his and gave me a dose of the famous Trump charm. I knew all about his longstanding affair with Marla Maples, but Marla was nowhere to be seen that night — and out of sight, out of Donald's wandering mind. We started talking about golf. Donald bragged that he had a scratch handicap, but he clearly had other sport in mind.

"You know," he told me, his eyes searching mine, "I just want to meet a nice, quiet girl who wants to have a family." He was about as subtle as a sledgehammer: Play my cards right, he was implying, and I might be that lucky girl.

As I laughed to myself about the whole situation, Donald handed me his phone number. That very moment, O.J. arrived and walked up behind me.

"Oh, look, honey," I said, taking the card and passing it on to O.J., "Donald wants you to play golf with him when you get a chance."

O.J. instinctively put his arm around me: *Back off, Jack, this belongs to me.* But I could see that he and Donald made a sort of boys' connection at that party. Birds of a feather . . .

Later on, when I told O.J. about Donald's advances, he shrugged it off. "That's normal," he said. "A guy sees a pretty girl, and he's gonna hit on her. But now he knows you're my girl, and he won't do that anymore."

A month later, I was working out of town while O.J. had a golf tournament in Pebble Beach. He called me and said, "Baby, you're not going to believe who's here."

"Try me."

"Do you remember that girl Robin?"

How could I forget — it was *the* Robin, the girl with the bedroom eyes whom O.J. had kept on ice the day we met.

"I'm out on the course with Donald Trump, and this girl comes out in tight, tight pants — you *know* they're not golf clothes," O.J. continued. "Every man out there turns around to look at her, and it's Robin. She goes up to Donald, and I realize she's with him."

Later we exchanged our usual I-love-you's and long good-byes, but I hung up with an insecure feeling. I wished I was in Pebble Beach that moment. I *should* have been there for O.J., I thought.

It wasn't that I didn't trust him. Since O.J.'s birthday celebration the previous summer, when he'd been so remorseful after kissing that girl, I'd had no reason to doubt him. But I couldn't stop thinking about Robin or the way she'd draped herself around O.J.'s chest — she was like a human warning flare.

I fretted the whole next day. I stared at the phone; it stared back. Finally I snatched it up, dialed the hotel in Pebble Beach, and asked for Donald Trump.

"O.J. tells me that he saw this girl Robin with you on the course yesterday," I blurted out. "Just put my mind at rest — please tell me that Robin is with you."

Dead silence. Donald was dumbfounded. What I didn't know was that Marla had picked up on the other line. The fur was about to fly in that hotel suite.

"I can't *believe* the feud you started here," O.J. told me the next day. I felt embarrassed but also relieved. O.J. was still my good, loyal guy. As he himself noted, why tell me about Robin if he'd had anything to hide?

By then I was counting down to Valentine's Day, when we'd be together in Palm Beach. During the week before our holiday, I had a job in Los Angeles, while O.J. had business in New York. He told me that he'd be sharing a room at the Ritz-Carlton for a night or two.

Wait a minute, I thought at the time. This is O.J. Simpson. He's on the Ritz-Carlton board of directors — why would he have to share a room? But as soon as my suspicion surfaced, I pushed it back down.

Later that week, O.J. called me at home and asked if I was planning to go to Palm Springs: "I heard Donald's having a big blowout down there."

I told him I hadn't heard about the party. Besides, I'd be tied up at work.

When we were apart, O.J. and I usually spoke several times a day, just to hear each other's voice. On Saturday, the night before Valentine's Day, I called the Ritz-Carlton from my condo at about eight, or eleven o'clock New York time. A man answered — O.J.'s roommate, I presumed — and told me O.J. wasn't back yet. That wasn't so unusual, as dinners often ran late in New York.

I tried again an hour later and got the same story. The man in the room was starting to sound nervous. By 2 A.M. New York time, I had a gut instinct that something was wrong.

O.J. called an hour after that. He'd been out with the guys, he said, having a good time.

"Fine, great," I said — I was overjoyed to hear he was all right. Now I could sleep.

I boarded a plane the next day and got to Palm Beach in the afternoon. O.J. had been due in before me, but there was no answer when I rang up to our room from the front desk. I rang again: no luck. That was strange, I thought. On the third try, after a number of rings, O.J. finally picked up.

"Hey, Peola, get on up here," he said. "I've been waiting for you, girl."

When I opened the door, it was like walking into a plant store — the room overflowed with flowers. I picked up a greeting card on the table and read the inscription: *I love you, girl. You're the only one for me.*

Something seemed off-kilter. O.J. was sitting in his bathrobe, but the bed was made as if he hadn't touched it. The room was spotless. When I visited the bathroom, there wasn't a drop of water on the floor; the shower hadn't been used.

Then there was that strange expression on O.J.'s face as he smiled at me from his chair. He looked like a guy who was getting away with something.

Unsettled, I called a friend of mine in Miami who I knew was alone that day. "Kim, we're here — would you like to have dinner with us tonight?"

"I *know* you're here," said Kim, sounding perplexed. "I saw O.J. at Sinatra's Bar a couple nights ago — didn't he tell you?"

I hung up and faced the smug man in the bathrobe. "Kim says she saw you in Sinatra's Bar," I said, trying to keep my voice low. "What's going on?"

"That's bullshit," O.J. said. Right away he was loud and animated — defensive, it seemed to me. He denied everything. "I've been in New York, like I told you," he insisted.

"That's not what Kim says."

"Who do you believe — her or me?"

I'm such a terrible liar that O.J. could catch me fibbing in a second. If I told O.J. I'd cooked something and it was really from the deli, I'd get so nervous that I'd break out laughing. But O.J., I began to see, was very good at lying. He was straight-faced and convincing. I wanted to believe him — but why would Kim make this up? Why was he making a fool out of me?

I looked at the lavish display of flowers all around — *Just like at a funeral home,* I thought.

"You keep your damn flowers!" I yelled, and I grabbed the first dozen roses I could reach and threw them at him.

There were two things that you could not do with O.J. One was to challenge some excuse he'd made up; the second was to spurn one of his gifts. O.J. glared at me, veins bulging from his neck. "You ungrateful *bitch!*" he yelled — and then he grabbed some chrysanthemums and threw some back at me. For a moment we were showered by a bunch of dripping, mangled stems.

O.J. and I were only getting started; we tested the hotel's soundproofing that afternoon. Then I abruptly retreated. I got very quiet, which is what I do to end a confrontation. I curled up into a fetal ball in the armchair and cried.

Still steaming, O.J. left to go out with Marcus. He said he'd pick me up at six for a party hosted by Dan Marino, the Miami Dolphins quarterback. Then he stalked out of the room.

I was outraged and confused and heartbroken, all at once. I was eager to get out of there before O.J. came back. I wanted to leave him a note reading, *"I don't want to see you, I don't want to know you — you're a liar."* Then I'd add something less polite.

I reserved about six different flights back home. But each time I gathered my things I'd sit down and start crying. I was so tormented, so torn, that I'd miss the flight, so I'd book the next one and miss that, too.

I guess you could say that I didn't know my own mind.

O.J. was a half hour late getting back, then an hour. I had too much time to think. It's the demons you don't know that make you crazy. I kept obsessing over the possible scenarios, none of them pretty.

Where had O.J. been when I first rang up to the room? Had

he slept somewhere else the night before? Did he have another girl in a second room at the hotel? *Stop it,* I told myself, splashing cold water on my face for the umpteenth time. *You don't want to go there.*

"You won't believe what happened," O.J. said when he finally returned with Marcus, two hours late. "We ran out of gas."

Did he need the time to tell the other girl good-bye — in that real sweet personal way of his?

O.J. was having a big laugh about something with Marcus. I wanted to confront him, but by then I was wrung out. I told him I'd need a few minutes to freshen up.

"Hurry up," O.J. said. "We're late."

At the party O.J. and Donald sat together. They seemed really pleased with themselves, like two tomcats after a big night in the alley. I ran into one of O.J.'s golfing buddies, who sort of smirked as he said, "Yeah, O.J. was anticipating your arrival so much that he couldn't sit still. He was in the room arranging those flowers the whole time."

I was simmering. I kept my distance from Donald and O.J.; if I got too close, I knew I might not be able to rein myself in. O.J. had not only lied to me, he was making me look like an idiot. I was about to boil over when a very cute, very southern quarterback started hitting on me.

"What are you doing with *him*?" the quarterback said.

Excellent question. If O.J. had lied, there seemed a good chance that he had cheated. I'd been there, done that with Dolph Lundgren, another man I'd trusted with my heart. The experience had leveled me, crushed my self-esteem. I'd promised myself I wouldn't stand for anyone else dragging my love through the dirt.

I smiled back at the quarterback and discreetly gave him my Los Angeles phone number: "If you can remember this, you can call me. . . ." I wasn't looking to date him or get some rise out of O.J. I did it to feel better after a major assault on my ego.

You're an attractive, desirable woman, I said to myself as the quarterback's interest sparked in his eyes. *You're still an okay girl.*

Driving back to the hotel, O.J. was quiet for a long time. Then he started to mutter to himself. "She wants the QB, she can have the QB. She can have the damn QB . . .

"You want the QB, is that what you want?" he burst out. "You want the QB, don't you?"

"What's a QB?" I asked, realizing I had turned the tables. This time it wasn't him walking out the door to "play golf."

O.J. went nuts. "*Quarterback!* You want the damn quarterback!"

"I don't even know his name," I said. Of course, I did. But I was just as mad as O.J., maybe madder.

O.J. flailed his arms as he cursed the QB, and we swerved all over the road.

"Forget about the QB!" I yelled back at him. "Why did you lie to me?" I wasn't holding my anger in anymore. I have never been a hitting girl, but I turned to O.J. and smacked him across the face as hard as I could with my open hand. It was great therapy; I wouldn't take that one back. It's a good thing, too, that O.J. could take a punch, or we might have run off the road.

Stunned, he gripped the steering wheel with both hands. He was seething. Clearly restraining himself, he said, "I'm not going to have that relationship again." A heavy silence settled over us.

That night I slept as far away from O.J. as a king-size bed allows. He tried to touch me, once. I roughly removed his hand; the old charm wouldn't work that night.

The next morning, needing some fresh air, I took a ride with the Benders. When we passed Donald's Mar-a-Lago mansion, we saw a gigantic party tent, and Bobby said, "Yeah, I heard there was a big party there over the weekend."

As soon as I got back, O.J. drove me to the airport. I couldn't get away quickly enough. As I left him I said, "You stay here with your flowers and I-love-you's," and I wheeled away before he could answer. What more could he tell me? When you've heard lie after lie, communication loses its meaning.

I was seething on that plane. Before takeoff the flight attendant asked if I wanted a cocktail. I ordinarily decline — alcohol and flying don't mix for me — but this time I said, "I'd love some champagne." I swigged a glass down, ordered a second.

Marcus Allen was sitting a couple seats over, next to some television actress he knew. When I overheard him mention O.J.'s name, I glared at him and said, "O.J. can take a long walk off a short dock!"

I can't say I was feeling no pain, but the champagne was starting to make it manageable.

A pair of golf pros, en route to a tournament in L.A., became my drinking partners. Somewhere over Texas they invited me to a dinner party with all their tournament buddies at La Dôme, a big show-business restaurant. I'd be delighted, I said. No grass would grow under *this* girl's feet.

Dinner picked up where we'd left off, with rivers of Dom Pérignon. Soon two other golfers, singer-actor Jack Wagner and football player Chuck Cecil, were furiously flirting with me and getting on each other. The contest was to see which of them I'd date the following night. I thought it was funny and flattering, but I was weary of men and wanted to go home. "Call me tomorrow and we'll work it out," I told them.

The next morning, my concierge buzzed up: "O.J. Simpson is here to see you." O.J. had followed me home. I felt a wreck — I had a rare hangover, and my eyes were about cried out — but resolved to put up a strong front. O.J. wasn't going to talk his way out of this one, I vowed.

He got right to the point: "You were right. I lied, and I'm really sorry."

Here was O.J.'s explanation: In New York he'd run into Sean Penn, who was taking some people to Miami in his private plane. O.J. had finished his work early, so he joined them and flew down ahead.

"Well, why didn't you just tell me?" I said.

"I didn't want to hassle with explaining it all to you," O.J. said, "and have you question what I was doing."

That made no sense. As far as I knew, Sean Penn was a nice, upstanding fellow with a girlfriend. Why would I object to O.J.'s hitching a ride with him? And why would he go to such elaborate lengths to keep the truth from me, unless something else was going on?

My phone rang in the middle of O.J.'s alibi. I'd ignored it, but now the message played over the speaker:

"Hey, this is Chuck —"

"And this is Jack —"

"And we're on our way to the golf course —"

"And we want to know which one of us you're going out with tonight."

At which point O.J. grabbed the phone and said, "Hey, this is O.J. I know she's beautiful, and I know she's funny, and I know she's nice — and I know she's my girl, so you better stay away from her, or I'm going to kick your ass."

I was glad the golf pros called when they did. Their interest might put O.J. on his guard, make him take me less for granted. (O.J. didn't hold a grudge; I later set up a game for him with Chuck and Jack in Panama City, and they all shared a good laugh about the phone call.)

But *was* I O.J.'s girl? He sure was acting the part, sweet and possessive and all that. But if he'd lied once, could I trust him now? I felt dizzy, disoriented. I didn't know which end of our relationship was up.

Over time I'd find out what really happened in south Florida that weekend. Donald Trump hadn't planned a party in Palm Springs, as O.J. had told me. The party was set instead for Palm Beach, and O.J. was fishing to make sure I didn't know about it. Donald hired two big buses to pick up the Elite models based in Miami, and O.J. wanted to be there to join the fun.

The "roommate" at the Ritz-Carlton — the guy O.J. had planted to cover for him — was part of a big, calculated plan.

If O.J. had told me about Donald's party, I might not have been overjoyed, as I was still a little worried about Robin. But I certainly wouldn't have told him not to go. If you trust a man, you have to trust him all the way.

And if you can't trust him, it doesn't matter where he goes or what he does. He can pick up a girl on a street corner as easily as at Mar-a-Lago.

O.J. swore that the party was an evening out, nothing more. I wanted to believe him; I *needed* to believe him. But why would he deceive me unless there was something more to it?

I couldn't prove that he'd been with someone else, however. And O.J. looked so sorry and sincere, and it felt so good to be back in his arms. . . .

When that sweet, southern quarterback called me later in the day, I had three words for him: "Sorry, I'm taken."

On the first weekend in April, we took Sydney, Justin, and Arnelle to Las Vegas. O.J.'s older daughter had been off at Brown University, and I hadn't spent time with her before. She was perfectly cordial but seemed to keep me at arm's length.

We saw the Cirque du Soleil, the modern circus without animals, and dressed up in period costume at the medieval-themed Excalibur. It was great fun, but I could sense Sydney pulling back from me.

At breakfast at the Mirage, with the kids off with Arnelle, O.J. was silent as a stone. After I drew him out, he let me in on his problem: Marcus and Nicole had been sleeping together. A few days earlier, he related, Nicole had come to him and said she wanted to end the affair but that Marcus wouldn't let her alone. If O.J. didn't do something, she was going to tell Cathryn.

Then Marcus came to O.J. and guiltily confirmed Nicole's story.

"I don't know what I'm going to do," O.J. said, tears welling in his eyes. Not only had one of his best friends betrayed him, but Marcus and Cathryn were soon to be married at Rockingham. And Nicole was helping to organize the event.

There was more. According to O.J., Nicole had said some things about me that weren't very nice. He wouldn't go into detail, but I could see that it bothered him.

"I don't understand what you're talking about," I said. "She doesn't know anything about me."

"Well, I guess she heard something somewhere," O.J. said blandly.

Looking back, it seems likely that Marcus passed on to Nicole what he'd observed on our plane home from Miami. Sensing there was trouble in paradise, Nicole had launched a campaign to get O.J. back, by fair means or foul.

Back in Los Angeles, O.J. told me that Nicole and her girl-friends had shown up at the Riviera for a golf lesson and that Nicole had spent the hour flirting with him.

A few days later, I dropped by Rockingham unannounced late one afternoon, as I often did. But this time O.J. looked pained.

"I can't stay right now," he said.

"What do you mean?"

"I've got to take the kids to dinner with their friends."

"Great," I said. "That sounds like fun."

And O.J. said, "No, Nicole's going to be there."

I tried to be cool and reasonable — "Okay, I under-stand" — but it was just an act. I left O.J.'s house crushed. Without even realizing it, I had become that pathetic, ridiculous cliché: the Other Woman.

Had I been thinking rationally, I would have blamed O.J. He was the person in control, after all, the one making the choices and hedging his bets. But I wasn't ready to admit that O.J. was choosing to discard me. And so I blamed my bruised heart on an easier target — I blamed it on Nicole.

Our blowup in Palm Beach notwithstanding, O.J. and I broke up not with a bang but a hundred whimpers, most of them mine. For weeks he sent mixed signals. One moment he'd be playing Mr. Family Man, the next he'd be calling up on a clear-as-glass spring day to say, "Come on, I want my girlfriend to ride bikes with me — I want you here with me." He invited me on a romantic weekend in Mexico, but at the last moment I came to my senses and canceled. That was just as well, seeing as how Nicole and the kids just happened to turn up at the same resort . . . which kind of ruined the fun for O.J. — and the girl he invited after I pulled out. (O.J. accidentally let that information slip when he was in jail.)

We broke up half a dozen times that spring; my life was in constant turmoil. There were some good times. But for every one, there'd be another crash landing — another fight, another falling out. I may have forgiven O.J. his trespass in Palm Beach (that was the only one I knew about), but I couldn't forget it.

Why keep taking more punishment? Why let O.J. back in the door? As I think about it now, I was living in a cocoon. My life revolved around my work and my apartment. I had plenty of friends but rarely made time to see them. In striving so hard to be independent, I'd become isolated as well.

Then I'd let this one man into my cocoon, my safety zone, and as the song goes, I'd grown accustomed to his face. I'd gotten used to his smile and his corny banter and his good-night phone calls whenever we weren't together. I relied on our daily routines; I couldn't sleep right without that phone call. I needed to know he was *there* for me, even when I couldn't roll over and crook my arm around him.

When you come down to it, I feared being alone again.

The funny thing was, I really liked spending time by myself. It was time I used for reflection, to get my bearings. And I knew as well as anyone that it's better to be by yourself than to hang on to a sick relationship.

I knew it . . . but I could not act on it, not for a long time. I just wasn't able to put my feelings in a jar and store them in a cabinet.

So O.J. and I struggled on. Breaking up and making up became part of the relationship, almost a weird game. When we were splitting, I'd walk about the apartment, crying and praying, "Please, God, take this feeling away from me. Make it stop hurting." I hoped the phone wouldn't ring. I didn't want to hear from our mutual friends, much less O.J. himself.

All his life, O.J. had fought for extra yards; he wasn't a man to give up easily. "Pick up the phone, pick up the phone, I know you're listening, pick up the phone," he'd call out over my answering machine. Hearing him go on like that was agony. Half of me shrank from answering; the other half was dying to pick up and tell him off, once and for all.

Usually I picked up the phone and told him off, only to have O.J. finesse my anger with one of his cute little tricks. He'd drop his deep voice another octave and say, "Girl, you're not going to say good-bye now. You're not going to hang up the phone on me, are you?" I loved that bedroom voice. I knew I was being manipulated, but I fell for it every time.

O.J. didn't stop there. Sometimes I'd answer the phone and hear, "I'm looking up at you, I know you're there, I see your light on."

I'd run to my third-floor balcony over Wilshire Boulevard. There in his Bentley would be O.J., murmuring into his cell phone. When things were relatively fine, and I felt like Juliet to his Romeo, I'd call down to him about how much I loved him. But when things were bad, I'd ask the doorman to tell O.J. I wasn't home.

"One of these days," I told the doorman, not quite knowing where the words came from, "I'm going to be shot."

My quarrels with O.J. hurt me twice — first in the bitterness of the argument itself, second in the distance it set between us. When the pain and frustration grew too much to bear, when I ached to reconnect with him — for him to truly understand me — I turned to sex to knock down and melt away those invisible walls between us.

Even as everything else was ripping apart, we had no problems with our clothes off. Through those long, dark nights, nothing else mattered — the sweet fit of our bodies took me back to a happier time. To the time when I thought we would love forever.

But the feeling didn't last like it used to. Like a drug, sex promised so much — bliss, peace, freedom from all care. I thought sex with O.J. would open the doors to communication; I longed for that safe harbor in his powerful arms. But drugs offer false promises, and sex can too. When our passion was spent these days, I'd feel emptier than before. We didn't talk much after sex anymore. O.J. would turn over and drop off to sleep, like a man falling off a ledge.

I'd lie there in the dark and wonder just who it was lying beside me, and why I still cared.

I took every job that came my way that spring. I was getting regular magazine work through Elite in New York and Miami, and TV commercials from my Los Angeles agent — I liked those the best, because you worked for several days with a real team. I was rarely at home for more than a day or two at a time, by my own choice. It was easier to miss O.J., I'd decided, than to confront what was missing between us. When I was offered a shoot on April 22 in the Grand Canyon, for a Japanese cigarette company, I jumped at it. You couldn't get much more remote than that.

I turned down O.J.'s offer to drive me to the airport, but I had a feeling that he'd show up there. On my way through the concourse I walked close to the wall, trying to be inconspicuous. But as I turned the corner toward my gate, there he was.

"We've got to talk," he said.

As we sat down in an empty conference room, I could see the anguish in O.J.'s face. Nicole was pushing hard for a reconciliation, he said. She was bombarding him with cassettes of love songs, with videos of their wedding and the children.

She'd also written O.J. a letter that basically said, "If Paula was to get pregnant, we'd lose our chance to get back together."

The campaign was taking its toll. It was raising the kids' hopes, and O.J. felt guiltier than ever about being a weekend dad. After he'd brought the children back to Nicole's condo one night, he tucked them in before leaving. "Daddy, I want you here in the morning," Sydney said. "I want you to stay."

That tore O.J. up. "I just don't know what to do," he told me.

"Look," I said, "I don't want to go through this anymore. It's not fair to me. I'm getting on this plane — either get on with me now, and we'll talk this through, or let's just call it quits."

I don't know what I expected. Had O.J. dropped everything, would we have lived happily ever after? As it turned out, he couldn't come, or wouldn't come. He had an appointment that afternoon, he said. He left me at the gate.

My ultimatum was left hanging. I think both of us knew that I lacked the courage to back it up.

To top everything off, my father called. Then a long-haul trucker, he was delivering something out my way, and he thought it was about time that he met O.J.

I was worried — no, I was petrified. Given my dad's closed mind about race, and the fact that O.J. and I were on the rocks, here was your classic no-win situation.

"I don't think we should do this," I said.

"What's wrong with you?" said O.J., his dander up.

"You don't understand," I said. "My dad would never approve of us."

But O.J. was convinced that my father would like him. Didn't everyone like him, after all? He wouldn't let it drop, so I made a reservation at La Dôme and crossed my fingers that we'd make it through dessert.

Once the plan was set, I began to hope that something good might come out of the dinner. Maybe my father would see that two people could be mutually supportive, regardless of their color.

Maybe I was hoping that O.J. would somehow see the same thing — that the two of us *were* close and connected. That we had something to save.

I picked Dad up at his truck stop, an hour outside L.A. I hadn't seen him in months, and the sight of him now — in his boots and his everyday Wranglers — wasn't something to settle my nerves.

But O.J. was ready. No sooner had we gotten to our table than three shots of vodka, Dad's drink of choice, materialized there. A minute later, three more — I was keeping right up with the menfolk, because I was scared to death of what my father might say next.

But it turned out just as O.J. had predicted. Properly lubricated, he and Dad hit it off just fine. My father was having a great time, especially after two young wannabe starlets — or high-class call girls, it was hard to be sure — came over to our table and began fawning all over him.

In Los Angeles, only the most powerful men dress casually at fancy places. When those girls saw O.J. making a fuss over Dad, they must have pegged my father as some big-deal producer. They laughed at his wit, admired his belt buckle. It was all pretty disgusting.

Then it got worse, as O.J. started flirting with one of the girls. Dad was in his own world; he didn't even notice what was going on across the table. When I heard O.J. start talking dirty about "a black stallion," I'd had enough — he was making a play right in front of me!

Livid, I excused myself to the ladies' room. I splashed cold water on my face. The woman in the mirror looked so haggard, so miserable. *What am I doing here?* I asked myself, again.

Coming out, I saw O.J. heading toward me with a big smile. Taking a solid stance in my high heels, I swung through with a roundhouse right. The slap landed flush on O.J.'s cheek, hard enough to leave fingerprints.

It was the second time I'd struck him, and the last time, and I made it count.

As O.J. staggered backward, he said, "What was *that* for?"

"You know," I said. "I'm leaving." And I did.

I was happy enough not to be invited to Marcus and Cathryn's wedding at Rockingham. To watch two people pledge their futures together — to participate in the hypocrisy — was more than I could bear.

When I called O.J. on the morning of the wedding to see how things were going, Nicole answered the phone; she was putting out the flowers. O.J. wasn't available, she said. The frost in her voice made me shiver.

"Just tell him that I called," I said.

By the time O.J. rang back, minutes later, I felt a new certainty. There was simply no room for me in his life.

I could never win out against Nicole — she had too many weapons for me to fight. She had history and two young children on her side, and the capacity to use them both.

I was more frightened than anything else. *Could she get him back?*

Sad to say, but at this point I turned the blame on myself. I tormented myself for not being desirable enough to hold on to O.J. — for not putting my pride away, for not making myself available when he needed me. With no career to juggle, Nicole was always available to O.J., day and night.

O.J. claimed it was Sydney and Justin who were pulling him back, that Nicole wasn't part of the equation. But what if O.J. was hiding the truth, trying to break my fall? All my ugly self-doubts, the ones I'd kept buried, rose up like ghouls in some cheap horror movie.

Once you give in to jealousy, there is no telling how low you can sink. Deep down, I knew that O.J. and I were splitting out of a loss of love and trust. Nicole wasn't really the issue — not whether they shared old secrets, not whether he liked her body better than mine (although she was working out and looking fine, while I was getting scrawny from stress). But the truth was hard for me to handle. It made me feel rejected, abandoned. Far better to blame Nicole.

In my misery, I *despised* Nicole. I would never say it aloud, not even to myself. But once the terrible thought had formed, it was easy to think it again . . . and go further.

Nicole was ruining my life, taking back the man I loved. What gave her the right? I wished she would *vanish from the face of the earth.*

⋆ ⋆ ⋆

In his own way, I believe that O.J. was as conflicted and torn up as I was. Sometime around Mother's Day he told me he was going up to see his family in San Francisco. He asked me to come with him — he wanted to show me where he'd grown up — but I had a job I couldn't get out of. O.J. seemed disappointed but not particularly upset.

His sister Shirley answered the phone when I called that weekend. "No, I see his bed was slept in, but he's not here now," Shirley said. "But I know that he was here."

I got the same report three days running. I couldn't reach O.J., and he wasn't returning my calls. I got frantic — we'd never gone this long without talking. Even when we were fighting, we tried to fix things before the night was out. What had I done wrong?

I called Cathy Randa, O.J.'s assistant, who knew everything about his schedule. She checked Nicole's place, to see where the kids were, but no one answered.

Later that day she took me to a church, the only place I felt safe. Then the awful realization hit me. "I just know he's with Nicole," I told Cathy, tears streaming down my face.

"No, I'm sure he's not," Cathy said.

I prayed as hard as I could — for O.J.'s safety, for my own sanity. I missed his smile and his scent and his companionship. That night my lonely bed was an ocean to drown in.

Five days after he left, O.J walked through the door of my apartment as if he'd stepped out for a quart of milk. I was too grateful to holler at him. I laid aside my gut instinct: that O.J. had lied to me again to be with his ex-wife.

I just ran to O.J. and threw my arms around his neck. I hugged him with all my might and I cried, "Are you okay? I've missed you — I *love* you."

O.J. smiled and shrugged. He said he'd been busy with Arnelle, who'd joined him in San Francisco, and then got tied up in a poker game with some friends who owned the 49ers.

It wasn't much of an explanation, but I was ready to let O.J. slide and just be in love again. Then I spotted something odd: a straw ring on his wedding finger.

"Why are you wearing that?" I asked him.

And O.J. said, "Oh, a lady on the plane back to L.A. came up to first class and said she'd made it for me to wear. Ask Arnelle, she'll tell you."

A fishy little story, but I didn't challenge it. I wouldn't ask Arnelle, of course. I wouldn't humiliate myself any further.

I just put my arms around O.J.'s neck again and held on for dear life.

Not long after his mysterious disappearance, O.J. took me to dinner at La Dôme. I somehow knew what was coming before I heard the words.

"I've got to resolve things with Nicole, one way or another," O.J. said. "I've got to give it a shot, for my kids' sake."

He'd decided to commit himself to a one-year trial reconciliation. Nicole and the children would remain in her condo — O.J. didn't want Sydney and Justin bouncing back and forth, in case things didn't pan out. But he'd be able to tuck them in at night and wake them up in the morning, just as Sydney had wanted.

It wasn't fair to hold me on a string, O.J. went on. He couldn't keep hurting me, so he'd stay away for the next twelve months. Until he knew what the future held.

I listened and nodded as my heart plunged through the floor. I didn't try to change his mind or ask a single question, though I suspected this was less than the whole truth. I knew O.J.'s concern about his children was real and deep-seated, but I wasn't so sure how Nicole fit in. And I thought he might be seeing someone else on the side.

But I also recognized that O.J. had to go back, or he'd never understand why he divorced Nicole in the first place.

There were mixed signals to the end. Even as he gave me the bad news, O.J. played with my knees under the table. He kept our champagne glasses filled. By the time the bottle was empty, we'd moved on to a lighter subject: a recent movie where a woman takes off her underwear in a restaurant and hands it to her escort.

"I dare you to do it, right now," O.J. said, laughing.

We'd been talking loud enough to draw the attention of a table across from us. The people caught wind of O.J.'s challenge, and now they were egging me on.

Hey, why not, I thought. If there's one thing a model can do, it's wriggle out of her clothes. In no time at all, I'd reached down for my panties and stuffed them into O.J.'s pocket. The other table cheered. O.J. beamed. I'd made him proud, one more time.

Why play such a twisted game? Beneath the drink and the heat of the moment, I think I wanted to leave O.J. a vivid memento of what he'd soon be missing.

And what he might one day return for.

We wound up in an empty nearby park, petting like a pair of teenagers, until the buzz wore off and I started crying. I threw my friendship ring into the grass and asked O.J. to drop me home. I said good-bye to him — the final punctuation, I feared, in our relationship of good-byes.

I went to bed knowing I'd be alone the next morning, and for many mornings to come.

6

Breaking Up

Our farewell dinner plunged me into depression. Nights were the worst. I waited for a call I knew wasn't coming. I missed O.J.'s voice, his smile, his body next to mine.

Sleep was impossible. I have no taste for hard liquor, but I bought a bottle of vodka — my dad's drink — and stuck it in the freezer. For three straight nights I sat at my dining room table, mixing vodka with tomato juice and gulping as much as I could stand.

For three straight nights I got sick, and then I threw the rest of the bottle away.

I'd always liked all kinds of food. Now the only thing I could get down was the Italian hoagy at Subway. You can only eat so many hoagies, and I began to lose weight.

I was mourning for lost love, a special kind of grief. As the months passed, time failed to heal my wounds. How could it, when I was still stuck in limbo, hoping that O.J. and I would reunite? I turned down any dates that came my way. How could I make someone else happy when I was so miserable myself?

I thought about O.J. incessantly — remembering the good times, glossing over the bad. I thought mean-spiritedly about Nicole. I wondered what their life was like, whether she was making O.J. happy.

My friends kept asking if I was all right. My mother worried about me no end, called several times a day. But the only person I'd let in was my acting coach, who put my torment to good use. The steam would be coming out of my ears or I'd be soggy as yesterday's washcloth, and my teacher would say, "Oh, great — we can use that."

He had a lot to work with; I was a mess. My weight had dropped from 135 to 117, when I'd stopped checking the scale. On the set of *Red Shoe Diaries,* a Showtime drama where I'd landed my first real part, they were mixing vitamins into Häagen-Dazs milkshakes for me.

My face was gaunt, my eyes chronically red from crying. My love life was nonexistent. I'd put O.J. out of my world, but I couldn't get him out of my head.

In fact, I was making real progress in my acting and tried to concentrate my modeling in Los Angeles so I wouldn't miss my weekly classes. Unfortunately, I was getting so thin that my West Coast bookings fell off. There wasn't much demand for swimsuit or lingerie models who had more angles than curves. (It would have been different in New York, where I might have been Calvin Klein's dream skeleton.)

My bills were getting paid by TV work, with clients like Finesse shampoo and Sunkist soda. My most memorable commercial was shot in a downtown L.A. studio for a Swedish cookie company. They submerged me in a bathtub filled with milk, until all you could see of me were my feet and my shoulders on up.

I was already feeling premenstrual and out of sorts — and then the milk became a milkshake. We'd been hit by the aftershock of a fairly significant earthquake; this huge camera looked ready to topple on my head. But the director never missed a beat, never offered to get me out of there. The show must go on, I suppose.

I stayed in touch with Cathy Randa, the one person who thought that O.J. and I could have a future. One day she told me that she'd ordered Rogaine for her boss.

"Why?" I said. "He's not losing his hair."

"No, he's got a problem in another area," Cathy said. She confided that O.J. was having trouble getting excited in bed with Nicole in the wake of her affair with Marcus. He'd heard Rogaine might help.

He never had that problem with me, I thought.

Ah, reality. What had driven O.J. and me apart was a loss of trust and therefore love. Now he was really getting to experience what a lack of trust can do to a person physically.

That was the first sign that O.J.'s reconciliation might not be working out. The next one was more direct. In October, while I was shooting a feature film called *The Dangerous* in New Orleans, O.J. sent me roses and tried to invite himself down to the set. But I told him I was too busy to see him.

In fact, it was more than that — I was feeling really good at the time, and wanted to stay that way. I had a stock role, and the movie was less than Oscar material, but it was good work for me; I was reaching down inside and figuring things out. I was eating right and working out at a gym and exploring New Orleans with the other actors. I seemed to be getting stronger by the day.

In late November, about halfway through the one-year separation we'd agreed to, O.J. called and said, "I made a huge mistake leaving you. I tried to make a go of it with Nicole, but it didn't work."

"What are you saying?"

"I'm saying that I'm sorry I hurt you, and I've got to see you. I'm doing the Thanksgiving game in Dallas — meet me there the day before."

Those were the words I'd imagined so long, but now they made me wary. How could I possibly believe him? How could I let myself get hurt again? I started to make excuses: "I'll be on my way home to Panama City —"

"*Please,* Paula," O.J. pressed me. "I promise I'll make things all right."

That was hard for me to comprehend. How could anyone fix a thing so badly smashed? Still, I needed to hear what O.J. had to say, though I doubted it could help.

I stopped in Dallas and spent the night at O.J.'s hotel. We talked and tried to get comfortable, but it didn't work.

Nor did our lovemaking. I couldn't count the nights I'd hugged a pillow and pretended it was O.J., but now our sex was cool and distant.

I was silently furious, mostly with myself. *Why am I back here?* I thought. *What am I doing?*

The next morning I awoke early. I said good-bye and I meant it.

Not four hours later, back home in Panama City, I turned on the NFL pregame show. There were Sydney and Justin on the sidelines, throwing snowballs at O.J. It would be more than a year later, when the tabloids ran photos of that family scene, that I discovered Nicole had been there as well.

She must have gotten to Dallas while my side of the bed was still warm.

Had O.J. called and sold her the same song and dance? That he'd made a big mistake, but now it was over with me, and he'd make everything all right?

He'd have been correct about one thing. It *was* over, my heart was sure of that.

Back to my gray life I went. I worked and I slept and got up the next day for another modeling job. Weeks went by without my answering my phone; I didn't want to give O.J. a foot in the conversational door. When I checked for messages I'd hear flurries of hangups, and I'd have the eerie sense that it was him. When O.J. missed me enough, he'd call just to hear my recording.

A week or two into 1994, on a job in Miami, the cell phone rang in my car. "Hey, girl, where are you?" O.J. asked.

On such-and-such street in Miami, I said.

"How are you?"

"Fine." I'd give him name, rank, and serial number, no more.

"Well, guess where I am?" O.J. said in his extra-cute voice.

"Where?"

"I've been following you — I'm at the restaurant at Turnberry's, just around the corner."

Ringed by water, Turnberry Isle is one of my favorite hotels, a place where we'd often stayed. I was in a quandary. As soon as I'd heard O.J.'s voice, my fixation spiked like a fever — I *had* to see him.

But how could I let him toy with me like this? Where would it ever end?

Instead of pulling over to make the turn toward Turnberry's, I merged onto the interstate, heading north. I was struggling with myself, my heart against my head; I kept talking to O.J. as I drove away from him. I wanted to believe it was over with Nicole — but could I be sure? I got all the way to Palm Beach before I turned the car around and told him — as casually as I could — that I'd try to drop by.

On the way I stopped at a very expensive boutique in Bal Harbour. I told the salesgirl, "I want an outfit that says, 'I shoulda never let that girl go.'" She pulled together a white silk blouse with little black cuff links, white riding pants, and some Norma Kamali lace-up shoes that crisscrossed up to where the pants began.

That outfit was pure "ouch." I knew it worked the moment I stepped into the restaurant and made eye contact with O.J. He was seated at a table with a friend, and when he saw me he crashed in midsentence — his jaw actually dropped, just like in the movies.

O.J. and I started talking as if we'd left off the night before. As I sipped champagne, I felt unguarded, reconnected. I was happier than I could remember. At one point O.J.'s friend got up and left, and neither of us noticed. I had forgotten how beautiful O.J.'s eyes were — deep brown and liquid, with those big, flapping eyelashes. I couldn't look away from them.

Short of kissing, we were as intimate as two people can be in a public place. He *did* love me, I thought, throwing caution to the ocean breeze.

We finished the bottle and took a second one up to O.J.'s room. Common sense was long gone, and my "ouch" of an outfit soon joined it. We took each other quickly, bluntly — we'd had all the foreplay I needed in the restaurant.

And then, when all was said and done, and O.J. was sleeping, I snapped out of the spell. Reality bit and nearly knocked me over. It was two in the morning and I was more than a little tipsy, but I couldn't get out of the room fast enough. I threw on my clothes and flung myself out the door.

It took a tremendous effort just to stay on the road back to Lagorse Island, where I was staying with friends. When I got there I jumped into the shower and scrubbed myself raw to get the dirt off. To scour off O.J.'s scent, O.J.'s touch.

The next morning O.J. called and said, "Where did you go? Why did you leave? You left the door open — I could have been robbed."

"I know," I said. "I made a big mistake." *And I'm talking to him right now,* I thought.

"I needed you," O.J. went on. "I wanted my Peola next to me in the morning."

In the face of O.J.'s sweetness, there was no way I could explain my revulsion. It made no sense, not even to me.

"I just needed to go," I said, and hung up.

My friends thought I should be dating. They reasoned that I couldn't put O.J. behind me until I had someone else to look forward to.

I tried, very tentatively, and without much success. I saw Mr. Negativity, a director I'd blind-dated years before. He looked like Kevin Costner but whined like Jerry Seinfeld, and time hadn't improved his disposition.

Then there was the actor who was so intense that he was

scary to be around; I could never feel quite safe when he walked behind me.

Finally, there was the dark-haired Adonis my brother Michael brought home. He seemed smart, too, like he had it together. We had a good enough time, and then he dropped me home, where my brother confronted me with more than normal interest.

"Did you kiss him?" Michael asked.

"Yeah, I kissed him good night," I said. "Why do you want to know?"

"Yes!" Michael said, pumping his fist. "That's twenty bucks. Did you do the nasties with him?"

I was aghast. "What are you talking about?"

"I get a hundred if you went all the way," he laughed, without a bit of shame.

My brother was treating me like a filly in the Kentucky Derby. I was too furious for words, too hurt for tears. It was all just fun for him. How could I keep getting betrayed, time after time?

How could I be such a fool?

In April 1994, I bought my white Bronco for $6,000 down. I'd always liked O.J.'s truck, but the purchase had nothing to do with him. Earlier that year I'd stopped at One Rodeo Drive to drop something off at my hairdresser's. Ten minutes later, when I came to retrieve my Toyota 4Runner from valet parking, it had disappeared.

When they finally recovered the Toyota, it was filled with hypodermic needles, pornographic magazines, and bullet holes. An out-of-work actor — he'd also left his 8x10 glossies behind — had stolen my truck, crashed it into a dozen parked cars during the police pursuit, and totaled the front end. When I got my insurance check, I decided to buy a truck more suitable for camping; I'd long dreamed of a trip to the Grand Canyon. That's where the Bronco came in.

As it turned out, my next camping trip would be to Big Bear, at a festival hosted by the Calvary Chapel, a nondenominational group with which I'd been studying the Bible. For three days I was inspired by the singing and praise for God all around me. I hadn't made a real commitment yet, but my eyes were starting to open.

It was around this time that O.J. and I began speaking again. He was in Puerto Rico, filming an NBC pilot called *Frogman*. Nicole had been supposed to join him there but never made it. That was an old sore point between them. Since Sydney's and Justin's births, Nicole had been able to join O.J. on location less and less, and he complained bitterly about it. That the children were now in school and it was hard for her to just pick up and go made no difference to him. He hated feeling lonely on the road.

In any case, O.J. promised me, Nicole was history: "I couldn't come to you any sooner — I'm sorry, but I couldn't hurt you, and I needed to do this first." He was telling me that he'd put in his year, held up his part of the bargain. And wasn't he a loyal, trustworthy person for not pursuing me in the meantime? (If you didn't count our lapses in Dallas and Miami, of course.)

"It's our time, girl," O.J. cooed. Then he asked *me* to come to Puerto Rico. I wasn't buying. I'd moved on, I kept telling myself. There *was* life after O.J., and it wasn't so bad. I was coping just fine, thank you.

On May 8, Mother's Day, when I was visiting Mom in Florida, O.J. sent her a huge bouquet with a card that read, *"I guess I can't call you Mom yet. . . ."* I was incensed — *How dare he!* I grabbed those freaking flowers and tried to hurl them over the balcony.

I had it on good authority that O.J. had been with at least two other women during the past year. ("Aren't you glad that's not you?" a mutual friend would say, trying to cheer me up.) O.J. always had backup — there was always another pretty girl in reserve.

(What I *didn't* know was that O.J. had yet to stop seeing his ex-wife. According to his civil trial testimony, he'd had "a great time" when they dated on May 4, and again on May 7.)

He sprang his ambush on Tuesday, May 10, my stopover day

in L.A. between jobs in Miami and Las Vegas — O.J. had a knack for learning my flight schedule through friends.

After getting off the plane from Miami, I was looking for my limo driver and wondering why he wasn't at the gate. I started walking toward the concourse, pulling my luggage behind me . . . when I caught O.J. in my peripheral vision, sneaking up alongside with a mischievous look in his eyes.

"Hey, good-lookin', what's cookin'?"

"I can't believe you," I said, trying to sound mad and failing abysmally. "You just take the cake."

O.J. had canceled my limo driver to pick me up himself. I loved his spontaneity in spite of myself. He told me again that it was all over with Nicole. When he asked me to dinner — sushi, one of my great weaknesses — I heard myself say yes, impetuous as ever.

By that point, O.J. and I were grooved in our dance. I'd withdraw; he'd maneuver; I'd yield.

But with hindsight, the evening was a watershed. If I'd turned away from O.J. at LAX, if I'd kept on walking and hailed a cab — if I'd kept saying no, and meant it — I wouldn't have wound up dating him the night before the murders.

And if we hadn't renewed our affair, I might have been able to sidestep the topsy-turvy horror show that just about destroyed me.

So why did I agree to try again? If I was thinking at all, it might have been that you can't hate someone without loving him, too. If I felt that violently toward O.J., there must be something there worth another shot.

Over the past year my life had closed up like a flower in a frost. I worked, I studied acting, I read or listened to music at home. I had so little connection to anybody that the idea of a niche in a relationship — even a once-failed relationship — was awfully exciting.

But while I might have been crazy, I wasn't stupid. I was not about to leap into romance and fall flat again. My fear of abandonment was real. We would take small steps, I told O.J., one at a time, and see where they led.

★   ★   ★

I didn't know if our relationship could be fixed, but I felt certain it had no shot without help. At our sushi dinner I'd told O.J. that I wouldn't see him again unless he agreed to meet with Dr. Barry Michaels, a therapist we'd gone to the year before. O.J. halfheartedly agreed.

I don't think either of us gave our all in this exercise. I was too bruised and mistrusting, and O.J. couldn't see the point of it.

When Dr. Michaels saw how angry I was coming in, he proposed seeing us one at a time. After hearing O.J.'s point of view, the therapist cautioned him, "Don't pressure her to move too quickly before you're communicating on other levels."

In other words: Don't try to rush me into bed.

But after I went in and voiced my hurt and distrust, Dr. Michaels had different advice: "I think it's time for you to move on."

As we drove off in our separate trucks, O.J. was in front of me. I could see him talking on his cell phone, no doubt complaining to some guy friend about the drudgery he'd just been through: *Oh, I had to do this with Paula to make her happy. . . .*

I wasn't quite ready to take Dr. Michaels's advice. But a sense of finality, of failure, began to sink in.

O.J. and I passed a night or two together after that, but they were spiritless episodes. I loathed myself. I beat myself up for not waiting for something — someone — better. Five minutes or so after our bodies disentwined, I'd be hunting for my underwear and the keys to my Bronco. I'd leave O.J. again, in a hurry, as I had that tipsy night in Miami.

From the beginning, we'd had a relationship of good-byes. Leaving was easy for me.

Regrettably, so was coming back.

O.J. wanted to go to Palm Springs for Memorial Day weekend and coaxed me into coming with him. I didn't see much point in the trip; I didn't see what it could change.

I was stuck at work Friday till midnight, shooting a cable television comedy called *The Newz,* in which I played a sadistic dentist. By the time we got into Palm Springs, at 2:30 A.M., I was exhausted. But I was looking forward to the morning. Maybe we'd have a special breakfast and a chance to weigh the burning issue of the day: why two intelligent people in love couldn't work things out.

No such luck. O.J. was up with the birds for his golf game, and I threw a fit. Once I'd seen his golf mania as an annoying but harmless quirk. Now it represented all the distance between us, everything that was wrong.

I had a lot of time to myself that morning. Time can turn doubts into shadows and big, scary things. I brooded about the past and all of O.J.'s lies. I'd *wanted* to start fresh and forget. But now I realized, again, that it wasn't possible.

When O.J. finally came back to our room, I told him, "Look, I just can't do this."

O.J. had heard this so often that he no longer took it seriously. At times he'd make light of my distress. At others he'd air his frustration, treating me like some irrational, demanding woman who could never be happy.

"What do you want from me," he'd say, "a pound of flesh?"

I resented that expression — if my last look in the mirror was any indication, I was the one losing flesh here.

The truth was, I didn't know what I expected from O.J. Not marriage, or to move in with him (he'd already asked, and I'd refused). Not to give up golf forever — I wanted none of those things. There wasn't any way O.J. could wrap the world in a bow for me. There weren't any magic words for him to say.

Because it wasn't the words that were missing.

It was trust, and when trust is missing there are no words.

I left him and flew back to Los Angeles. That evening O.J. rang up to my apartment; he'd cut short his weekend to follow me home again. We talked for hours, to no result.

I can't do this, I kept saying, to myself more than to him. Knowing that I'd have to end it if I was ever to be free.

*   *   *

They say that if you don't like what one therapist tells you, try another. Upon the advice of a stylist friend of mine, I'd been seeing a hypnotherapist for several weeks before O.J. and I got back together. She was a really smart woman who'd helped me understand things.

I'm walking down a huge stone staircase with a giant bag of sand on my shoulder. The bag is very heavy, but there's a hole in it. With each step I take, the load gets lighter and lighter on my shoulders. Until I reach the bottom, a beautiful garden, and feel positively weightless. . . .

In my hypnotic state, the bag of sand represented O.J. and my hurt. Each time I walked down the staircase, it seemed a little more possible that I could leave him behind me.

"Step carefully," my therapist warned me when I told her that O.J. was trying to get back in my life. "I would love to meet him — we could see if he's workable."

When I passed that on to O.J., he accepted the invitation. I think he took it as a challenge. He figured he could outfox the therapist and win our debate. He felt sure that he could make better points for staying together than I could for splitting up.

If our session revealed anything, it was how far apart we'd drifted. I raised my main concern: the lies O.J. had told me and how they'd damaged my trust in him. When I brought up the trip to Disneyland he'd taken with Nicole, O.J. had a quick counter.

"I don't have a problem with it," he said, "the kids don't have a problem with it — you're the only one with the problem." Yes, he'd lied to me on Valentine's Day, he was sorry, but it was over. "There are some things we can't fix," O.J. argued. "It's happened, it's done, we've decided to stay together and you've got to let it go."

At the end of the hour, my therapist told O.J. that my feelings were valid, and he had to think of them first.

If we decided to stay together, she added, our past could not be allowed to come into the present. We had to start fresh or not at all.

Walking us out the door, she whispered to me, "I think he's workable."

O.J. and I agreed to see her again, but we never did — we got caught up doing more "important" things. Besides, I knew that O.J. could always outflank me. He was so convincing, so reasonable — and so shameless. "*All* men cheat," he'd insist.

O.J. was so persuasive that there were times I'd wonder if I *was* asking too much from him. Maybe he was right and I was wrong. Maybe my questions had no answers.

Maybe "complete" love, I thought sadly, lived only in songs.

In my visits to Rockingham that May and June, I noticed something missing: Michelle, O.J.'s jewel of a housekeeper. Earlier that year Nicole had ended an argument by slapping Michelle, a tiny woman who might have come up to Nicole's shoulder. O.J. urged Michelle to file a police report; she quit her job instead.

Around the time we saw my hypnotherapist, O.J. told me that Nicole had wrecked her Ferrari while she was under the influence. And he got real concerned when he dropped his children off at Nicole's condo and found Faye Resnick staying there, "wired out of her mind."

In refreshing contrast to Dolph, O.J. steered clear of drugs. I never saw him do cocaine, a big plus. After witnessing how coke had hurt my brother Michael, I knew that I could never live around drugs again.

During the time I spent with him, in fact, O.J. took nothing stronger than Motrin, which he needed daily for his arthritis. (When I later read claims by Faye Resnick, and then a Buffalo drug dealer, that O.J. was a heavy cocaine user, they were talking about someone different from the man I knew.)

One day I was at Rockingham when Nicole called. As soon as O.J. picked up, even I could guess she was furious — O.J. was trying in vain to calm her down. It was all about Nicole's friend Faye

2/1/68
My brothers: Michael, age three,
and Vinnie, age five.

11/69
I'm almost three.

Second grade.

My stepfather Bill and Mother on their wedding day. They were married on the beach in a simple ceremony. That's my stepbrother, Lee, in the background.

A day on the boat:
Mother.

A day on the boat:
Bill.

This is how I remember my father most, always a
pretty lady on his arm.

Seventh-grade cheerleading.
Dad couldn't be there and Coach had his
three daughters to escort, so good-hearted
Thomas did the honors. It was
a very sad night.

Azalea Trail Queen.

Moments before the announcement that
I had been chosen Sweetheart of the
Beach. Mother, in her role.

Playing in the wardrobe on the set of Roman Polanski's Pirates *in Tunisia*

Seventeen years old, in Venice, on my first Italian photo shoot.

On a modeling shoot in Africa.

Dolph Lundgren tricked me into a date that lasted three years, with the help of photographer Firooz Zahedi.

Dolph and I on the beach in Panama City.

This was taken by Terrance Donovan and is Mother's favorite picture.

Modeling furs for Grosvenor.

Modeling for DeBeers Diamonds in London.

Taking a break from the collections on the streets of Paris.

My brother Vinnie.

Italian Bazaar cover photographed by James Moore.

My favorite cover — Australia was so peaceful compared to the hustle-bustle of New York and Paris. Even today, it's highly unusual for a man to appear on the cover of a woman's magazine.

COSMOPOLITAN

DECEMBER 1988 $2.80
NZ $3.95 (inc G

Free pull-ou
**COSMO MAN
CALENDA**

**101 knockout
Christmas ideas**
Gifts! Food! Fashion!

Andy Warhol's party book

**The beauty secrets of the
million-dollar cosmetic queens**

Cocktails with Tom Cruise

<u>WIN</u> a fabulous trip to New York,
a Hawaii stopover <u>plus</u> spending money!

WILL YOUR
MARRIAGE
LAST?
Take our test

Resnick, who'd recently told O.J. that she wanted to be friends with us, too. Now Faye had invited herself along to an upcoming dinner at Cedars-Sinai that we'd be attending.

O.J. didn't think Faye was really the issue for Nicole. He'd told me how sad Nicole felt when O.J. and I got back together.

After hearing Nicole out, O.J. said, "Look, I didn't invite her. She invited herself. I don't care if she goes or doesn't go." He was talking loud, as usual, but he sounded more exasperated than really angry.

O.J. was already put out with Nicole. She'd tried to fudge on the IRS by keeping Rockingham as her legal address, which would give her a big tax benefit. O.J. was one of those by-the-book businessmen, and he didn't want the IRS coming after him. He had his lawyer send Nicole a letter saying she could no longer use the Rockingham address.

Those small incidents aside, Nicole seemed very much in the background in those first two weeks of June. O.J. hardly talked about her. He had enough to worry about with me and our therapy.

On June 5, we took Sydney and Justin to a high-profile pediatric AIDS benefit. I spent most of my time with the kids, stayed as far away from O.J. as I could. It reminded me of our first time in public, two long years ago, at Magic Johnson's birthday party.

But this time I wasn't dodging the cameras; I was dodging the man who'd brought me. "Are you Daddy's best friend?" Sydney asked me. I didn't really know what to tell her, but her words rang in my mind throughout the trial.

O.J. was used to winning, in everything. He was sure he could charm me back. Earlier that spring, he'd sent me a card:

I guess this is just a process we're going through. I just pray that when we are old and laying around together, we can look back on this and laugh.

On Friday, June 10, I picked O.J. up at LAX with a smile. My tension had dissolved, because I'd finally made up my mind.

My bag of sand was almost empty.

*   *   *

On Saturday morning I saw my hypnotherapist and broke the news. I told her I'd felt a lot healthier and stronger before O.J. and I had tried to reconcile. It was time to lighten that bag of sand some more. For that matter, it was time to dump it off my back. I was ready to be in the world again; my mourning period was done.

"How are you going to tell him?" my therapist asked, and then I realized that I hadn't thought that through.

"This is going to hurt him," she went on, "and you have to do it in a very delicate way. It can't be out of anger or blame — you know what will happen if you tell him the way you *want* to tell him."

I knew exactly what she meant. If I made specific complaints, O.J. would just resume our debate. He'd trot out all his old tricks, work overtime to win me back.

My therapist knew the truth as well as I: that O.J. was a man who had trouble letting go.

It was one of the many things we had in common.

On Saturday night, O.J. and I had a longstanding date at a black-tie fundraiser in Bel Air to honor Leah Rabin, the wife of Israel's prime minister. I knew how much O.J. was looking forward to the evening. I think he saw it as an opportunity to make things up to me.

I didn't have the heart to spoil it for him.

When O.J. picked me up in his Bentley for the party, he had one word: "Wow."

Gold sequins can do that to a man. The dress was real daring for me; I'm usually low-key in public. When I'd called O.J. that afternoon to ask him about it, he said he thought it "might be a little too much."

But when I saw the look on his face, I knew I was fine.

My sequins set the tone for the evening, which was magic from start to end. The party was outdoors, in a cozy Italian garden. The night was balmy, and O.J. and I were sweetly in touch again, as if we'd turned back the clock to relive our first infatuation.

For the first time in weeks, I felt at ease with him. I was receptive; O.J. was attentive. When he greeted someone he knew, he'd tell them, "This is my girlfriend, Paula." I'd never much liked that title and the pigeonhole it put me in, but for now I basked in it. I was happy and proud to be on this magnificent man's arm.

I was included in each conversation, and we talked about everything under the sun — everything, for a change, except our own dreary problems. Then the people drifted off, leaving O.J. and me at our table, alone in our euphoria. In between little kisses, we watched the human carnival around us: the man who kept dribbling food down his chin, and the lady next to him — his wife? — who seemed so discontent; the brunette in an advanced state of décolletage, making eyes at a guy who was with someone else.

We could joke about those people because we felt so different from them. Our eyes were only for each other.

"Can you imagine," O.J. said, gesturing at the huge house in front of us, "filling all these rooms with babies, you and me?"

I laughed and thought about my fantasy for when I grow old, a funny dream I'd shared with O.J. I'd be in a rocking chair, my man right beside me. Neither of us would have any teeth left, but that wouldn't matter. I'd just lean over and say, "Come gum me, baby!"

Barely an arm's length away from us, Natalie Cole began to sing — a few jazz tunes, and then that wonderful ballad her father once sang.

"Unforgettable, that's what you are . . ."

I leaned back on O.J., smiling and sleepy. Having made my big decision, I could relax with him at last — the pressure was off. He was such a pretty man in his tuxedo; I know that I must have looked deeply in love. It wasn't a pose. I felt all the warmth I'd ever felt for O.J., all the closeness, all the comfort of his arms.

I'm not usually one to deny her feelings. But for these few brief hours I decided to take each moment as it came — no analysis, no dissection, no what-are-you-thinking-and-why.

After so much grief and anxiety, I thought, we deserved one night for its own sake.

Natalie finished, and we left the party early, around ten o'clock. O.J. had to be up for golf, of course. As the Bentley sailed up to my apartment, the spell was broken — I was relieved when O.J. didn't ask to come up.

I'd already told him that I might be flying to Las Vegas the next day. I never informed him why I was going. If I told O.J. about Michael Bolton, it would only hurt him and confuse things. Michael wasn't the reason we were breaking up.

O.J. would be flying to Chicago on business Sunday night, after Sydney's dance recital. We kissed good night, and I casually promised to call him.

A few minutes later I was talking to Michael, sharing my excitement for the day to come — and confiding that I had one last piece of unfinished business before I left.

On Sunday, June 12, I didn't pick up my phone until seven in the morning. By that time, O.J. figured to be on the third fairway, with his cell phone back in his car. There would be no one to hear my voice except O.J.'s computerized answering service.

I knew it was a cop-out to say good-bye in a phone message, but I didn't know how else to do it. If I spoke to O.J. directly, it would have been a big confrontation. We would have argued for hours. At best, I would miss my flight to Vegas; at worst, I'd lose my nerve and be back at square one.

Our track record, after all, wasn't so great. I had trouble saying no, and O.J. wouldn't take it for an answer.

This time had to be different from all the other breakups. This one had to stick. I wasn't rushing from his bed in disgust this morning. I was turning the page and closing the book, and wishing him well as he did the same.

It was terribly hard to make that call. I slowly punched in

the number and uttered a small wish: *Please don't pick up, please don't pick up* . . . After four tense rings, I heard O.J.'s lighthearted recording and then my starting gun, the beep.

"I know you've been trying to work things out," I began, just as I'd rehearsed, "and I've been trying very hard, too. But between work and golf and the kids and my schedule and your schedule, there isn't enough time to figure out all these things that hurt so much.

"I just couldn't get the answers I needed. There's no one to blame — we're just two people in different worlds.

"The pain is too much for me. I can't go on sleeping with you and then moving to the couch and crying for hours — the feelings are tearing me apart."

I told O.J. that I deserved to have a family, but that it couldn't be with him — "You already have two families, and you won't want to start a third, even though you've said you would."

Once I got started, I went on for quite a while, maybe fifteen minutes. Toward the end, I remember telling O.J. that if he truly loved me, he would let me go. It was painful for me, too, but I thought it for the best. I told him I'd be gone for a while and that I wouldn't be answering my phone.

I closed with words I hoped O.J. would accept and understand, both for what they were and what they weren't:

"I love you."

I was so excited when I hung up that phone, and proud of myself, too, that I'd been able to go through with it. I'd taken back control of my life. It was such a huge thing, and I'd somehow done it the right way.

The bad time was over, I thought, as I gathered my luggage.

I was flying so high that I barely needed a plane.

7

In the Beginning

You might say that O.J. was a mistake from the start — that it was *supposed* to be Joe Namath.

When I was a little girl in Florida, I'd tell my friends, "I'm going to marry Joe Namath when I grow up." I'd heard that Joe had won the Super Bowl, but I loved him for himself: for his cleft chin and cocky grin and rakish sideburns. He was about the cutest thing on television this side of the *Brady Bunch* boys.

That Alabama drawl of Joe's didn't bother me, either. I was the first person in my family born down South — my big brothers could make me bawl by calling me "Johnny Reb."

My mother, Mary Ann, was raised in a well-to-do Connecticut family, the Cartenutos. Her parents, one generation removed from Italy, owned two prosperous florist shops and a comfortable country-style home in Shelton.

My mother married her Army sweetheart. They built a gracious house of their own and were set to go into the family business. But they grew apart, and to her parents' dismay, my mother got divorced, then married a salesman named Vincent Barbieri: my father.

Dad was the kind of guy, they said, who could sell iced tea to an Eskimo. He was also the black sheep of the Barbieri family, a man given to drinking, philandering, and violent rages. In 1964, my mother left him and took my two big brothers — Vinnie, then two years old, and Michael, just a baby — to a new life in Florida. Dad followed soon after. The result of my parents' reconciliation, a girl born on New Year's Eve of 1966, was me. Grandfather Cartenuto was enraged by Mom's departure. When it was clear that she wasn't coming back, he took a bulldozer and rolled over the storage shed with all the possessions she'd left behind.

My family settled in West Palm Beach, where my father became a truckdriver, in tune with his wandering style. I grew up with this image of him as a Clint Eastwood character, a guy who drank two fingers of vodka for breakfast and could beat up any man, anywhere.

The difference was that Clint Eastwood never hit a woman. I was still an infant when Dad lost it one day and pushed Mom against a piece of furniture, cracking two of her ribs. Then he just left us, leaving his sanitation truck company — the family's main source of income — in the lurch.

Mom had to save the business, so she took a leave from her law office and went out to work. Setting me next to her in my baby basket, she drove that garbage truck with its fourteen forward gears to all 500 stops on the route. Our customers would come out and try to help Mom; they knew what a fix we were in.

My parents got divorced when I was three years old, and I didn't see Dad much after that. He'd be on the road, or with one or another woman.

Mom remarried two years later to Bill, the owner of a local barbecue restaurant, and like her a transplanted northerner. Bill was a charmer with an uproarious sense of humor and a wide range of talents. He was an easy man to fall in love with. A superior chef, he was also a crack mechanic. He could fix anything from a coffee pot to a convertible; he could take things apart and put them back together.

When I was seven years old, my stepfather sold his restaurant and we moved to Panama City, then a sleepy beach town. After his discharge from the navy, Bill worked in advertising at the *Miami News*. In Panama City, he returned to advertising, and found us a three-bedroom cinderblock house in St. Andrews, a working-class neighborhood.

The best part of the house was a huge backyard, where my brothers and I would play our endless games. A far corner served as final resting place for the various pets who came and went over the next years, each of them buried with the solemnity and dignity of a real person. Until, that is, Mom found her passion for gardening. She started with a row of green beans, then came strawberries, tomatoes, eggplants, watermelons, squash, even peanuts. Our playground was getting a lot smaller.

The front lawn, meanwhile, was reserved for a huge treasure of a houseboat with a rusted-out hull that Bill worked on whenever he could. Our games were squeezed out into the quiet dead-end street.

It wasn't long before Bill left the newspaper. As my father never paid child support, Mom was carrying the whole family on her salary as a supervisor with a land-title company.

There wasn't much money, but we made do. We lived off the garden and out of the Gulf, where Bill would take us fishing. We feasted on oysters, shrimp, and blue crabs — I could eat spaghetti and crabs every week when they were topped with Mom's marsala sauce. One summer we caught loads of king mackerel, which we ate every way imaginable. To this day I can't look at one.

We lived in a town that felt safe and small. I could fish with my friends among the cranes and herons or build forts in the woods across the street. When the weather got hot, we'd invade the motels and go swimming. We called it "pool-hopping" — when we got thrown out of one place, we just moved to the next.

Transportation was no problem. Bill found an old ten-speed, sanded it down, and painted it the prettiest silver you ever did see. He added racing stripes and glitter, and I wound up with the sharpest bike in the neighborhood.

There were times, however, when I'd feel a little deprived. My great passion in life was Chick-O-Sticks, a crunchy peanut-butter candy. Before I got my bike, I'd walk fourteen blocks down to the little convenience store and plunk down my nickel for a Chick-O-Sticks fix. But there were many days when I didn't have that nickel. So I'd hang around until I saw some grown-up loading up on candy at the counter. I'd crowd in real close and stare soulfully at the Chick-O-Sticks. In my most pitiful Little Orphan Annie imitation, I'd say, "I sure wish I could have some of *that*."

It never worked.

My mother made my dresses until I was ten years old. They were summery, cotton things with floral prints, and I thought they were beautiful. My only pants were polyester, until one day in fifth grade when I got to borrow my friend Sandra's Levi's.

At reading circle that day, James Yon, the cutest boy in the class, kept edging over till he was sitting right next to me. I was startled when I felt him playing with my backside.

"What are you doing?" I said. I was genuinely baffled. No boy had ever paid me a second look.

And he said, "Oh, I was just trying to get your Levi tag with my pen."

On our way home after school that day, James stopped and gave me a kiss — my first kiss.

It was my initial glimpse at the power of fashion.

By then Bill was getting into his bourbon earlier in the day, till he was pouring a "bump" into his breakfast coffee. The more he drank, the meaner he got. He'd be sweet and loving in the morning, peevish by lunch, a red-faced bear by dinner.

Later on I'd understand how damaged Bill had been, how he'd been packed off to a brutal military school when he was seven years old, after his mother died. But at the time I could only fear him.

Sometimes he'd take me along to the bar, with strict instructions. Whenever we saw a good-looking woman, I'd recite, "You sure are pretty, ma'am."

After returning to St. Andrews, Bill would tinker with his latest greasy motor at the kitchen counter, drinking the hours away. It might be long after dark when my mother finally made it home, exhausted after another day at work.

One night I came in for dinner and found my mother sitting quietly at the kitchen table with a cocktail in her hand. She was the picture of dignity — except for the tomato sauce dripping off her nose and the blue crab legs embedded in her hair, sticking out like some crooked antennae.

"Mother, what happened?" I cried.

"Bill just admitted," she calmly replied, "that he hates spaghetti and crabs."

She never raised her voice to him that night, never said a word. Bill was a big man — six-two, 240 pounds — and she feared to fuel his fire.

But as my brothers got older, they began standing up to Bill, and the result could be a bare-knuckled brawl. I remember one day after a big rainstorm when twelve-year-old Michael picked up a two-by-four and squared off against Bill in the carport. After staring daggers at each other over the family sedan, the two of them moved their standoff to the front yard. Bill lunged at Michael and slipped and fell in the mud. It was a turning point of sorts, the first time Bill had been defeated in their confrontations.

Then Bill delivered an ultimatum to my mother, one I'd hear many times: "Either he goes or I go."

Those conflicts would make me feel so helpless; I couldn't fight, and I couldn't leave.

Shortly after we moved to Panama City, I found my home away from home.

A young man with a shy smile knocked on our door and asked my mother if I might like to go to Sunday school at a new, independent church across town. Though my mother was Catholic, she probably sensed that I needed a haven from the chaos at home. That young man's love of God shone through him, and she wanted me to share it.

Come Sunday morning she stood with me at the corner, waiting for the yellow bus — "the JOY Bus," it was called, for *Jesus* first, *Others* second, *Yourself* last. Among several dozen kids from all over town, I took my seat for my first trip to Sunday school.

I liked everything about the Church of Christ. I loved the stories and the songs and the warm family feeling I'd get when I joined the congregation for services. I felt fully accepted, never out of place.

I was awed when people took their little glasses of grape juice to signify the blood Christ shed on the cross. I was only eight years old, but I knew I needed to be baptized before I could take my glass. I understood how serious it was even then.

I liked it most of all when that young man I'd met in St. Andrews — the minister, Jack Reece — took me in hand and told me how Jesus loved me. I could hardly wait for the next Sunday. I'd get mad if Mom and Bill made me leave church early to go fishing.

By the time I turned twelve, I'd drifted away from the JOY Bus and the Church of Christ. But those serene Sundays had planted a seed, and it would grow inside me all the same.

Most girls I knew growing up in Panama City still live there today. It was rare for someone to leave the state, unheard-of to leave the South. My more ambitious friends planned to be teachers. But for some reason I was different — I'd say I wanted to be an actress, and I didn't care who laughed.

I'd work hard in ballet class, then come home to devise my own dance routines. I practiced with a tape recorder I'd gotten as a bribe to stop biting my nails.

The early returns were not real encouraging. In sixth grade I entered a talent contest — a brave act, since I had no apparent talent at the time. My dance teacher helped me put together a routine to "Shake Your Booty," by K.C. and the Sunshine Band.

On the big day I dressed up in my little red-and-white fringe outfit, and whenever the chorus got to "Shake, shake, shake," I would wiggle and gyrate with all my might. I remember Vinnie and Michael sitting in the front row and slumping down lower and lower as I kept on shaking — they were mortified.

The judges were similarly unimpressed.

I longed for Dad to show up at these occasions and was invariably disappointed. Now and then I'd visit him for a week or so in the summer back in West Palm Beach. I remember tickling his back while he read the newspaper over his morning shots of vodka, and how he liked to call me "Button."

Dad was never mean to me, but I'd hear some wild stories about him. One time he stuck his new wife's head under a running faucet, spoiling her carefully teased beehive and all the while insisting that *she* was drunk. The poor woman, a no-nonsense bartender, got so mad that she shot my father in the behind.

"Can you believe Dad got shot in the butt?" Michael said gleefully.

Or as my cousin Melissa put it, "You have the most *colorful* family."

Every so often a job took my father through Panama City — whenever I saw a white truck, I looked into the cab to see if it was him. Many were the nights I lay in bed crying, till my mother came in to soothe me.

"Is my daddy dead?" I'd ask her. "Why doesn't he call me? Why doesn't he *love* me?"

"You'll see him soon," Mom would say.

She was almost always wrong.

When I made my sixth-grade midget-football cheerleading squad, Dad swore he'd be there to escort me at our homecoming game. I waited till the very last minute of halftime; I watched all the other girls take their proud fathers' arms.

Dad never showed. Finally one of the players offered to escort me. I remember how disheveled the boy looked, with one sleeve up and one sleeve down on his windbreaker.

I was crushed, as only as an eleven-year-old can be. It might have been kinder if Dad had left my young life for good and stopped getting my hopes up.

Soon I was looking elsewhere for a father figure — to a house across the street, next to the Gulf Coast Community College athletic dorms, where the Whitehouse family moved the summer after my sixth grade.

Coach Whitehouse was a remarkable man. He ran both the high school and community college baseball teams and somehow raised five children on his own after his ex-wife moved to a different town.

Through junior high I'd have dinner most nights with my surrogate family. The coach was always there, making sure there was meat and two vegetables on the table. He always made room for me. Before long I was calling him "Dad."

The coach's eldest daughter, Marsha, became my best friend. She was sleeping over one night, in my tiny corner bedroom, when we awoke to a rocking explosion. Marsha and I grabbed our blankets and ran outside as the fire trucks arrived to douse a blazing car by the dorms.

Later we learned that the car belonged to a white girl who had climbed into a black player's bedroom window. That wasn't done in Panama City. Our schools were integrated, but interracial dating was unheard-of. Too many people in town shared the sentiments of my father, who'd long ago told Mom: "If you are ever raped by a black man, don't come home."

Race perplexed me when I was young. I remember being chased down my street by some black children chanting, "White cracker, white cracker, white cracker!"

Meanwhile, the white students in school would point at my oversized lips and snidely tease that I had "black blood" in me.

I always seemed to be in between things.

As I entered junior high school, a kind person might have called me a late bloomer. But I was convinced I was the ugliest girl on the Gulf Coast. I had those big lips and a chipped front tooth from a bike accident. I was tall and bony. Worst of all, I'd stayed flat-chested when every other girl in school seemed to be developing.

My brothers, ever sensitive, would croon a takeoff on the seventies song "Brickhouse": *"She's a brick wall, she's flat."* I'd cry and want to strangle them, all the more because I knew they were right. With my ruler-shaped body and mop of curly hair, I looked like a Q-tip.

In school I found my niche as class clown. I played the same part at home. Relentlessly cheerful, I tried to divert everyone from Bill's rages — not least Bill himself.

Later on, in family counseling, I learned that each of us had played a textbook role. Michael was the rebel, the one who defiantly fought back. Vinnie was the one who ran away — at seventeen, he left home to surf in St. Augustine.

I was the joker, laboring for a laugh.

And Mom was the silent person, the one who just took the abuse and took it and took it.

Never stable, her marriage was getting downright dangerous. Bill would disappear for weeks at a time. At night I'd lie frozen in bed. I'd hear dishes broken and my stepfather's rough harangue, and then an ominous silence.

I remember being afraid to cry or cough or make the slightest sound for fear that Bill would hear and come in and start on me. I lay still as a statue, hoping that the sounds would stop. Wishing that Bill would go away, disappear.

Sometimes Mom would gather her three children and flee with us to a motel down the street. She had a standing arrangement, and for a while we averaged three nights a week there. It was an adventure for my brothers and me, even when the four of us had to share one bed.

My mother didn't always get away in time, however. One morning, after spending the night at Marsha's, I found Mom lying on the living room couch, facing the wall with her back to me. I remember how her arms were stretched over her head. She used to tell me to sleep that way, that it would make me grow taller.

I was chattering away, all excited about something, but Mom wouldn't turn around. "Please *look* at me," I said.

Then I saw what she'd been hiding — one whole side of her face was black and blue. The night before, Bill had lost it again. The police finally had to knock down the front door to get in. They took Bill away, but not before Mom suffered a concussion.

"Why do you stay?" I pleaded with her. "We can leave — let's just go. We don't have to come back here *ever*."

But for all those years Mom put off moving on. I think she was afraid to lose her third marriage. She kept hoping things would get better. She kept hoping the brilliant, charming man she had fallen in love with would resurface.

She was afraid, finally, to be alone.

It wasn't until I was much older that I began to understand why it took so long for Mom to leave. When you place a man at the center of your life and define your happiness through him, it's a very tough thing to let that man go. Even when he makes you feel as if you're on a roller coaster nine days out of ten, it gets hard to trust that you could ever be happy without him.

What amazes me about Mom is how she sustained her relationships with her children. Every now and then, whenever the weather turned especially cold or stormy, my mother would skip work and let us skip school. She would cook up a big pot of spaghetti or stew, and we'd all cuddle in bed together and watch movies. That was "Huggy Day."

Our lives finally changed in 1981, when I was set to enter high school. One day my mother came home with a big smile and said grandly, "Well, I've got us that swimming pool you always wanted."

By then a licensed Realtor, she had bought twelve raw acres in the countryside, subdivided them into one-acre parcels, and sold them on installment plans. Then she traded in the mortgages for a small motel called the Thomas Drive. We had not only a fabulous pool, but a new home — and a separation from Bill.

For me our new life was a fairy tale, though I sometimes felt like Cinderella before she got her glass slipper. We never had a maid at the Thomas Drive. It was a mom-and-pop operation, without the pop. Michael and I cleaned the rooms and the pool, and helped check people in when we weren't in school.

High school began to open my eyes. My humanities teacher, Mrs. McKelvin, introduced me to Mozart and Dante and Michelangelo. Most of all I liked the French Impressionists — I felt like I could step into their paintings and land on a Parisian boulevard.

I ached to travel. I wanted to go everywhere and I hadn't been anywhere, just one visit to my cousins' in Connecticut and a short trip to Disney World after Mom and Bill got married.

Even within Panama City, there were places I could not go. In high school I mixed for the first time with people from Bay Point, the gated, wealthy neighborhood that straddled a golf course. Bay Point lay just three blocks from our motel, but it seemed another world — a place for *normal* families, where people didn't drink and fight and call the police every other night.

The Bay Point kids were nice enough. One of them, a doctor's son, would give me a ride to school in the morning. But I still thought they were different and that I wasn't good enough to go out with them.

In tenth grade I began to emerge from my geeky stage. I even heard a few wolf whistles when I passed the college boys down for spring break. Then my big brothers stepped in to ruin my budding social life. They were the big surfers in town, the tough guys, and soon word got around: *That's Michael and Vinnie Barbieri's little sister — don't mess with her!*

I thought I'd finally broken through when the captain of the football team — just the coolest thing that ever walked — started flirting with me in math class. All my girlfriends had already gone much further than I, and when he finally asked me out, I thought, *This is it — he's really going to give me a big old kiss.*

When my date arrived, Michael intercepted him at our door. By the time we got in the car, the guy wouldn't even look at me. He stared straight ahead all evening, even more nervous than I was. When he dropped me off, I exploded: "What is it — what's wrong with you? What's wrong with *me?*"

And the football captain said, "Your brother told me if I touched you, he was going to break both my arms."

I marched into the motel, grabbed Michael's beer bottle out of his hand, and flung it at him: "How dare you? He'll never ask me out again!" And he didn't, of course.

Not until junior year did I have a real boyfriend. He was very dramatic. Whenever I was late for my first class, which was just about every day, he'd call me on the phone and say, "If you're late tomorrow, I swear, I'm just going to shoot myself!"

After we'd dated for a few weeks, I was ready to break up with him. But I kept putting it off — and then I got a phone call. My steady had smashed his motorcycle into a parked truck and fractured both his legs.

I rushed down to the hospital and sat there with him almost every day for a month. There was no way I could leave the boy now. That would be the easy way out, and I saw how much he needed me.

After he came home, he spent two more months relearning how to walk. Meanwhile, I missed the Christmas Ball and all the football parties. I was out of circulation for three months, an eternity for a fifteen-year-old, but I didn't feel right dating anyone else.

It wasn't until my boyfriend returned to school and seemed healthy and strong that I broke up with him. The girls in my class were appalled: How could I do such a horrible thing to such a sweet boy?

So I wound up feeling guilty about a situation I should have avoided in the first place.

It was a pattern I'd repeat, at much greater cost, with a man named O.J. Simpson.

For some time I'd assumed that I would go to the University of Florida and eventually to law school. My mother had worked in law offices for years — I think she would have become a lawyer herself, except that my grandfather believed that girls had no place in higher education.

When the local Sweetheart of the Beach pageant rolled around, in February of my junior year, a woman from the garden club, Kay White, encouraged me to enter. I did it on a lark; I certainly had no hope of winning. After all, I'd been rejected as a football cheerleader five years in a row. It got to the point where Mom wouldn't even ask me how I'd done. I'd just shrug my shoulders, rub my eyes, and get over it.

I always thought a person had to keep trying. It didn't matter where you wound up as long as you put forth an effort. For me that meant captaining the dance team at football halftimes, where I got to make up the routines with my girlfriends.

I had no idea of how to prepare for my first pageant. Most of the competitors had their hair in curlers, with manicures and pedicures to boot. I'd never even heard of a pedicure before — I was a tomboy who loved to run around barefoot, and I'd been busy cleaning the bathroom upstairs in Unit No. 7!

My curly hair fought me, as usual, so I brushed it wet and hoped it would stay out of my eyes. I didn't wear any makeup. I just soaked up the experience and tried to stay out of the tougher girls' way.

The pageant was staged at the civic center on the beach. All the moms and dads were out front, armed with cameras. They announced the third and second runners-up, and I felt happy just to be a part of the show.

Then they announced the first runner-up — and Mom's photo shows me beaming like the sun when I heard my name. After so many rejections, so many times of "No, no, no," I'd finally gotten a "Yes."

The following month I entered the Azalea Trail, a much bigger to-do, with 300 junior and senior girls from all four area high schools. The winner was supposed to represent young Southern womanhood, and we were presented in antebellum dresses and hats.

Once again I came fresh-faced, unadorned. While certain I was out of my league, I barreled ahead. I have another picture, taken when they named me Azalea Trail Queen, with my hand raised to my face. I remember that moment — it was the first time in my life that I'd felt *pretty*.

Years later, I learned that a number of judges were concerned that I was too "sexy" to be a proper queen. That would have seemed ridiculous to me at the time. I was still your basic brick wall; a 32-B cup would have meant progress. But those grown-ups must have spotted something I couldn't yet see in the mirror.

That spring I got to meet my first celebrity: Eddie Money, in town for a March of Dimes Walk-a-Thon. Life sure is changing, I thought. Of course, I had no idea who Eddie Money was, but I knew he had to be important.

A local DJ picked me up in a limousine, a huge thrill in it-self, and took me out to where Eddie Money was staying. I delivered breakfast to his door, decked out in my little crown and pants suit.

Judging from how Eddie sounded that morning, he'd had quite a party the night before. He slid into the limo, and I'll never forget what he said to me en route to our public appearance: "So, what concerts you been to?"

"I'm sorry," I said. "I've never been to a concert before. My mom won't let me go."

"Ain't never been to a concert before?" he rasped. "She must be a virgin."

I just wanted to sink into the seat of that limousine and melt away — because he was right, of course.

In my senior year, now fortified by lip gloss, blue eye shadow, and my new set of hot curlers, I won Sweetheart of the Beach. A month later, my friends Terri and Debbie heard about a fashion show at the Panama City Mall. They kept coaxing me to go and get "discovered."

Not thinking much of it, I agreed to join them. At worst, I thought, we could do some boy-watching. I was strolling through the crowd, minding my own business, when an urgent voice rang out: *"Stop that girl!"*

I looked around with a sinking feeling . . . and then I saw Mary Lou Ton, of Mary Lou's Model School in Pensacola. Her left hand held a microphone; she had just interrupted her own fashion show.

Her right hand pointed unmistakably at me. I turned red — I felt like a total spectacle in front of all these kids from my high school. But Mary Lou would not be denied. She pulled me to the side and told me we had a month to prepare for "something big in Atlanta": the four-day IMTC (International Model Talent Competition), also known as "the Facefinders' Olympics."

I went along with Mary Lou — not because I saw the IMTC as my big break, but in the modest hope of winning one of the smaller scholarship prizes there. My mother thought it would be fun for me, but she was busy at the motel and didn't get all that involved.

I proceeded to take a crash course in "poise, carriage, facial expressions, makeup, hair, dress, and a dozen other female femalities." To gain confidence I modeled at Mary Lou's shows. For $50 I'd drive the four-hour round trip to Pensacola, which used little of the gas in the baby-blue Mazda RX-7 Mom had bought me.

When we arrived in Atlanta, I was awestruck. It was the biggest city I'd ever been to, by far. My hotel was built around a lofty atrium, and I rode up to my room in a glass elevator. I'd never seen anything like it.

As we entered the convention center, power was humming through the air. All the major agencies were represented — "the Big Four" from New York, the most famous names from Paris. Soap-opera casting people from Hollywood scanned the scene with hawks' eyes. Hundreds of stunning young models milled about, men and women both, all vying for the recognition and contracts that would go to the winners.

Mary Lou had limited experience at this level, and I was truly clueless. In the photography competition, I had to go onstage in front of a huge screen for a simulated photo shoot. With no idea of what to do once I got up there, I just absolutely winged it.

At one point I put my hands to my head and stopped; the auditorium erupted in applause. I sat on the floor, leaned forward, and got comfortable, just did what came naturally. The crowd went wild.

I wound up winning that category.

In the runway competition I tried to do everything Mary Lou had taught me: to walk as if a string were pulling through my body, from my seat to the top of my head, making me as tall as I could possibly be. I made nonstop eye contact — the greatest runway models, I'd heard, seem to be making love to the entire room.

I was still green and self-conscious on the runway. The only way I could handle all the stares was to imagine the audience sitting in their underwear and think, *Oh, that's a great outfit!*

I won that category, too.

By then I'd been tagged as a comer. While the other girls from home went out on the town for fun, Mary Lou and I were snatched up in a whirl of high-powered business lunches and dinners. Top headhunters from Ford and Prestige and Elite, the cream of the cream, sought our company. We were wined and dined, wooed to the max.

Midway through the contest, Dominique and Jacques Silberstein, the world-renowned fashion photographers, had my hair cut to my shoulders for a special shoot. All of a sudden, I thought, I looked very European.

Barely turned seventeen, the world lay at my feet. Elite wanted to get me an apartment in New York. Eileen Ford was ready to take me into her own house. Other agents urged me to go to Paris first, then sweep into New York as the New European Girl.

That sounded good to me, especially after they tossed free plane tickets to Paris into the kitty. I was dying to see Notre Dame and the Louvre and all the other places I'd learned about in humanities class. I'd lived too much of my life in books and fantasy; it was time to do it in person.

For the final night's awards dinner, my mother had found me a gorgeous off-the-shoulder white gown with a fitted top and a silk bottom that trailed to the floor.

When I was named the overall winner, I thought I might just float away.

But when the contest was over, I still had modest goals. I planned to finish high school, work in France over the summer, and save money for college in the fall. I told only my closest friends what I was doing, but word got around. I could hear some girls mocking me behind my back — "Oh, *she* thinks she's going to be a model in Paris and New York."

Back home the notion seemed so unreal, even to me. I'd always thought there were girls in school much more beautiful than I was. Only two years before, a number of them had been chosen to model for Gayfer's, the biggest store in town, and to serve on Gayfer's Teen Board as fine examples of local youth.

But I wasn't all that popular, I didn't dress preppy — I just wasn't a Gayfer's Teen Board girl. So I was rejected, once again.

And then, almost overnight, I'd been picked as one of the top young models in the country. Before I knew where I was headed, I'd arrived.

8

Into the World

I believe you are very special and, therefore, should be with a special agency," wrote an Elite vice president shortly after my return from Atlanta. After sorting through a raft of similar courtship letters, Mary Lou and I settled on Prestige in Paris. We'd been won over by Claude Haddad, one of the more prominent agents we'd met at the IMTC.

At a convention of suave operators, Claude had stood out. He was tall and tanned, with wavy black hair, a picture of French finesse. At dinner he claimed to be forty-five, and though we guessed he was ten years older, why quibble with such a charmer?

Claude agreed to pay for two round-trip tickets to Paris and to house me in an apartment with other models. Mom scraped together $300 for spending money, and in June of 1984 off I flew, with Mary Lou at my side to help me get settled. Claude was there to meet us when we landed. In the thrill of the moment, my first time overseas, I barely heard his suspicious welcome: "Baby, your apartment is not ready yet, you must stay with me — it's okay, I take care of you."

Claude had a spacious flat in Pigalle. An older newcomer from Mary Lou's modeling school, a tall blonde named Felicia, had already made herself at home. I thought something strange was going on, but all was fine until Mary Lou returned to Florida a few days later.

Within hours the locks had disappeared from all the doors — a big problem, I realized, when Claude walked in on me in the bath and refused to leave until I started crying.

Claude's phones blocked calls to the States. I felt trapped. "It's no big deal," said Felicia, as though she were some jaded woman of the world. "That's just him."

Still fighting jet lag, I slept soundly that night. It was dark when I snapped awake to see Claude at the foot of my bed, holding up the blankets to gaze at me in my T-shirt and panties, ready to climb aboard.

When I cried out, Claude dropped to his knees and served up a practiced line. "I love you — you have made me crazy in love with you," he swore. "Do you have a boyfriend? Have you ever been touched by a man before?"

This guy was completely nutso, I thought. I burst into tears and somehow prevailed upon Claude to leave.

The next day I met him in the living room, grateful to be fully clothed. Claude launched into his rhapsody of passion as I measured the distance to the door. As soon as he went to the kitchen for coffee, I grabbed my things and dashed into the street.

Not knowing how to use the pay phone outside, I asked the first man I encountered for help. My high school French must have failed me, as the man grabbed his crotch and started chasing me. Panicked, I ran into a pharmacy and jabbered at the people in hysterical English; they promptly threw me out.

Finally I found a Good Samaritan who helped connect me with Eileen Ford of the Ford Agency in New York; I didn't know who else to call. She directed me to her colleague Jean-Luc, Claude's competition in Paris.

I went straight to Jean-Luc's office, and he couldn't have been kinder or more helpful. He said he had a place for me to stay on the rue de Blanche — "No, it's your own apartment," he assured me. "Your roommate is from West Palm Beach, she just got here a few months ago, you'll love her. Her name is Marie."

Jean-Luc escorted me to the apartment, gallantly opened the door — and there was Marie, butt naked on the floor with two gorgeous male models.

I sure wasn't in Panama City anymore.

I went to my room and sank into a huge depression. The apartment was paid for by the agency, but Claude had kept nearly all my spending money for "safekeeping." With but a few dollars left, I determined that the cheapest meal in Paris was a baguette with Brie cheese. I lay in bed and ate those cheese sandwiches morning, noon, and night.

Still jet-lagged and homesick, I was sleeping all the time in a bed filled with baguette crumbs. In no time at all I had put on ten pounds, up to 130.

After a week or so I roused myself to venture out to "go-sees" at magazines and catalogue companies. There might be ten appointments a day, and I'd feel fortunate to land one of the ten. I'd jump the Métro turnstiles to save a few francs, grapple with my maps, pray I wouldn't miss my stop or turn off at the wrong street.

The clients had to check you out in person, to see if your eyes sparkled and your skin glowed. But I'd lose most of my glow on the way; just reaching my destination would wipe me out. My attitude was, "Here I am, here's my book, here's my pictures, thank you very much, I'm ready to go home and get into bed now."

I kept gaining weight by the day. Too heavy for the runway or most editorial work, for the trips with topflight photographers that would gain me those precious tear sheets, I found myself doing lots of bride jobs. In the car with Jean-Luc one day, I was reaching for another croissant when he frowned and said, "Don't you think you need to worry about that a little bit?"

No, I didn't. I'd never thought about my weight back home, where I could wolf down a whole Domino's pizza. (It hadn't hurt, of course, that I'd been working out with the dance team five hours a day.)

Concerned about my hermit lifestyle, Marie pulled me along to a dinner party in a fashionable part of town. "You need to eat dinner, anyway," she said. I was really hungry that day, and tired of Brie and baguettes, so I agreed.

When we got there, everyone was drinking. I was introduced to our host, a genteel man with a strong accent. "Would you like a glass of champagne?" he asked me.

"No, thank you, I don't drink," I said.

"A cigarette?"

"No, thank you, I don't smoke."

I must have seemed just off the boat, but my new acquaintance was unfazed. He even told me about a nonsmoking, nondrinking associate of his, a movie producer, whom he wanted me to meet.

Our gracious host turned out to know a lot of movie people. He was Roman Polanski — which might have impressed me more had I known the name.

Roman became a good and loyal friend at a time when I badly needed one. He was a remarkable man who'd escaped as a boy from the Nazis in Poland and made a great success in Hollywood, only to have his wife, Sharon Tate — a woman he'd loved with utter devotion — brutally murdered when she was expecting their first child.

How do you pick up the pieces after that, I wondered. How do you brush yourself off?

Later on I'd hear all the stories and gossip about Roman, but with me he seemed to have no ulterior motives. He had a striking girlfriend who made him happy, and he got a kick out of playing the matchmaker. At his next dinner party he arranged for me to meet his producer friend, Tarak Ben Ammar, who was a nephew of the president of Tunisia.

At thirty-five Tarak was twice my age, but we hit it off and talked into the night. The next evening we all went out for Chinese food, where Tarak taught me how to handle chopsticks. On the way back he told me to use his car phone — another first for me — to call my mother.

"Hi, Mom, it's me," I said brightly.

"Are you okay?" I could tell Mom was worried; she had yet to get my first postcard.

"I'm fine," I assured her. "I'm with my friends, Tarak Ben Ammar and Roman Polanski!"

I'm surprised she didn't pass out.

Now that I'd found a crowd to play with, Paris took on a different light. Marie and I and some other girls went out dancing at various nightclubs, and I'd never had so much fun. Back home I'd been inhibited on the dance floor. I'd step to the side and snap my fingers, and that was about it. But in Paris, after a few flutes of Dom Pérignon or Roederer Cristal (champagne wasn't so bad after all), I became a *great* dancer. We'd go well into the morning — between the clubs and my go-sees, I was wearing out my shoes.

When I wasn't dancing or working, I was eating, only now I was taken to the fanciest French restaurants. I was coming of age in a hurry, thrown into a grown-up world.

I was also getting bigger. My weight climbed to 135.

Looking back, I'm amazed at how reckless I was in those days. The Paris club scene could be a dangerous place, especially for teenagers with AMERICAN stamped across their foreheads. One night Marie went to a club without me — she was a girl who lived on the wild side — and didn't come home. I heard a rumor that she'd been drugged. I told the agency about it, but I never saw her again.

With the coming of August, as Paris prepared to shut down, Roman and Tarak invited me on a trip to Italy and Tunisia for preproduction work on the movie *Pirates*. After deducting expenses, my agency paid me $300. I was back where I'd started.

In Rome, while Tarak worked, Roman took me on a tour of the Sistine Chapel, the Spanish Steps, all the places I'd read about. I was overwhelmed by the Pietà — so much power and tenderness to be captured in stone. And I met the producer Dino de

Laurentiis, who had the most amazing eyes. He could see things about people that others missed.

In Tunisia I went along with my friends to a spectacular Mediterranean beach, only to be scandalized when Roman's girlfriend joined the crowd and took off her top. I could never do that, I thought . . . but I also felt more and more stupid as the day wore on.

After a couple of weeks on holiday, I grew restless. Tarak and I had slept together one night, but there was no passion — the sex felt clinical, removed, a sign that something was missing. Besides, I'd gone abroad to *work,* and up till now I had little to show for it. My portfolio was a lot slimmer than I was.

In Atlanta I'd met a Folio agent who'd offered to pay my way out to Japan whenever I was ready. Now I took him up on it. I knew I'd made the right choice as soon as the hired car dropped me at my Tokyo apartment — I had cable television! The working conditions were miles ahead of what I'd seen in Paris. No more wrestling with subway maps; a driver took me to each appointment. I walked in fresh and confident, and soon I was snapping up jobs by the handful.

In Japan they strove each time for perfection. Before the shoot itself started, I'd be treated to back and facial massages. Then they'd cleanse my face and spend an hour on makeup and another hour on my hair. No detail was left to chance.

I never paid for a meal in Tokyo. I just flashed my agency "comp" card, and everything was on the house. It's hard to gain weight on sushi, but I ate so much of it that I managed. I filled out to 140 pounds. My pants split at a disco. At one appointment a client measured my hips and then exclaimed in Japanese: "Ooh, she's a big girl!"

But still I worked every day solid for months. The jobs paid so well that I put off college. Not so long ago I'd been stretching a five-dollar allowance and saving for weeks for my next pair of jeans. Now I was making commercials for clients like Wella Balsam shampoo and getting $40,000, counting residuals, for one day's work.

Money was still abstract to me. I'd never know exactly what I made, since my agency took out its expenses before depositing the rest in my savings account. I sailed through that period with a bank card and a pocketful of cash.

By November 1984, I was ready for my next big step: New York.

The cabdriver was losing patience. Fresh from the airport, I'd asked him to take me to Zoli, my new agency in New York, at Lexington Avenue and East 56th Street. As much as I liked Eileen Ford, the Ford Agency was known for its blond and blue-eyed all-American girls: definitely not my type. Elite took on more "exotic" models, but I couldn't quite see myself as exotic at the age of seventeen. Meanwhile, Zoli's Debbie Lang had delivered a great pitch to Mary Lou and me in Atlanta. She seemed convinced that I could be a star, and I was eager to find out if she was right.

But as the cabbie slowed to drop me off, I saw a bunch of young guys in white loitering by the corner with their bicycles. I'd read about New York City street gangs, and my long plane ride had me just about hallucinating anyway.

"Please go around the block again," I begged the driver, for the eighth time.

"Lady, you're here, you need to get out," he said.

"But you don't understand," I said, my voice quavering. "There's a gang on the corner there, and I'm just a girl by myself."

"Lady," the cabbie said wearily, "those are the pizza-delivery guys. Now please get out of my car."

I'd come to crave that pizza — nothing better than a New York slice, folded over, unless it was a bagel from Bagel Nosh. But carbohydrates were definitely out of favor at Zoli. When I went up to see Debbie Lang, the agent I'd met in Atlanta, she took one look, put me on the scale, and pronounced, "We need to go on a diet."

That rubbed my fur the wrong way. I rebelled. Over the next

several months, Debbie put me on the scale every time I saw her. The minute I left, I sped around the corner to Carvel Ice Cream. I ordered the biggest cone on the menu, with a double helping of sprinkles.

The fact was that I felt healthy and strong at 140 pounds. Cindy Crawford had established a new vogue of voluptuous girls; she'd proved that star models didn't have to be anorectic. At five-nine, I thought I could carry the weight, and the clients seemed to agree. In my first week in New York I was booked by Jordache: one day, $7,000. As soon as I got my check I marched into Trump Plaza and bought a $1,500 teddy bear.

Now I cringe to think how careless and extravagant I used to be. I sent money home to Mom and my brothers, but I also bought whatever I wanted whenever I wanted it. A model's life can spoil you that way. You work hard, granted, but the agency takes care of all your basic needs. You don't even see the bills. *Budget* isn't part of your vocabulary.

With steady bookings from a gigantic German catalogue company called Otto Versant, my annual income rose well into six figures by the time I was nineteen. Yet I didn't have a single credit card or even a checking account. I was so bad at handling money that I couldn't pay the airport tax after an expense-paid trip to Israel. A nice stranger behind me gave me the five dollars.

Still, I wouldn't trade those years for anything. From my base in an apartment in Gramercy Park, I lived and worked on six different continents. I learned to speak French and Italian and a little German and Japanese. I never regretted missing out on college, especially after a brush with academic life on the eve of my Jordache job.

A boy I'd dated after high school had invited me down to visit him at the University of Florida. His fraternity was throwing a Viking party, so I found a cute little outfit in New York. As soon as I walked in the door I knew I'd made a wrong turn — back on Madison Avenue.

Each frat member had brought a bottle of grain alcohol to pour into the punch, and soon I was in the middle of a full-scale panty raid. People got so loaded that they started hurling their drinks at each other, leaving bright red punch stains on my pricey rented costume.

What was I doing here?

Worst of all was the food fight. A monster turkey drumstick struck me smack in the eye, which turned several shades of purple the next day. I saw my Jordache job going up in flames.

We wound up able to do the shoot, thanks to the wonders of modern makeup, but I never dated that boy again.

After two years in New York, I'd begun to make my mark. I was featured on several European magazine covers. Editorial work paid only $90 a day, but the exposure was invaluable. Those big lips I'd once hated now became my trademark. They set me apart.

(I was mortally insulted, in fact, when a tabloid later claimed that I'd enlarged my lips with silicone injections. I knew they were all mine — and that I'd put up with enough grief to earn them.)

I was treated respectfully in my work, with one notable exception. At a dinner I met a well-known photographer, and we arranged to do a test the next day. When I showed up on the set, no one else was there.

"Take off your clothes and go lie on that black leather couch," he said abruptly.

My instincts told me to bolt, but then I felt silly and ignorant — here was one of the best photographers in the world, asking me to do what I'd been trained for. Why was I so nervous? But by the time I was naked I was crying, and soon I grabbed my clothes and left.

I didn't neglect New York's club life. One night the artist Keith Haring gave me a T-shirt with one of his famous stick-figure designs. After I put it on, he took scissors to the edge of the shirt, cutting small pieces out around my waist — an instant Haring original.

It sounds glamorous in the retelling, but at the time I felt out of my league in such sophisticated company. And I mostly steered clear of the drug scene. The druggie girls soon burned out their careers; the clients got tired of morning no-shows.

One summer I went back to Italy with a girl named Becky, my Zoli roommate in New York. With sunglasses and Walkmen in place, we'd hop on the subways in Milan and pretend we were detectives, cooking up suspicions about our fellow passengers. As we babbled away in English, no one had any idea what we were talking about. We did little girl things in a big old world.

I linked up with a young man named Fabio Borghese, whom I'd met in New York. He came from a very good Italian family; he was, in fact, a prince. In between my shoots in Milan, Fabio showed me Capri and Sardinia. We kissed and held hands, but that's as far as it went — just a summer fling with a sweet boy who was always nice to me.

I didn't know it then, but my life was about to get a lot more intense. And a lot more complicated.

In 1987 I went to Los Angeles on a bathing-suit shoot for the Jimmy Z surfer campaign. I was supposed to be there for just a couple of days, and then my brother Michael got into the act.

Michael was divorcing his first wife at the time. To cheer him up, I invited him to share my luxurious, prepaid hotel room. One evening we went through a Wendy's drive-through, with Michael at the wheel of my rental car. He dropped a slice of tomato in his lap, looked down, and promptly plowed into the truck in front of us.

Though my West Coast agency had signed for the car, they held me responsible for the damage. As a result, I had to stay in Los Angeles and work off my debt. To get me jobs, they sent my book out to a number of top photographers, including the great Victor Skrebneski in Chicago.

Victor was world renowned for his powerful work in black and white. He discovered Cindy Crawford, created the Willow Bay campaign for Estée Lauder, and shot one of the most amazing pictures of Bette Davis ever taken.

Now he wanted to hire me.

We began with a little catalogue job in Palm Springs. I adored Victor from the start. He was such a polite, distinguished man, so well dressed and well spoken, as gentle and caring as any father.

We were just getting to know each other when he had me stand upon a rock, maybe two feet off the ground. Then he asked me to close my eyes; Victor has a strong feel for artistic detail, even in his catalogue work.

The only problem was my fear of heights. As soon as I closed my eyes, the old terror gripped me and I tumbled to the ground. Victor brushed me off, and from that point on he called me "Baby." He booked me on the spot for an Italian *Vogue* photo essay on Hollywood.

That job would push me to a new tier. Suddenly I found myself working with established star models like Sandra Freeman and Renee Simonson, who was on the cover of just about every *Vogue* in the world.

The highlight of my Italian *Vogue* shoot was a profile nude shot in front of the famous Hollywood sign. I'm holding a *Variety* and wearing hot pink shoes, with the mountains and the city behind me. It was sensually artistic and technically perfect and kind of funny, all at the same time.

It was also my first nude, which made me nervous. But when you work with a master like Victor, there is no room for self-consciousness. You lose yourself totally in the process.

Another shot was staged at Universal Studios, where I was asked to stand on King Kong's hand. My phobia hit me full force as soon as I lifted my foot off the platform to climb up. By the time Victor shot me, tears were streaming down my face. I didn't have to fake my fright of the great ape that day.

But the picture that changed my life was a group shot in a hotel room with Renee and Sandy and Dolph Lundgren, who was fresh from *Rocky IV* and *Masters of the Universe*. The four of us were in bed together, seemingly naked but strategically covered by a sheet.

Dolph was bare-chested. Renee and Sandy and I were wearing a million dollars' worth of Bulgari diamonds, the real deal.

Victor had me lying back against Dolph, with a stone the size of a robin's egg on my finger. Then he put me over the edge: He told me to put my hand on Dolph's firmly muscled thigh.

Oh my *goodness,* I thought. I had never seen a man to measure up to Dolph Lundgren. He was a full six-foot-five, with shining blond hair and shoulders big enough to hold up the entire world.

After skipping a beat I damned the torpedoes and placed my hand as instructed . . . and for the first time I knew what it meant when they said "Time stopped."

At that moment I lost track of the diamonds, the guards, Sandy and Renee, even the commanding Victor Skrebneski. All I could see was this Michelangelo sculpture in the flesh. All I could feel was the heat of Dolph's tanned leg — so hard, so smooth — and a tiny trembling in my fingers. As if my hand were conducting some strange flow of energy.

Victor and his assistant, Dennis, picked right up on what was happening. They were as tickled as they could be.

Baby was in love.

I didn't try to kid myself; I knew I'd gone head over heels. But I put Dolph off once he got my phone number and started asking me out. Besides, I had all the work I could handle after the Italian *Vogue* shoot, up to two weeks a month with Victor alone. I needed to focus on my career. My infatuation with Dolph was so intense it had scared me.

And maybe I sensed, even then, that something was wrong with this drop-dead gorgeous picture, this fantasy I was spinning and repressing at the same time.

Dolph kept calling over the next month, and I kept turning him down. I was working in Miami one afternoon, miserable with the flu, when I got a call from Tom Hahn, at the time a booker for my Los Angeles modeling agency. He'd confirmed me on a job in Malibu the next morning.

"I'm too sick, Tom — I just can't make it," I protested. "I can't get on another plane."

"Look," he said, "they're paying you ten thousand dollars for the day to do a simple kissing shot with this guy. Just get on the plane and rest up on the way, and they'll have a car there to take you to the job."

That flight was one of the worst travel ordeals of my life. I had a fever and the sweats and barely found the strength to collapse into the car at LAX. In Malibu I met the photographer, Firooz Zahedi, and told him I couldn't do a kissing picture — "I'm going to get this guy so sick, it's not fair."

The photographer smiled and said, "That's okay, just go and tell the client. He's out there by the beach. I'm sure we can work something out."

I straggled out to the beach, and there at water's edge stood Dolph, large as life. "I couldn't get a date with you," he explained, "so I figured I'd have to pay you to come see me."

As sick as I was, we wound up taking some of the most beautiful pictures in that shoot. I leaned on Dolph through the whole day. He fed me vitamins, nursed me through.

"I just thought of something," I said toward the end. "Do you have a Jacuzzi?"

"As a matter of fact, I have two."

We went to Dolph's Mt. Olympus house, and the Jacuzzi drew the flu clean out of me. As I lay in the swirling water, relaxed and at peace, I knew it was no use fighting something we both wanted, something I *needed*. I knew I couldn't leave him.

From that day on, as long as it lasted, Dolph Lundgren would be my world, my life.

There is nothing like young love when you've never known lies or cheating. With Dolph my heart was unconditional: childlike, innocent, trusting. We were lovers and such good friends at the same time. He took care of me, looked after me. For someone like myself, who'd always carried the burden for my family, every day felt like vacation.

We're made for each other, I thought. *We complete each other.*

Though both of us were busy (Dolph made two or three movies a year), we were constantly planning our next romantic getaway. Once Dolph took me shopping in Paris for a dress, and we ran into his ex-girlfriend Grace Jones. While I knew they'd had a long and stormy affair, I saw nothing to be concerned about. Grace was with her new husband. She and Dolph were civil and distant. They'd both turned a page, I thought.

I forgot all about Grace Jones when Dolph and I headed back to the Crillon, past the Sienese marble foyer and into our courtyard suite. We plundered our refrigerator for the Taittinger stocked on ice there, and when we touched I felt the heat of the first time we met, when our bed was filled with diamonds.

Dolph came to see my family in Panama City; I met his mother in Stockholm. We got off the plane there to a hail of fireworks, which seemed to happen to us all the time, in bed and out. "You know I ordered this just for you," Dolph would say.

Some months later, after the Thomas Drive Motel was destroyed in an electrical fire, my mother temporarily moved into my rented place on the Pacific Coast Highway, while Dolph and I leased a house overlooking the water on Malibu Beach Drive.

I treasured our every hour there. We'd work out and jog on the beach, then dash in to make love any time of day or night. One morning I was booked to fly out at seven for a job in Cabo San Lucas. Dolph and I rose early to have breakfast together, and at some point I realized that I had no intention of going anywhere. I called my agent, blew off a $6,000 day with a major-league photographer, and nestled back into Dolph's arms.

Playing hooky had never felt so good.

Even a perfect romance, of course, has room for improvement. One time Dolph seemed unusually pensive and I asked him what he was thinking.

Big mistake.

"My friends like you," he began, "my family loves you, everything is wonderful. But do you realize that we go out for every meal, that you don't cook at all?"

I knew this was no small complaint. Like many large people, Dolph was serious about his food.

I burst into tears and the first thing I did was call Mother. To my surprise, she got mad. After years of hearing her say, "Watch how I cook this or someday your husband's going to bring you back to me and say, 'What did you teach this girl?' " instead she was saying: "He ought to get you a cook." The second thing I did was read *Betty Crocker's Cookbook,* front to back. The next evening we dined on burnt chicken, but I learned. Before long I'd be dashing back from a shoot for Speedo or *Town & Country,* throwing on an apron, and whipping up Veal Oscar for a dinner party of twelve. I even made *samlur,* a Swedish puff-pastry cake filled with almond paste and fresh cream, then topped with powdered sugar and hot milk. The result was heaven, and it took about as much time as building a suspension bridge.

I did it gladly. I would do anything, *be* anything for Dolph. I strained to make him happy; my days would hinge on his approving smile.

But toward the end of 1987, just as we seemed at our closest, I started falling short. Dolph would be inexplicably late — hours late — for one of my gourmet dinners. Infuriated, I'd tell him off and call my mother to pick me up. (Mom, who adored the man, would say, *"Now* what did you do?") I'd be packed and off in five minutes, leaving a sobbing Dolph behind.

Drugs proved a more serious wedge between us. I'd moved in circles where cocaine was plentiful and tried it myself. But I couldn't trust people when they were high. I'd learned from hard experience that the coke would be talking, not the truth. When you grow up with an alcoholic father and an alcoholic stepfather, it takes the glamour out of drug use.

On the other hand, I knew that Grace had done a lot of drugs with Dolph — for him it was, "If you love me, you'll do them too." So I tried for a while to keep up, but there was no way. Dolph was so much bigger than I was, for starters. But it was more than that: When I looked in the mirror when I came down, I didn't like who was staring back.

In November we managed to set our issues aside. In Namibia to shoot a film called *Red Scorpion*, Dolph asked me to join him for his birthday. To mark the occasion, I picked up a chocolate cheesecake from the Cheesecake Factory, our special favorite. I changed planes with that cheesecake in London, Zurich, and Johannesburg.

In Namibia I felt goofy in love, just nutsy for the man. Dolph seemed to be with me, step for step. When I got home I rushed to the phone to call his hotel room — I couldn't wait to hear his deep voice.

Instead, a woman picked up. Even before she identified herself and made it plain what she was doing there, I knew it was Grace.

Dolph was cheating on me. Up till then I'd refused to believe people could do this. If you truly loved someone, how could you hurt them that way?

A few weeks shy of my twenty-first birthday, I'd had my first real heartbreak, and I took it hard. Dolph scrambled to make amends. He sent me three dozen red roses a day for weeks and a flood of tearful letters. I tossed out the flowers and didn't write back. I was angry beyond words.

On December 10 Dolph mailed out a classic, one for the Cheaters Hall of Fame. Grace had come to Namibia at his urging, he confessed; he'd done a horrible thing and felt very bad about it.

But wait, he'd had his reasons. I was getting "too possessive." I was losing my "individuality." I must learn, Dolph wrote, "not to fully give yourself to anyone unless you're perfectly sure. Always keep a part of you to yourself, which makes you more mysterious and attractive anyway. *And,* unfortunately, never trust a man."

He closed with, "Paula, try a smile," and drew a little happy face by his signature.

Try my foot up your bottom, I thought. As far as I could see, Dolph's letters were the ramblings of a guilty conscience, the fancy footwork of a man who'd called me his fiancée but had yet to come up with a ring.

Dolph was saying I cared too much, but I'd always thought that was impossible. How could you care too much, or love too much? How could you fence in your heart?

Now I was starting to second-guess myself.

One day, months after our blowup, I finally answered my phone before the service picked up. Dolph and I talked for hours. For a long time after that — too long — we tried to patch things back together. But it wasn't the same.

It didn't help when Dolph kept insisting that it was "normal" for men — and just about mandatory for Swedish men — to have mistresses. Rather than lash back, I would retreat to the bathtub and sit and reflect.

I was the cleanest girl in Los Angeles in those days.

In the end, there was too much guilt on Dolph's side, too little trust on mine. I thought I could forgive, but I couldn't quite forget. I could never feel secure with a man I considered unfaithful. What would happen when we both got older and the latest crop of girls stayed as young and fetching as ever?

We made one last trip together, to Australia, where we both had work. I'll never forget a runway show where I had to extend my arm and freeze as they cut the lights. In the blackness I felt a powerful set of lips smooching up my arm. It was Dolph, who'd bought a front-row table and brought along his costar, Lou Gossett Jr. That little surprise nearly knocked me off the stage, but I thought it was very sweet.

By then Dolph had figured out his problem: long separations. "If we're apart for more than two weeks," he said, "that's when the trouble will start."

The test came when I flew back to Los Angeles for Mom's gall-bladder surgery. I returned to Australia two and a half weeks later. Dolph had been true to his warning. At a Rolling Stones concert in Sydney during my absence, he told me, he'd met a girl and slept with her. It was no big deal, Dolph said, just a one-night stand.

The next day I left him, for the last time.

* * *

It was 1989, a year for change. Mom was ready to move back to Florida. She was lonely in Los Angeles, and her arthritis had flared up there, till she couldn't put her stockings on some mornings. So I bought us an airy, skylit house in Bay Point, the gated neighborhood that once had seemed so intimidating. Our backyard faced out on a duck pond and golf course. My mother moved in that winter, to the home she'd long deserved.

I needed a new base for my modeling as well. Los Angeles was impossible. Everything there reminded me of Dolph, and I dreaded the thought of running into him. It was time to go back to New York. I took an apartment in Gramercy Park, then called Elite and told them, "I'm ready to go to work."

Elite represented the ultimate career move. I'd put it off for some time; I'd been content working with Victor and living with Dolph. I had a regular set of clients — the German catalogue company and Victoria's Secret, among them — and made a good living without driving myself too hard.

But Elite would demand total focus on my work. The perfect therapy, I thought, for a woman scorned.

It turned out to be the right move at the right time. Through Elite I came to such master photographers as Albert Watson and Guy Bourdin, the best of the best. For catalogue and advertising work I could now command up to $10,000 a day. Add on a few lucrative commercials, and my annual income peaked at several hundred thousand dollars. I put some of it into a money market fund, but I was still a free spender — I was just living for the day.

Few models age gracefully within the fashion industry. By 1991, now going on twenty-five, I knew I was closer to the end of my career than to the beginning. For some time I'd been studying acting, my first love. The more I worked at it, the more I wanted to learn.

Tom Hahn, now working for Jon Peters at Columbia Studios, told me about a wonderful acting coach. Roy London taught Geena Davis and Sharon Stone, as well as a number of other talented actors. I moved back to Los Angeles to audit his class. A few weeks later, ready or not, I was up for a part opposite Billy Baldwin in a feature called *Machine Gun Kelly.*

Since I knew next to nothing about acting, I figured I'd get help from someone a little more seasoned. So I rang up Jack Nicholson, whom I'd met at several private screenings over the years, never thinking about what an extraordinary thing I was doing.

"Sure, come on over," Jack said as if we were old friends. I drove out to his place on Mulholland, and he spent more than an hour with me. I knew his reputation as one of Hollywood's leading seducers, but he was nothing but professional with me. Jack's main piece of advice: "Be natural."

Billy Baldwin had approval over who got to be screen-tested. When I met him in at a hotel piano bar in Santa Monica, I was so nervous that my hands were shaking.

"Are you cold?" he said.

"Yes, I am," I said, rather than admit to "stage" fright. "You know, they say the warmest parts of your body are between your knees or under your arms."

I was just babbling, but Billy looked at me seriously. He took my hand and placed it under his arm, where it stayed for the rest of our conversation. At the end he asked me upstairs, but I begged off. "I have to get back to my stuffed peppers," I told him.

I wondered if I'd ruined my chances, but that night I got called with good news: My screen test was scheduled for the next day. It went well enough to make me a finalist for the part, along with Molly Ringwald and Diane Lane. *Machine Gun Kelly* never got made; Billy had a play-or-pay deal, and his contract expired. But I felt thrilled just to have been in the game. I felt that I was growing in Los Angeles, moving in good directions.

That first month back I bought a one-bedroom condominium on Wilshire Boulevard's "Golden Mile," in Westwood. It wasn't a palace, but it had a balcony and a doorman and a lobby with fresh flowers and modern art. Most of all, it was *mine,* the fruit of my hard-earned independence. I'd lost Dolph, and there was no other man on the horizon. But I had a real life, and that condo was the proof of it.

Back in Florida, Michael was working at a parasail ride on the beach. One day the apparatus was drifting back toward the sand where some children were playing. When Michael went out to retrieve it, a gust of wind lifted him fifty feet into the air before he could react.

Michael wasn't strapped in, and his grip on the bar started slipping. He knew if he fell he'd be dead or hurt badly — but he also knew that the longer he waited, the worse it would be. When he let go, people on the sixth floor of a nearby apartment building were looking up at him.

When my brother hit the sand, he shattered his femur. I rushed home from a shoot in Sicily and reached the hospital just as Michael came out of surgery, screaming in agony.

"Can't you give him something more for that pain?" I asked the nurse.

"He can't have too much too soon," she said.

"Just *give* him something — if he gets an addiction, we'll deal with it later."

More than once I'd think back to that exchange and shudder. After his first operation was botched, Michael had to undergo a second painful procedure. He wound up on a morphine drip for eighty-two straight days, and by the time he left the hospital he was indeed addicted.

While living at my house in Panama City, Michael turned to cocaine. When Mom couldn't handle it anymore, I persuaded my brother to fly out and enter a drug program in southern California. I knew I was in for trouble as soon as I picked him up. Michael had found a girl to party with on the plane and stayed high the whole way.

Since I didn't know what my brother might have on him, it was a big relief to leave the airport without getting arrested. I told the limo driver to go straight to the rehab place, but Michael insisted on stopping along the way. He literally fell out of his seat when he got out for one last snort.

Three weeks later, the program called to inform me that they'd kicked Michael out for breaking the rules. I felt devastated but agreed to enroll in their family week to learn more about what I was dealing with.

That week opened my eyes. Back in Florida, Mom was calling the program director in a panic: "How could you do this? He's going to die — how could you kick him out?" But after speaking with the counselors, I saw that everyone wanted Michael to get clean except for one person: Michael. By giving him a home and spending money, I was simply enabling him to do more coke.

It was time for a dose of tough love. The counselors told me to leave Michael on the streets, to force him to face his own reality. I did it, but I can't tell you how hard it was. As I drove off, I saw Michael in my rearview mirror. He was standing there with a cheap duffel bag and no idea where he'd sleep that night.

There was intense family backlash. My mother, my father, my brother Vinnie, Michael's girlfriend — all were agreed that I was stone-hearted, stubborn, and generally out of my mind. Finally, after holing up in a hotel for four days to dodge their hysterical phone calls, I relented and flew Michael back to Florida.

Meanwhile, my father was jobless and just barely hanging on. I'd asked Mom to let him move into a Panama City townhouse she owned, a huge request, but it was either that or pay rent for Dad somewhere else.

My father continued to nosedive, just locking himself in to drink. "You need to look for another place to live," I told him. "You've got to get out and do something." Dad got even more depressed. He had his beloved cat put to sleep. He sat at the kitchen table making a noose: more guilt for his guilt-ridden daughter.

I was a wreck. To top things off, Dolph made one more play for me. We had a few less-than-wonderful dates, then a final explosion. Dolph was sitting in my apartment when Apples, my Yorkshire puppy, crawled up on the back of the couch to kiss his cheek. Dolph, that buzzard, flicked the back of his hand and knocked my puppy to the floor, all three pounds of her. That was the last straw. You can mess with me, but keep your hands off my dog.

It was at the gym, just after Thanksgiving 1991, that I met Dean Hamilton. An independent movie producer, Dean seemed to be that rare breed in L.A.: a normal guy. He wanted a family, he wanted his dog — he wanted to fill his house in Malibu with life and love.

I was under severe strain. Every day brought new ripples of hostility about Michael, whom I'd recently sent home. I felt guilty and fragile and nearly jumped through my skin whenever the phone rang.

Dean was an answer to a prayer. We'd hardly begun dating when he stepped in as a buffer with my family. "You need to stop this — you can't hurt her anymore," he'd tell them, gently but firmly. After hanging up he'd come to me and say, "I wish that you didn't have to feel all this hurt. I wish I could take it all away from you."

Boy, that's a great idea, I thought. Here was a man who would take responsibility for a change. Who wouldn't use me, as Dolph had, or love me for my money, as Michael had. Who just loved me for *me.*

On Friday, December 13, 1991, all of two weeks after our first encounter over a StairMaster, Dean and I hopped a plane to Las Vegas and got married at a twenty-four-hour wedding chapel.

On the day we got back to L.A., my husband called Mom and asked for a list of my assets. Flabbergasted, she told him, "Pound sand, sonny!"

Undaunted, Dean came to me and laid it on the line: "I need a check for eight thousand dollars or I'm going to lose my house."

A zillion-watt lightbulb switched on. Now I understood why we'd rushed to the chapel. Dean was in a fix, and he needed a loan.

By running pell-mell from my greatest fear, I'd found it lurking in my honeymoon bed.

I felt like I'd fallen through the surface of the earth. Had Dean told me about his money problem beforehand, I most likely would have helped him, and we might have gone on from there. Instead, he had played me for a sucker: typecasting.

Feeling more shame than anger, I gave Dean the $8,000 anyway. (He has since paid me back.) Then we filed for an annulment.

I lacked the nerve to go back to Margaret Paul after that. The diagnosis would be all too obvious. Once again, I'd used sex as a drug — to dull my pain, to deny reality and paper over my problems.

As I looked back on it, I'd tried to change by abstaining from sex after Dolph, only to go into the equivalent of withdrawal. On the surface, I seemed to be getting a grip on my life. In fact, I was an overdose waiting to happen.

Enter Dean Hamilton, so kind and helpful and urgently marriageable. If you viewed it this way, our wedding was a two-way street; Dean and I had used each other. I covered Dean's mortgage, and he handed me an out, a respectable way to go off the wagon. You can't tell a bride to stay celibate, after all.

I'd like to say that I learned a big lesson from Dean. That I went forward, sadder but wiser, and changed the poison patterns of my life. That I learned to put sex in its proper place: as a secondary part of a healthy relationship.

I'd like to say all of that, but the rest of my story would suggest it was not quite true.

9

Ports in a Storm

From the first time we met, I knew that Debbie and Terri Whitehurst would be my friends for life.

I was in tenth grade; Debbie was a year older, Terri a year or so younger. Like thousands of other young people, they'd come to Panama City for spring break, a wild time in my hometown. They came up to me at a beach party, and Terri said, "You have the prettiest hair — she looks just like Marianne, doesn't she, Debbie?"

I learned that Marianne was the oldest of four Whitehurst sisters from Bolivar, Tennessee. Their parents, Billy and Judy, owned a famous flight school there. I was impressed that they trusted Debbie and Terri enough to let them stay on their own at a family friend's beachfront hotel.

The girls liked Panama City so much that they came back every spring and summer vacation through high school. Mr. and Mrs. Whitehurst eventually bought a house and several condos in the area, and before long I'd been adopted into the clan.

They were the kind of family I'd always dreamed about: stable, loving, reliable. I knew they'd always be there if I needed them.

After the Bronco chase, with O.J. now in custody, I needed them badly.

As Debbie and Terri met me at the gate in Memphis on the morning of June 18, I felt so conspicuous — I thought every stranger's eyes were on me. I wished I'd had my novelty-store red wig and come in disguise.

My friends were sweet and affectionate, as always, and knew better than to mention O.J. The previous day's events soon seemed far away.

Until we stopped at a McDonald's drive-through. We passed a newspaper box, and there was the *Memphis Commercial Appeal*'s banner headline about O.J. His arrest was treated like World War III.

It was then that I started to realize that I could fly away, but I couldn't hide.

I slept most of the sixty miles to Bolivar. I was in a tunnel of fog, grateful not to talk. I awoke as we pulled up to a gracious country house on top of a wooded hill.

I'd never been to the ranch before, and it exceeded anything I'd imagined. The Whitehursts owned eighteen hundred acres, as far as I could see. Their land stretched out below me like a quilt of greens and yellows and browns. They had soybeans and corn there, and a wetlands preserve.

I remember looking out that first day and spotting dozens of light brown specks clustered across the plain. I looked again through binoculars and the specks turned into deer — I might have been back in Africa.

The sight was awe-inspiring and made me feel hopelessly out of place. Just like Pigpen, the *Peanuts* character with the cloud of dirt over his head, I'd brought my mess of bad energy into this pristine environment.

Billy Whitehurst had been a pilot for Eastern and later in the military. He'd brought more than ten thousand students through his flight school, without a single fatality, before selling it in 1992.

He was also an ideal dad, strong and unflappable. "We're going to get through this," he'd say, and while he was comforting me I actually believed it.

Needing more sleep before anything, I was ushered into Debbie's old bedroom. It was the most beautiful room I'd ever seen: floral prints, a gilt-framed mirror, a thick Oriental rug that made you want to go barefoot.

Best of all was the lace-canopied bed — it gobbled me whole. I felt like a princess in a perfect world; I felt like I'd clicked my heels like Dorothy and come home.

My friends drew the shades and unplugged the phone, and I plummeted into sleep.

I'd given Cathy Randa my number, and O.J. called me from jail that night for the first of a thousand times. Mr. Whitehurst picked up and tried to encourage him, and then he passed the phone to me.

"I'm so sorry for scaring you that way," O.J. said. "I should never have put you through all that." He sounded mortified. He was plainly remorseful about having taken off in the Bronco with a gun.

"That's all right," I said, and it was — I was just so glad to have him on the line. It was like talking to a ghost; I'd thought I'd never hear that voice again. "Are you okay?"

"I'm not okay," he said, "but you don't have to worry — I'll never try anything like that again."

After a few minutes we said good night. Someone gave me a wonderful pill that knocked my socks off. I went back to my canopied cave and was out until morning.

During the three weeks I stayed in Tennessee, I spoke to O.J. several times a day. We'd always know it was him calling; the operator would say, "Collect from the County Correctional Facility."

At the start we had no time limits. We talked endlessly, for hours at a stretch. I put our past issues aside; they seemed so trivial now. All that mattered was getting the man I cared about through to the next morning.

All that mattered was that O.J. was still alive.

O.J. told me about the daily strip searches, and how chilly his cell was — he needed a warmer sweater, he said, and some thermal underwear. His arthritis had flared up; his bed was so high he had trouble getting into it.

When O.J. talked about the bars staring back at him or his cold metal bench, I was right there with him. I melted into the jail, as I had into the Bronco during the chase.

No, it was more than that — I felt as if I *should* be in the jail. It would be so much easier if it were me instead of him.

Wasn't I the one who had wished Nicole gone?

When O.J. was especially depressed, and I'd said all I could think of but nothing was working, I'd pass the phone back to Mr. Whitehurst. A staunch Christian, he'd often quote from the Bible. I remember a verse he liked from Hebrews: "Faith is the substance of things helpful, yet not things."

"You have to put yourself in God's hands," Mr. Whitehurst would tell O.J., "and if you're innocent, He'll take care of you."

After we finished our call, I'd sit in a big upholstered chair in the master bedroom and look to Mr. Whitehurst for some words of wisdom. Early on he asked me, "Are you sure you want to be involved with this, Paula?" But he never told me I was nuts. He never pushed me to change my course or to stop answering the phone.

He and Mrs. Whitehurst simply gave me all their love and support. They treated me like the innocent girl they'd met years before in Panama City. In their eyes, I still was that girl.

They were more experienced in suffering than I'd known. A few days after I arrived, I saw a picture of Marianne and remarked that we did indeed look alike.

Then Mrs. Whitehurst told me the story. Two weeks before I'd met her two daughters, she said, they'd been in a car with Marianne at the wheel. A log flew off a truck in front of them and smashed through the windshield.

It also went through Marianne, who died instantly. The family doctor suggested that Debbie and Terri go away for a while, which was why they'd come to Panama City. All these years they'd kept their story bottled up.

I understood why they hadn't told me. As I was discovering for myself, it didn't always ease your pain to talk about it.

In between phone calls, I prayed and watched CNN in the den and smoked Mr. Whitehurst's cigarettes with unsteady hands. I kept waiting for the authorities to come on and announce, "This has all been a terrible mistake, and O.J. Simpson has been released."

Instead, I was confronted by the stern face of Marcia Clark, the assistant district attorney assigned to the case. "It was premeditated murder," she told the media on Monday, June 20, just three days after O.J. was arrested. "It was done with deliberation and premeditation."

That sure is some nerve, I thought. How could Clark be so sure, so soon — when I knew she was so wrong? I worried about how her statement would affect O.J., who'd looked so weak at his arraignment that morning. When he'd stood to plead not guilty, I worried that he might fall down.

I cried a lot that day. I felt like the world was flooding through the chintz-curtained windows and drowning me.

My theatrical manager, meanwhile, was pressing me to talk to *PrimeTime Live* out at the Whitehursts' ranch. I'd already turned down a million-dollar offer from the tabloids. The atmosphere seemed so inflamed that I didn't see much point to an interview, even with a legitimate journalist.

I told him, "Tom, I'm not ready right now."

"The press is driving me crazy, you've got to do something for me," Tom persisted. "Just talk with Diane Sawyer. If you don't like her, you don't have to do a thing."

I reluctantly gave in. We arranged for one of Mr. Whitehurst's pilots to pick up the *PrimeTime Live* crew in Memphis the next day and bring them back to the ranch.

When I spoke to O.J. that night, I didn't mention Diane. I felt guilty about hiding it, but I didn't want to upset him. Besides, I still doubted that I'd go through with the interview.

Then I spoke with Diane, and I changed my mind, as Tom thought I would. She was one person, I decided, who could get my story across without destroying my integrity. I was still anxious about putting O.J.'s case at risk. But how could I hurt anything as long as I told the truth?

The interview reflected my total commitment to O.J. — my empathy for his pain, my conviction that he was innocent. "I'm hurt where O.J. is right now," I said. "I don't think it's fair that somebody could have their life just ripped away from them in a second."

When Diane asked why O.J. hadn't put forward his innocence the day after the murders, I proposed that the shock of getting hauled down to the police station in handcuffs — not to mention the loss of Nicole — had devastated him.

While sidestepping Diane's questions about the nature of our relationship, I described O.J. as "sensitive" and "spiritual." He wasn't a drinker, I said. And he certainly wasn't a violent person: "He's never hit me."

"Has he ever yelled at you?" Diane said. "Have you seen the rages?"

"He's never yelled at me like that," I replied. In my mind, he never had. We'd had our share of shouting matches, sure, but I couldn't remember any of them being really scary.

I wasn't thinking about our fight in Laguna, or O.J.'s fit about "the QB" in Palm Beach. I had blocked those incidents so far out that they no longer existed.

It was a time when I remembered only the good things.

Toward the close of the interview, I voiced my indignation: "When this is all over, I think there'll be a lot of apologies. There better be."

When the interview aired on June 23, I felt relieved — I'd made the right choice. In a delicate time, when I might have been publicly shamed or ridiculed, Diane had treated me fairly.

That weekend I should have been in San Francisco, where

Becky, my old New York roommate, was getting married. Instead, I stayed holed up in Bolivar and fended off the press. Once people had noticed the limo carting the *PrimeTime Live* equipment out to the ranch, it was just a matter of time before I got tracked down. The night the show aired, we were startled to see a woman squinting through the Whitehursts' back window, then tapping at the door.

"Is Paula in there?" she said. "May I talk to her?" It was a reporter from the *Commercial Appeal*.

When Terri said it wasn't possible, the reporter got incensed: "Just because I'm not Diane Sawyer!" She wouldn't take no for an answer, until the local police escorted her off the property.

After that I stopped answering the phone, and the Whitehursts told people I was no longer staying there.

To Tom's chagrin, the media kept peppering his answering machine. The Sawyer interview had only whetted their appetite; he was getting hundreds of calls per day. He got so frustrated that he took to sending people out on costly wild-goose chases. He told one photo crew I'd flown out to the Swiss Alps, another that I was working in Alaska.

I worried that O.J. would be angry when I told him about the interview, but he was surprisingly philosophical: "Well, it's done now, isn't it?" A few days later, as he heard good reviews from his friends, he passed on their compliments. He was *proud* of me, and that felt so good, like it had when he used to compliment my dress or hair, only more so.

I wanted to do more; I wanted to shout out my faith in O.J. to the whole world. If people could know him as I did, I thought, he'd be out of jail tomorrow.

During the first weeks after the murders, media coverage was up and down. The tabloids actually started out in O.J.'s corner, offering rewards for information about "the real killer." But the June 27 issue of *Time* was a blow — a low blow.

When I first saw O.J.'s darkened mug shot on the cover, it

didn't strike me as sinister, as it did many. I found it heartbreaking, instead — *What terrible shape he must be in,* I thought. If people focused on the color of O.J.'s skin, some might see darkness or shadows or mystery. But I looked at O.J.'s eyes, and they were very telling.

They told me that this person was shattered, maybe beyond repair.

When O.J. found out that the cover had been "enhanced" by computer, he was irate. He thought he was being railroaded — not only by Marcia Clark, but now by the press.

Perhaps I was naive, but I didn't see the *Time* photo as racist. America had loved O.J. for the way he ran and then for being O.J. If ever a person was colorless, it was him.

The press had sold a lot of magazines and newspapers by making O.J. a hero. Now they'd sell a lot more by destroying him. As O.J. said, "They love to build you up so they can tear you down."

I was just learning how the game was played, and they were hard lessons, every one of them.

By the first week of July, O.J. and Bob Shapiro were looking to add a lead trial lawyer to their team. The Whitehursts and I rooted for Gerry Spence; Cathy Randa was crazy about him, too. Judging from his TV appearances, Gerry had both exceptional smarts and the skill to reach a jury emotionally.

But it became apparent early on that O.J. leaned toward Johnnie Cochran. "We need someone who can communicate with black jurors," he told me. O.J. was concerned about the media hype with the perception that he'd moved away from his inner-city roots. He didn't think that Gerry's cowboy hats and leather fringe would fly in Los Angeles.

Later on, when I heard Johnnie in action, I knew that O.J. had made the best choice. When Gerry Spence is speaking, it comes from Gerry Spence and no one else. But when Johnnie spoke, I heard O.J.'s voice right through him. The two men shared the same language, and I think the jurors trusted that.

* * *

I took Excedrin P.M. to sleep at night, and usually it worked. But one time I awoke in the dark — and saw a young woman staring at me through my bedroom window. Her face was aglow, as though she held a flashlight beneath it.

"Terri!" I screamed. I was in a cold sweat. *"Terri!"* My friends came running into the room and checked the window. My curtains were drawn, as usual. There was no one there.

That nightmare was just one sign that I wasn't coping so well. Then there was my inability to eat. When Ozella, the Whitehursts' cook, asked if I'd like one of her specialties — cornbread, black-eyed peas, a heavenly sweet-potato pie — I'd say, "Sure, I'd love to have that." Soon wonderful aromas filled the house. I'd be craving Ozella's cooking right up until it faced me on my plate, and then I couldn't touch it. Maybe I was running on too much adrenaline. Whatever the reason, my appetite had flown.

I never wanted to leave the house. I was afraid to miss a single one of O.J.'s calls; I knew how much he counted on my sympathy. But Terri and Debbie kept coaxing, and finally I agreed to a trip to a shopping mall in Jackson, thirty miles north. As I bought a floppy hat there, Debbie heard the murmurs in the next aisle.

"That's Paula Barbieri — that's O.J. Simpson's girlfriend!"

We moved on to a health-food store, and this time a woman asked me to my face: "Aren't you O.J. Simpson's girlfriend?"

I was ready to go home.

Another time we went to a supermarket in a little bitty town, the kind of place where you figured nobody watched Ted Koppel. We started grabbing pies and gallons of ice cream, all these great things that I normally loved but now couldn't bring myself to eat.

As we piled our baskets high, our butts hanging out of the freezer compartment, I got the weirdest sensation. I stood up and turned around . . . and everyone in the store was staring back in total silence.

After that I mostly stayed in. I felt protected in the house up on the hill, where the only creatures you could see were cattle and raccoons. I felt safe there, even when a tornado passed within fifty yards and drove us into the basement one night.

I could take natural catastrophes in stride. It was the man-made kind that wrecked me.

In Tennessee I had stopped the world and gotten off. If it had been up to me, I might have stayed forever. But when I heard that a hurricane was headed smack at Panama City, I knew I had to help Mom with our house in Bay Point.

The storm, I think, was a wake-up call — a sign that it was time to stop hiding and pick up my life.

I was too paranoid to fly home; I couldn't stand the idea that I might be spotted. So I borrowed Mr. Whitehurst's Jaguar and raced the clouds down to the Gulf.

At one point O.J. got through on my cell phone. He was really upset at the risk I was taking. "What are you doing?" he said. "What am I going to do without you?"

As I pulled into our driveway, my mother was moving the porch furniture into the dining room. Though we prepared for the worst, the hurricane fizzled into just another big wind.

But I still had my own stormy weather to steer through, and the forecasts in Los Angeles weren't so optimistic. The day I came home, Judge Kennedy-Powell allowed the murder-night evidence from Rockingham, including the bloody glove, despite the detectives' lack of a warrant.

The next day, the judge ruled that O.J. must stand trial.

Then there was the wrangling over how many hairs the district attorney's office could get from O.J. for analysis. The whole business made me mad. I remembered how Juanita used to snip out O.J.'s gray hairs. Now he was no more than a laboratory animal, a subject for experiments, fair game for any and all invasions.

⋆   ⋆   ⋆

For weeks I locked myself up in my bedroom. I stayed glued to the phone and the television, just as in Tennessee.

The difference was that here the media had me cornered, and they knew it. The security guards kept a special eye out for me, a good thing. Once they rousted a reporter from the bushes in a vacant lot across the street.

But there wasn't much the guards could do about the journalists who checked in at the nearby Marriott and drove by our house with cameras on their roofs.

My mother and I lived in terror. What if the murders in Brentwood had been drug-related? What if I were the next target? I had the house alarmed and perimeter floodlights installed. I kept the blinds closed, night and day — I sensed the eyes out there prying all the time.

From early on, the tabloids treated me as the Famous Man's Bimbo. I'd never read these magazines before. I always assumed that they made their stuff up. Now I found out I'd been right.

For example: *"O.J.'s Bizarre Jekyll & Hyde Obsession Drove Girlfriend Into Therapy,"* in the July 5 *National Enquirer*. Quoting an anonymous "friend" of mine, the story reported that O.J. had proposed that we have three-way sex with A.C.

The *Enquirer*'s sick fantasy left me muttering to myself. What did they think I was trying to do — make alphabet soup?

Every time the phone rang, I'd run downstairs. I'd stand by my mother as she took the call, all nerves and suspicion. All my life, my mother had been my closest confidante. I told her everything; we'd whisper and giggle like schoolgirls. Mom had always been on my side, and that's where she remained. When O.J. was having a particularly rough day, she'd take the phone and tell him a story out of the Bible.

But the upcoming trial drove a big wedge between Mom and me nonetheless. My mother knew that I'd broken up with O.J. just before the murders, and now she was watching my life erode.

I couldn't work; I couldn't eat. Mom didn't understand, and she worried about what would become of me.

I couldn't explain what was happening inside me — not to myself, much less to Mom. All I knew was what I heard on the phone each day: a man so distraught that he sounded like a wounded animal. Our old problems belonged to a life I could barely remember. When you've loved someone who gets into a terrible car crash or comes down with a grave disease, you don't think about the person's faults. You don't dwell on what may have driven you apart. You're reminded instead of why you loved each other, and what a hole would be left in your heart if the person was gone.

If I walked away from O.J. now, I was sure he would break. He might not have a gun anymore, but he would break inside, for good. I had to keep talking, talking, talking to him — when I heard how desperate he sounded, there just wasn't a choice. No other friend could support him the way I could. No one else could say, "I love you," and have it heard the same way.

"Oh, thank God I got you," Cathy Randa would say as she hooked me into a conference call. "He's really bad right now."

Usually it was I who arranged the three-way calls. Often it would be with one of the attorneys for whom O.J. had a life-and-death question, or at least what felt that way to him. When the lawyers weren't at home, O.J. would get grouchy and frustrated: "They're out at their fancy dinners, signing autographs, and here I am in jail."

No one had to tell me that nothing I heard could be repeated to anyone outside "the team." The stakes were too high. I could take no chances.

So I kept secrets from everyone, even Mom. The only time I opened up — the only time I came alive — was in talking to O.J. His evening call wasn't a duty anymore. It was the high point of my day, a brief reprieve from the jails that had swallowed us both.

Tom Lange, one of the lead detectives on the case, was working overtime. He rang my mother and left a message for me to call back. The next time he called I happened to pick up. "We'd just like to talk to you," Lange said.

I politely told him to call my attorney, Michael Nasatir, who'd been referred to me by O.J.'s business lawyer, Skip Taft.

In fact, I might have talked to the police had they come to me aboveboard. It might have been worth it just to get the heat off. But Lange, under pressure from Marcia Clark, proved to be a sneak in the first degree. He got hold of my phone records, and my mother's as well. He called everyone he could find, from the Whitehursts to old friends from high school. He asked them intrusive, insulting questions, mostly along the lines of "Did he ever hit her?"

Grasping at straws, Lange went to a local policeman, a former classmate of mine, and asked him to arrange a meeting with me. When the officer came to my house to tell me about it, I was furious. I was madder still that a police car was parked in my driveway in broad daylight.

So much for my low profile.

Later on, I'd see the police act the same way when they subpoenaed Marguerite, O.J.'s first wife. They tripped her car alarm and then banged on her door, shouting, "Your car is being robbed!" When she opened the door, they threw the subpoena inside.

And then the prosecution wondered why so many witnesses were less than cooperative on the stand.

My mother was alarmed at how much weight I'd lost. My clothes hung off me; bones stuck out of my neck. When Mom looked at my raw, gaunt face she wanted to cry.

She made all my old favorites — blue crabs and spaghetti, key lime pie from scratch. But she had no more luck than Ozella. How could I eat when I heard what O.J. was served in jail? His dinner came in layers: a salad on the bottom of his plate, then some creamed corn and chocolate pudding mixed together, then a cold chunk of mystery meat. They'd mush it all together and put a second paper plate on top.

What I wouldn't have given to trade places with O.J. To eat his gruesome slop as penance for my feelings for Nicole — *or for setting O.J. off? But I couldn't think that, couldn't go there. . . .*

On July 22, I stood by the television as O.J. was arraigned again, this time for trial. When I heard him say, "Absolutely, one hundred percent not guilty," I felt gladdened by his strength and sureness. He no longer looked like a man with nothing to live for. He'd come a long way in the past month.

Some people attacked O.J.'s plea as rehearsed, as the opening line of a Johnnie Cochran Production. But I'd spoken with O.J. and Johnnie the night before, and the plea never came up. From what I knew, there was no plan. Just an innocent man, speaking the truth.

My tenth high school reunion was on the horizon that summer, and I'd decided to sit it out. My social circle at the time had about six people in it and three of them were O.J.'s lawyers. A trip to the hardware store was a major act of courage. Go out to a party with hundreds of people? It was inconceivable.

Besides, my life was already public property. I couldn't quite picture my old classmates asking, "So what are you doing now?"

But an old friend named Nick Patronis wouldn't give up on me. "You've got to come," he insisted. "This is a once-in-a-lifetime event."

I compromised. I passed on the disco dance, as it wouldn't do O.J.'s morale much good if he heard I was at a nightclub. But I went to the beach party and to the more formal dinner in Bay Point — and I felt just fine. I hugged everyone within reach and had a great time.

I wasn't a Martian after all.

No one threw stones at our reunion. I found lots of women in bad relationships or trying to bounce back from them. A girl

I recalled as sort of spoiled had been humbled by a flagrantly cheating husband. Several others were divorced and raising children as single parents.

There'd been a time — before Dolph, before O.J. — when I'd heard similar stories, or when I thought back about what Mom had gone through, and smugly wondered why women chose men who hurt them. Now I was one of those women. I still didn't understand the syndrome, but I had a lot more compassion for my fellow sufferers.

A few horror stories made the rounds. The most popular and athletic girl in the whole class — she was so outgoing that we used to call her "Miss Congeniality" — had died of anorexia a few years before.

Then there was my friend Tim, the sweet doctor's son from Bay Point who used to drive me to school so I wouldn't have to chase the bus. After Tim's mother died and was quickly cremated, his father was charged with murder.* Tim told his girlfriend that he couldn't live knowing his father had killed his mother. Soon after that he committed suicide.

How I'd envied those "normal" Bay Point families. I'd assumed they were immune to the violence I grew up with in St. Andrews. Now I saw they were more like us than I knew.

While I didn't take pleasure in other people's pain, it was a relief to be able to think, "Poor them, poor them," instead of, "Poor me, poor me."

If only for a day.

Still shying away from airports, I had a car sent in August for the six-hour drive to New Orleans, where I'd be finishing voice-over work for a feature film, *The Dangerous*.

I remembered how good I'd felt when we'd shot the film — when my life was so full that I'd had no time to see O.J. Now it was all in reverse. I had no time for anyone or anything

---

*As of the date of this book, the case has not yet gone to trial.

but the man in that chilly cell in Los Angeles. No time for anything but my guilt and repentance — and a chance, just a chance, to retrieve a lost love.

Like a lot of people, I turned toward God only when desperate.

In my modeling years, as I ranged the world, I didn't see how attending church made you a better Christian. I found God on a Pacific island or on the plains of Africa or in a winter's first snow in New York — wherever I found beauty, I felt blessed and said a prayer.

Looking back, I wasn't living a Christian life at all. I was living with a man I wasn't married to. I drank champagne whenever it was poured. I was carefree and self-absorbed; I certainly wasn't doing much to make the world better.

Over time, I came to sense I needed something more.

It was during my dark summer in Panama City, I do believe, that the Lord stepped into my life — right in Melanie Smith's beauty shop. Melanie had known me since grade school, and she could tell how depressed and stressed-out I was.

"Paula, you have got to go see Jack Reece," she said. Melanie was a member of the Church of Christ, the independent church I'd attended as a young girl on the JOY bus.

"Yeah, I'm sure you're right," I said. "I do need to talk to somebody." But I knew I wouldn't seek Jack out. I was just trying to appease Melanie, make her think I'd be okay.

A few minutes later, I walked out toward the parking lot of this little shopping center — and into the path of a silver-haired man coming out of his doctor's office next door.

"Jack?"

"Yes?"

"My name is Paula Barbieri — I don't know if you remember me."

But Jack Reece did remember: "Yes, you lived in St. Andrews." He reminisced about the JOY bus and the songs we'd sung. Before

I knew it, we were singing those Christian songs of my girlhood, right there by the parking lot.

When it was time to say good-bye, I couldn't stop myself. "I'd love to come by your office and see you," I said in a rush. "I really need to get back to my Bible."

More than happy to receive me, Jack agreed to get together on August 15. As the date approached, I got apprehensive about what I would say about my life and how Jack would respond. To that point I'd kept my feelings inside. I wouldn't say anything to bring O.J. down or to further worry my poor mother.

In truth, I was full of pain, body and soul. I spent countless hours meandering aimlessly around my house, from one tissue box to the next. I felt caught between two powerful emotions: my fear of jumping into O.J.'s case, and my guilt if I were to abandon him. Where did my true course lie?

I had no idea what I should do next. I saw no one to turn to. The people in my life — Cathy Randa, the attorneys, O.J. him-self — had their own pressing agendas. They were all doing what they had to do, and I accepted that.

But whom could I trust to guide me through *my* trial?

That's why I went through with my meeting with Jack: to find some peace of mind. I was so weary of my burden that even a drop of support would be worth the getting.

I didn't know it then, but Jack had whole gallons on tap at the Church of Christ.

Typically, I began that first meeting by asking for help for O.J., rather than for myself. Was there anything in the Bible about persecution, some scripture to help a man unjustly accused? Or maybe it was for me after all. I *had* to believe that O.J. was being persecuted, that the D.A.'s office was out to get him for their own malicious reasons. I saw O.J. as a martyr, because a martyr was innocent by definition.

Because a martyr was not a monster, and this martyr had shared my bed.

Jack was wonderful. While giving me the verses I asked for,

he steered clear of any talk of O.J. As Jack pointed out, "The only person you have control over is yourself, and lots of times you don't even have that."

We focused that day on respecting God's boundaries, or what Jack called "staying inside the fence." He referred me to Deuteronomy: "And the Lord commanded us to do all these statutes, commandments, rules, and to fear the Lord our God *for our good always.*"

Those last four words were underscored in Jack's Bible. Our Heavenly Father wasn't oppressive or abusive, Jack explained. He set boundaries not to inhibit or restrict us, but to protect us.

As we read through the Ten Commandments, one jumped out at me with new meaning: *Thou shalt not kill.*

"If everybody agreed that we're not going to murder," Jack said, "think of how much more comforting our society would be, how we could live with much less fear."

I'd never thought I'd know a murder victim, much less get involved in a murder trial. Ever since hearing that first awful newscast, I'd shrunk from even saying the word. Hearing Jack pronounce it was a slap, jolting me out of denial.

Jack's lesson wasn't pointed specifically at me. But as he recited the Ten Commandments, I heard them with fresh ears. They had never seemed so real and important. "That's so right," I kept saying. "That's so right."

Then Jack turned to the New Testament, to Galatians 6: "Do not be deceived: God cannot be mocked. A man reaps what he sows."

Every action has a consequence, Jack said. You can better your harvest once you stay inside the fence and start planting good seeds. But it's a slow process, he cautioned. An oak doesn't grow overnight.

As our hour flew by, I didn't feel as if Jack was lecturing me or delivering some heavy sermon. I felt like that little girl again, holding the minister's hand and being told that Jesus loved me.

I felt as if I'd returned to a safer place, the one I'd been seeking all along.

As the summer unfolded, O.J. began cajoling me to come out to Los Angeles. "I can't wait to see you," he'd tell me. "I just need to know when I can put you on the visitors' list." The plan, he explained, was to add me to the list of material witnesses, whom he could see every day.

Then one day he said: "We're going to Judge Ito and get him to sign the papers, so in case you come next week, it's all ready."

He was prodding me ever so gently, but I couldn't miss the excitement in O.J.'s voice whenever he talked about my coming. It was the only time he sounded like his old self.

For a long time I put him off. "I don't know if I'm ready yet," I kept telling him. I felt safe in Panama City and as happy as I could be, under the circumstances. Los Angeles didn't feel like home anymore — it was the belly of the beast, the heart of everything that had gone tragically wrong.

But with each passing week I felt guiltier about not being there. To stay in Panama City was the easy road, but I don't believe I could have lived with it. How could I abandon O.J.? We'd shared so much, before and after June 12. How could I cut him off now?

While I wasn't O.J.'s girlfriend anymore, I knew I was more than just another friend. I simply *loved* him, beyond categories.

When I told him I was coming, in mid-August, he was almost giddy. He started planning every detail, as if we were going to Hawaii: Cathy would make the arrangements, they'd try to get me in the back way, and on and on.

I was excited, too. It wasn't just guilt and responsibility that were driving me to L.A. I *missed* that man. I'd grown accustomed to his face.

When I finally reserved my flight to Los Angeles, I booked my ticket under an assumed name: "D. H. Lawrence," the author of *Sons and Lovers,* an old favorite of mine. Everything went smoothly out of Panama City. But when I walked to my connecting flight in

Atlanta, I felt creepily on display, as if I were in a glass jar for public inspection.

As I handed my ticket and driver's license to the Delta counter person, I said softly, "You understand?"

The woman smiled and said, "Oh, yeah, I understand."

I didn't realize it at the time, but I wasn't just losing frequent flyer miles with my fake name.

The instant I boarded that plane to Los Angeles, I lost my identity.

10

Imprisoned

You couldn't miss O.J.'s new address. It was squat and beige and ugly, with a billboard of a sign in bright orange letters: LOS ANGELES COUNTY SHERIFF MEN'S CENTRAL JAIL.

Shielded by a concrete fence, rimmed by a few scrawny trees and a line of pay phones, the jail sat in one of downtown L.A.'s saddest neighborhoods. From what I could see of the empty storefronts, the only people doing business were the bail bondsmen.

To dodge the media, Cathy Randa had parked her car at the lower level of the jail's garage. But the reporters were one step ahead of us — they'd stationed a lookout there. By the time we'd taken a dozen steps, fifty cameras were mobbing us.

They were determined to get the big news of the day: my first visit with O.J.

As we neared the jail's entrance, the craziness pitched into chaos. The reporters barked out questions I pretended not to hear. One woman shouted a real clunker: "Are you here to see O.J.?" I never saw her again; I figured she got replaced.

One of the cameramen stayed just ahead of us, walking backward really fast. I saw him about to miss a step and I started to say something, but nothing came out. The man tripped and went down, hard, and three or four others fell on top of him.

Sweating like mad, I was ready to fall down myself. Then Cathy guided me through the door, and we passed into total silence. My gauntlet was over — the journalists weren't allowed inside.

Cathy led me into the next room, where Bob Shapiro was waiting. We went up to a guard in a booth of bulletproof glass, and I handed him my passport for identification.

While waiting for the go-ahead, I took Bob aside. Making sure I wasn't overheard, I said, "Before I go in there, I've got to tell you something."

For weeks my biggest fear had been that I'd wake up one morning to hear my "Dear John" message blasted over the airwaves. If O.J. and I had broken up on the day of the murders, it meant he no longer had a woman in his life. And if that were the case, it could support the theory that he'd killed Nicole in a jealous rage — really bad news for the defense.

"I'll put someone on it," Bob said. As it developed, neither Bob's detective nor the press ever turned up my message; O.J.'s computerized answering service may have automatically erased it.

It was time to go in. I stepped through a metal detector. A thick steel door swung open, then shut behind me. I felt a strange sort of relief. Nothing outside — not the media, nor my family, nor the prying eyes of strangers — could touch me now.

As a second steel door opened and I faced out to the inmates in the visiting area, I had a more ominous sensation. Whatever might happen inside here, these people couldn't just walk away from it.

Most of all, though, I was feeling excitement — I was about to see O.J. for the first time in ten weeks. I craned my neck to find him; a dozen heads swiveled toward me. To my right were two rows of inmates at open tables, conferring with counsel.

To my left were half a dozen glass-enclosed privacy rooms, for those requiring special security. A deputy kept watch on either end.

O.J. was seated in the farthest glass room.

As I made my way down the narrow corridor for visitors, the inmates stared at me through the glass. I'd been undressed by men's eyes before, but never with such weird intensity. My conservative pantsuit might have been made of cellophane. I recognized a Menendez brother, either Erik or Lyle — I'd never learn to tell them apart.

I put on my biggest grin and opened the glass door to the last cubicle. It was a tiny space, with barely enough room for three chairs across. O.J. and I were separated by a gray Formica counter with a three-foot-high panel of glass on top of it. We weren't allowed to touch.

But we were seeing each other's eyes and breathing the same stale air. For a starved and lonely person like me, that was a feast.

O.J. welcomed me with a self-conscious smile. Rubbing his face, he broke my heart as he said, *"Look* at me."

He was wearing a navy blue short-sleeved jumpsuit — he'd always looked nice in that color, I thought — with L.A. COUNTY JAIL stenciled on the front. A short prison buzz cut made his head look even bigger. His coloring was awful under the fluorescent lights, a sick-looking yellow.

I could see that O.J.'s canvas Reeboks had no shoelaces and that his legs were shackled to iron rings on the floor. I forced myself not to look down, not to wince or stare — I wanted O.J. to know I was okay with this.

"You look good," I said, almost too perkily. "I thought you were going to look a lot worse, I really did."

"I look terrible," O.J. said. "But you look great."

He put his hand up to the glass and I did the same. For the rest of that visit and every visit to come, our palms or fingertips would stay as close to touching as the rules allowed.

We shed a lot of tears over the next two hours. O.J. was putting up his best front, but his torment was never far beneath the surface. Behind his forced smile he was a man who'd lost everything but his pain.

We talked about our families and the lawyers and how much we'd missed each other. It was like old times, in the best sense.

Then O.J. drifted away from me. His pauses grew longer; I could tell he'd stopped listening. His forehead creased and his mouth turned down, and he let out an anguished howl from deep in his belly.

"Why is God doing this to me?" O.J. wailed. "I didn't do it. I never killed anyone — I can't understand why this is happening."

I pressed my hand to the glass so hard my knuckles got white. I wanted to reach through to O.J., to hold him and tell him everything was all right.

But I couldn't, and it wasn't.

As the clock struck eight and visiting hours were over, O.J. asked me to leave first. He didn't want me to see the guard lock his wrists back to his waist or lead him away in a slow prison shuffle.

He's still got some pride left, I thought.

It was so hard to go. I walked back down the corridor, maintaining eye contact with O.J. through the glass partitions. I wanted to ask someone, "Can't I just go get a sleeping bag and come back and camp out for a while?"

O.J. kept looking at me until the steel door slammed shut.

"What did he say?" the media chorused as Cathy and I left the building. If anything, they were wilder than before, but it was too dark to get much decent footage.

My first week back I stayed at Rockingham. It was where O.J. wanted me and where I thought I'd feel safest. At night I'd lie down on his big bed, on the left side, where I'd always slept. It was like being on the edge of some yawning cavern; O.J.'s absence felt so strange to me.

Whenever he called, I'd reach over to the right side, his side, to pick up the telephone. In a strange way, the phone replaced him. It was all that was left of the vivid man who'd once lived here.

Despite the driveway's locked gate and O.J.'s twenty-four-hour security, I felt spooked all the time at Rockingham. Day and night, a constant stream of traffic crawled by the house. The rubberneckers were out in full force.

What if the murders *had* been a drug hit, and Rockingham was the next target? It wouldn't be hard for someone to storm the perimeter fence and take out the two night guards. The front door had just one lock on it, easy work for an Uzi.

I couldn't count on much help inside. Although Arnelle and Jason, O.J.'s grown children, were staying in the attached guest rooms, the only other person sleeping in the big house was Gigi, the housekeeper.

The guards lent me a walkie-talkie to keep in touch with them outside, but I got more and more frightened as the week wore on. The smallest night sound startled me. At one in the morning, I'd be calling down to the guards, "Are you there, are you still there?"

One night I actually locked myself into the bedroom's walk-in closet — a full-scale dressing room, really — just to get one more door between me and any assailants. I curled up with a blanket on the recliner and slept better than I had in days.

The following day I told Jason how scared I'd been. He had some friends with him, and soon afterward the tabloids printed a hideous story about my having heard Nicole's ghost.

As O.J. would remind me after that dismaying incident, "You just can't say anything."

On August 25, I came before the grand jury investigating Al Cowlings for his role in the Bronco chase. I arrived to find Tom Lange and Philip Vannatter in the waiting room.

"Nice to see you." I smiled at the detectives, knowing full well why they were there: to pick up on any careless remark I might make. *I'm no dummy,* my eyes said. *Don't treat me like one.*

I entered the grand-jury room in a state of total tension. I could feel every beat of my heart; my diaphragm was so tight I could barely breathe. It was a simple room, with the jurors seated in rows. I thought they looked pitiless.

Christopher Darden, the assistant district attorney in charge, brushed my fur wrong from the start. I didn't like his body language, the way he stood there all jittery with his hands in his pockets. He looked at me like he was going to chew me up and spit me out.

And like he'd enjoy every minute of my ordeal.

Darden's abrasive style made me feel unsafe. I instinctively shut down on him from his very first question: "Are you O.J. Simpson's girlfriend?"

"I'm his *friend*," I replied sharply. I wasn't playing games with the prosecutor; I made a real distinction between the two terms. You don't hurt your true friends or lie to them or desert them for someone else.

But *girlfriends* were something else again. In my experience, men gave them little respect. I didn't want to be one ever again.

Darden wouldn't let the issue rest. He kept repeating the question and I kept echoing my response. It wasn't just my pride talking. Here was my problem: I couldn't answer with a simple yes or no and feel sure that I'd been truthful.

Even if I accepted Darden's definition of *girlfriend,* I had to consider my phone message of June 12. I'd broken up with O.J., or at least I thought I had. I was pretty sure that he'd gotten the message, but I couldn't know whether he'd taken it seriously.

Had I acted like a girlfriend when I went to O.J. at Kardashian's house? No — I was responding to someone on the verge of suicide.

"I need to talk to my lawyer," I told Darden. It was the third time in the last five minutes that I'd retreated to the hallway. Michael Nasatir was unfazed. "If you don't feel comfortable answering that question as yes, then don't," he said.

"On the advice of my attorney," I told Darden, "I respectfully refuse to answer that question."

The assistant D.A. blew up. He threatened to move me to another courtroom, to hold me in contempt and have me jailed.

I broke into tears — now Darden had an all-out emotional female on his hands. I looked up at the flag hanging from the wall and I wondered how an American could have so little protection. I had no lawyer in the room to stop this man from badgering me. The judge was just letting it go. The jurors seemed indifferent, if not bored.

There was no one to stand up and shout, "That's not right!"

And then I saw one juror in the front row, a black woman, look at me and clench her fist. As if to say, "Toughen up, girl, you're gonna make it."

That helped me compose myself — that, and the diamond-and-sapphire cross that I was clenching. The cross had been a gift from O.J. two Christmases before, a companion to my antique ring. It reminded me of higher laws.

After one more hallway conference, I told Darden: "We were dating, and I went to be with my friend."

That was the first hint Darden missed, my use of the past tense with the word *dating.* Sometime later, when he pressed me about whether O.J. had taken a black tote bag to Kardashian's house, I dropped a more obvious clue.

"I haven't traveled with him in some time, so I couldn't say what luggage he carries, really," I testified.

Had Darden followed that up — "When was the last time the two of you traveled together, and what happened after that?" — he might have led me to my "Dear John" message. While I wasn't about to volunteer this information, I wouldn't have lied under oath.

But Darden was like a bulldog with bad eyesight. Once he latched onto something, he couldn't let it go, even if he missed something better. (Or even if it blew up in his face — as we'd see later on with a certain famous glove.) As a result, Johnnie Cochran would be free to spin his sugary tale of O.J. and me as the perfect couple, right up to the night of the crime.

Had Darden been more perceptive, my grand-jury testimony might have been pivotal. It might have changed everything.

(When O.J. read the transcript, he couldn't stop laughing. "This is just so *you*," he exclaimed. "I can't believe how much you had this guy pulling his hair out.")

A.C. was never prosecuted, of course. In my opinion, the authorities never intended to charge him. The public saw A.C. as a hero who'd saved O.J.'s life. People wouldn't have stood for his arrest.

It was no coincidence that Darden was chosen to handle the proceeding. His boss had sent him out to get an edge in O.J.'s trial before it even started. The grand jury was one big fishing expedition.

Unfortunately for the district attorney's office, Darden went out with holes in his net.

As O.J. would tell me, "You're the first voice I want to hear in the morning and the last voice I want to hear before I go to sleep."

That was how I lived my life, from one call to the next. As pre-trial motions and discovery dragged on through the fall, I settled into a routine. At eight sharp O.J. would call and wake me. I'd lift the phone in a haze, groggy from my nightly Excedrin P.M. (I'd asked Dr. Huizenga, O.J.'s personal doctor, for Valium, but he was afraid I'd get addicted.)

O.J. had already been up and grumbling for three hours — without golf as an incentive, he loathed his 5 A.M. reveilles. We'd say our good mornings and how much we cared for each other. We couldn't talk long, as the deputies would be rushing O.J. off to the van and to court.

If he was able to sneak F. Lee Bailey's cell phone into the courthouse holding cell, O.J. would call again later in the morning: pep-talk time. We'd take turns, based on who was feeling the bluest that day.

As I watched the televised preliminaries, and later the trial, I might call one of the detectives with some idea or talk to O.J.'s family. No matter what was going on in court, I tried to stay optimistic. We all propped one another up.

During lunch break I'd run my errands. That usually meant

driving out to O.J.'s office on San Vincenti. After checking in with Skip Taft, I'd pass through the private office, where memorabilia covered the walls. I never got tired of gazing at a picture of O.J. in his USC jersey of bright burgundy and gold.

He was so young and proud in that photograph, and so beautiful. *I'd love to know that man,* I'd say to myself. *He just looks like a tower of strength.*

Cathy Randa's office was connected to Skip's. It was always good to see her; she never ran out of encouragement for me. We'd go for lunch to the Cheesecake Factory, but mostly I'd watch Cathy eat. I'd lose my appetite when I thought about the food O.J. was getting in the holding cell. Like the dreaded lunchmeat special: a slice of bologna on one side of the plate, two slices of Wonder bread on the other, hold the mayo, hold the mustard, hold the lettuce . . .

Sometimes O.J. would call my cell phone at lunchtime. He'd often be feeling gloomy and left out, especially when his lawyers lunched at a place that was famous for its hot turkey sandwiches.

Looking back, I didn't do all that much when I was out. Mostly I was in a fog, just going through the motions.

I'd go home for more Court TV through the afternoon. The hours couldn't go by fast enough; my whole day revolved around my visits to O.J. Aside from the times when Judge Ito ordered restrictions, I'd go down to the jail every day during the week. On Saturdays and Sundays, when the visiting area was moved to the musty jail infirmary, I'd visit twice a day.

By four o'clock I was headed into the shower and then to change into an outfit I knew O.J. would like. By four-thirty I was on the road. From Rockingham I'd drive east on Sunset Boulevard, south on the 405 freeway, then east on the 10 and south on the 110. If I left from my house (I was splitting time between the two now), it would be west on Wilshire Boulevard to the 405, and ditto the rest of the way.

I had my routes down to a science; I knew all the best lanes to navigate through rush-hour traffic. I could put myself on autopilot and get to the jail in twenty-eight minutes flat, and yet those drives never failed to upset me. I'd reach a point that O.J. had passed in the Bronco chase and I'd relive a piece of June 17. It would be eerie and heart-wrenching, every time.

I'd wonder about O.J.'s desperate state that day. Why had he felt so hopeless? How could he have tried to take his life? They were questions that led only to more questions, and I'd feel relief when I pulled into the jail by five o'clock.

Depending on when court had adjourned, O.J. would get back between five-thirty and six, so I'd wait by the checkpoint. Over time the deputies' faces became familiar. One of them, a tall black man, was just the sweetest person. As I surrendered my ID, he'd read my face and tell me how sad — or, less often, how happy — I looked. "Keep your chin up," he'd say.

Another guard, who worked off-hours as a trainer, consumed thirty boiled eggs a day for protein. He'd get after me to eat more.

Even the media became less fearsome as I got to know them as individuals. At first I wouldn't say boo on my way into the jail. But after a while we began chatting about other things in the news, like the latest earthquake. I came to realize that the reporters were just doing their job. Some had covered the Gulf War; O.J.'s case was but another tour of duty.

Far from acting hostile, the mainstream journalists would warn me when a tabloid crew made the scene. "Be careful, that guy's from *Hard Copy*," they'd say. Or: "Watch yourself, that's *A Current Affair*, and they've got a camera going."

During my first weeks back in L.A., Cathy arranged rides for me downtown. When that got too complicated, I had to start driving myself. On my first day on my own, I came out of the jail and climbed into my Bronco. Try as I might, my engine wouldn't start — I couldn't work the bypass switch.

The camera crews went on filming and filming and filming. Tears streamed down my face; I tried to hide under the steering wheel.

Then I heard, "Everybody turn off your cameras." A brawny cameraman set his equipment down, opened my door, and said,

"Let me do that for you." He inserted the little key perfectly and shut my door.

"Okay, everybody, turn 'em back on," my Good Samaritan instructed. I drove off, waving a thankful good-bye.

I always went straight home so I could be there when O.J. called. Often the phone would be ringing as I walked through the door. We'd pick up the conversation where we'd left off in jail. It was better that way, when there were no gaps in my life. When I had less time to think and worry.

Those night calls were partly postmortems. O.J. would be eager to review what had happened in court that day and to plan ahead for the next. I'd play operator and put through a conference call to Johnnie Cochran or F. Lee Bailey at their homes. Though I'd keep quiet when the lawyers were on, O.J. wanted me on the line. It was our way of staying together for every possible moment.

When O.J. was feeling low, Bobby Bender was our best bet. He took the bleakest situation and put a funny spin on it. Bobby could be really outrageous, but his caring always came through.

After our third party hung up, O.J. and I had our private time. I might put the Winans on the stereo and crank up the volume so O.J. could hear it. Or we might watch a movie or TV show over the phone together — O.J. on the small set he could squint at through his bars, me on the big screen in O.J.'s living room, where we'd snuggled many a time.

This might sound strange, but my favorite program was *Unsolved Mysteries,* where they'd review an unsettled crime and invite viewers to call in with information. Maybe it comforted me to think that even difficult crimes *could* be solved. The guilty would be brought to justice, sooner or later — which meant the innocent would be freed.

O.J. and I both enjoyed a good Clint Eastwood shoot-'em-up, but I was appalled when the deputies put on a rented video of the jail movie *The Shawshank Redemption.*

"That's not very encouraging," I complained to O.J. I suggested something lighter — wouldn't *Mary Poppins* be a nice change of pace?

We were at the guards' mercy, of course. Lots of times they'd switch in the middle of a show to something ridiculous. O.J. would holler out in frustration, "Come on, man, that was a good movie!"

As we got close to ten o'clock, when the phones would be shut down, O.J. took his sleeping pill and I gulped my Excedrin P.M., so they'd kick in at the same time. Then we'd start saying our good-byes, the toughest part of the day.

"I miss you," O.J. would say. "I sure need a hug."

"Well, I'm hugging you through the phone," I'd tell him.

Or if I was going through PMS or I'd just had a weepy day, he might say, "Give the pillow a hug."

Sometimes O.J. tried to hang on after closing time. He'd desperately beg the guard, "Please, I just want to say good night to my girlfriend. Leave me alone for five more minutes."

The guards didn't like that. Some of them got aggressive, right up in O.J.'s face: "Get off the phone right *now*." They held all the cards. If you bucked them you lost your privileges, and that was that.

When O.J. got really agitated and itched to fight back, I'd tell him, "Just stop it — just relax a little bit. You know you can't win if you go toe-to-toe."

I'd hear him sigh and say good night, and then he'd hand over the phone. And just like that, with the dial tone, I'd break. Those disconnections killed me. I'd lie there crying in O.J.'s bed, wondering when my pill would work, waiting for morning and the sound of his voice.

As I look back, I wasn't even conscious of how we were sliding back into our old verbal intimacy. Once I'd resolved to forget the past and ignore the future, my feelings of the moment held sway. Because I *did* love O.J. I'd never stopped loving him — not when he'd behaved so badly in Palm Beach, not when I left that message on the morning of June 12.

And now, under the most horrific circumstances, I'd been handed a chance to reclaim our love. To erase the failure of our romance. To be together once again, for as long as it lasted.

*   *   *

By the time of my first visit, jail life was taking its physical toll on O.J. His knees were getting worse. The poor lighting strained his eyes — O.J. was devouring five novels a week for escape, and he needed reading glasses for the first time in his life.

Basic hygiene was a constant issue. O.J. was humiliated when I saw his toenails, which had grown long and grotesque. It took several weeks and a court order to get him a nail clipper, just as it would for his thermal underwear. Then O.J. developed an excruciating fungus on his feet.

But what worried me most was how skinny O.J. was getting. His once-sturdy physique had been whittled away until his prison jumpsuit sagged off his collarbones. "I'm even losing my bottom," he'd say sadly. That was a heavy hit at O.J.'s self-image; he'd been proud of his great derriere.

Dr. Huizenga told me how important it was for O.J. to exercise. Eventually the doctor got a little stationary bike put in the cell, but O.J. never used it much. The workout got him too winded to talk on the phone, his lifeline.

As far as I could tell, O.J.'s celebrity status mostly worked against him inside the jail. He was totally isolated, in theory for his own protection. When O.J. was taken out of his cell and down a corridor, the other inmates were ordered to turn their backs and look away. The guards didn't even want them making eye contact.

(One fellow prisoner did connect with O.J., through a note that basically said, "Hang in there — Erik Menendez." O.J. was disinclined to write back. "Oh, that's perfect — me and the Menendez boys," he said ruefully. "That's just what I need to read in the tabloids.")

When the general population played basketball on the roof deck, O.J. watched from a nearby cage; his own "recreation" consisted of an hour of sunlight and fresh air per week. O.J. would have given a year of his life to get into a game and shoot a few hoops.

But what they couldn't take away was O.J.'s charisma. He'd be stuck in that rooftop cage, and the other inmates would trot by and say, "Juice, hang in there. You're gonna make it. You're gonna be all right." O.J. might start singing an Aaron Neville song and the players would join in. For those few minutes they were all together.

Around Labor Day, however, O.J. had a less friendly contact on the roof. A prisoner walked by and taunted him about a six-page pictorial in the October issue of *Playboy*.

The girl in the pictures was me.

I'd done the shoot in Kenya, back in July of 1993. I saw no stigma in appearing in *Playboy* — if Kim Basinger could do it, why not me? Working in the nude didn't bother me. I trusted the photographer, Peter Beard, an artist who wouldn't do anything trashy. Besides, I wasn't being hired as the open-legged centerfold girl. I wouldn't have to show the sun, the moon, and the stars. I could stay within my comfort zone, or at least so I thought.

The money was nothing special: $15,000 for a week's work, at a time when I could make $10,000 a day modeling. But I wanted to see Africa, and the timing was perfect. My strained relationship with O.J. was wearing me out. I needed to get as far away as possible. A week with the lions and giraffes was just what the doctor ordered.

I got paid for the job, but *Playboy* chose not to use Peter's work. I wasn't "showing enough," they told me. The pictures weren't as "sexy" as they'd expected.

But after O.J. was arrested, *Playboy*'s criteria changed. They'd shelved the photographs because I "wasn't known at the time," the magazine's spokesman said. "She became known in an unusual way, so we decided to run the shots."

The enormity of what I'd done sunk in while I was stuck in bumper-to-bumper traffic on Wilshire Boulevard one evening. In the next lane was a guy in a baby blue Jaguar with *Playboy* spread out on his lap. Sitting high in my Bronco, I could see him flipping back and forth between me and the centerfold, a girl who was showing whole constellations.

I felt raped and humiliated, and terrified. If the prosecution ever got me on the stand, you could bet they'd use *Playboy* to tear me down.

Bob Kardashian brought a copy of the magazine in to O.J., who was the soul of understanding. "Don't cry, now," he told me on the phone. "You don't have anything to be ashamed of. I thought it was really tasteful."

To this day, I still get photographs from the *Playboy* spread sent to me for autographs. It never fails to mystify me — do people expect me to sign my belly button?

If I was struggling against the whirl of the waterspout, O.J. was chin-deep at its spinning core. Jail demanded all of his considerable willpower to keep his head above water — to stay sane.

By nature a man of action, he now had time to burn in his cell. To reflect on every legal detail. To agonize about the course his life had taken, and where he might have gone wrong. Sometimes he'd get lost in the brambles of second-guessing. But even in his low moments, and there were plenty of them, O.J. never resembled the lost soul I'd seen in Encino. When he told me about his suicide attempt in the Bronco, he seemed ashamed of himself.

"I think I'm still here for a reason," O.J. told me. He was letting me know that he'd never try anything like that again, and I was grateful.

It takes a lot of energy to fight for your life; it was natural for O.J. to turn inward. But he could still break through his self-absorption on occasion. He'd get on me to eat more, or ask why I seemed so somber that day.

I'd never felt quite so flattered as I did when I walked into the visitors' room. O.J.'s eyes would light up every time. "Turn around and let me see you," he'd say. "You look awful pretty today."

I'd blush and do a little twirl in my dress, the one I'd settled on after three changes, knowing O.J. liked them short. I'd show him the legs he'd loved to stroke. It felt as if we were dating again, when O.J.'s approving smile could make my day.

We had some lighter times in that glass cube, too. O.J. might launch into a soliloquy from *Romeo and Juliet,* until he lost himself in the rhythm of the words. I'd just sit there, tapping my fingers on the partition, trying to be polite. When he finished, I'd say, "Very romantic, I get it now."

When the lawyers came in to discuss the case, they'd usually ask me to leave. But I'd stick around for visitors. As you might expect, O.J.'s circle of friends shrank after his arrest, but the few that hung in were steadfast. A.C. and Bobby Chandler, his old Buffalo teammates, were tremendous. Don Ohlmeyer, the president of NBC, came by almost every week. So did O.J.'s golfing buddies, particularly Craig Baumgarten, a movie producer.

(When the prosecution made a big deal about O.J.'s little spat with Craig on the morning of the murders, I knew they were barking up the wrong tree. O.J. would jibe at *anyone* who sulked after a bad shot — including President Clinton, with whom he played a round in California during the year of our breakup. As I heard it told, O.J. hit a long drive and bragged, "That's why they call me the Juice." President Clinton followed with an even longer one and countered, "That's why they call *me* the Prez.")

We'd have a high time when Cathy Randa and O.J. harmonized a medley of show tunes. And it was always a great day when O.J.'s mom came down from San Francisco. Mrs. Simpson had heart trouble, and O.J. was worried about her getting through the trial. He'd tell her, "I'm doing fine, Mamma, the case is going real good," and then he'd give her some bit of positive news from the defense team's detectives. "We're going to win this one," he'd say.

"That's right," his mother would agree. "That's what's going to happen here." O.J. needed to hear that. Nothing can match a mother's reassurance, no matter how old the child.

Mrs. Simpson couldn't climb the stairs at Rockingham. When she wasn't in her downstairs bedroom, she watched TV in the kitchen. The chairs there weren't right for her, and I knew she missed her rocker from home. One day I went out and bought her the Cadillac of rocking chairs, with cushions to fit. With my own mom so far away, the gift made me feel closer to O.J.'s mother.

She was always very sweet to me. "Thank you for being there for my boy," she'd say.

I blushed at the praise. I loved spending time with Mrs. Simpson, or with Shirley and Carmelita, O.J.'s sisters. When we were together, I felt less alone and frightened. I felt almost like part of the family. Almost like I belonged.

In October, the deputies found contraband in O.J.'s cell: a yellow highlighting marker he'd absentmindedly pocketed after a session in the attorneys' room.

Stung by flak from the media that O.J. was getting special treatment, the sheriff's office suspended his phone privileges for three days.

O.J. was furious. "If that's not the biggest crock of bull over a pen!" he roared at my next visit. "What did they think I was going to do with it?"

For O.J., it was three days of hell; the phone lines were his veins and arteries. It was hard on me, too. I missed O.J.'s morning wake-up call and his sweet good night. But I had it easy, I thought. I wasn't trapped behind bars. How awful it must be for him in his cell, with all those feverish thoughts and no one to share them with.

How is he doing right now? I wondered a dozen times a day.

I'd been drawn to O.J., way back when, by his strength and independence. At last, I'd thought, a man whom *I* could lean on for a change.

Now I had to carry him. The load was huge and getting heavier all the time. My back was stooping under the strain.

And I'd never felt more proud and needed in all my life.

11

Betrayal

Going into October, our big concern was the blood evidence at Rockingham and what the DNA tests would reveal. Bob Shapiro braced us for the worst.

"It's going to come back against you," he told O.J. "It's just something we're going to have to deal with."

But even with fair warning, I was stunned to hear the test results: Spots of blood in O.J.'s Bronco had been traced to O.J., Nicole, and Ron Goldman. After O.J. finished talking to the lawyers that evening, he called me to say good night. He sounded flabbergasted, worse than he had in weeks.

"I didn't do this," he said — and I felt so bad for him, that he needed to affirm himself to me. In fact, I'd already written the evidence off — to police chicanery or incompetence or whatever rationale I needed to keep the faith. I aborted my questions before they were asked.

"Why am I here?" O.J. went on, all choked up. "What did I do to deserve this? I've always been a good guy all my life. I've always done unto others, like Mamma raised me."

At ten o'clock the guards cut us off, before I could make sure he was all right. It was a bad night all around.

"What is O.J. doing in that cold, lonely room — pacing?" I wrote just after our call. *"No, I'm sure he's got his head in both hands and he's crying."*

After he had a day or two to digest the bad news, O.J.'s mood brightened. "It's like a football game," he said. "They just scored, and now it's our turn with the ball."

I told myself that the test results made sense — hadn't Bob predicted them? I shared the lawyers' distrust of any evidence gathered by the LAPD. These were the same detectives who had scaled the wall at Rockingham without a warrant, using the flimsy excuse that they'd feared for O.J.'s safety.

In one call I set up for O.J., Alan Dershowitz, the Dream Team's Constitutional expert, was vehement that the detectives had violated O.J.'s rights. "They've opened a huge door for an appeal," Alan said.

Hearing that, it became clear in my mind that the D.A. would do anything to win, fair or foul.

My suspicions were confirmed in another three-way call, this one with Dr. Henry Lee, the Connecticut criminologist. Dr. Lee told O.J. that it looked like someone had tampered with the evidence. I had tremendous respect for Dr. Lee's integrity. If he'd thought O.J. guilty, I was certain he would have pulled back.

I could draw only one conclusion: O.J. was being framed, plain and simple. It just wasn't *logical* for him to have killed Nicole — who would raise his children while he traveled all over the country? O.J. had nothing to gain and everything to lose by Nicole's death.

I didn't consider the possibility that logic had nothing to do with this crime — that it might have been an act of passion. I'd embraced O.J.'s claim that he and Nicole had no emotional ties as of June 1994, and that he'd returned to his family for the children's sake. Though O.J.'s suicide note had indicated otherwise, I *needed* to keep believing that. It would be too hurtful to think otherwise.

I wasn't complacent in my belief in O.J.'s innocence. I constantly sought confirmation and assurance. One day I asked Dr. Huizenga, "Wouldn't a person be covered in blood from head to toe if they cut someone's jugular?"

"Yes, of course," he replied. "There wouldn't be any way to walk out of there without a lot of it on you."

And yet O.J. had been driven to the airport just minutes after the crime, and no one had seen any blood on him. How could he possibly be involved?

That fall I did some sleuthing of my own — to help O.J.'s case, of course, but maybe to put my mind at ease as well. With Peter Neufeld, one of the defense attorneys, I retraced the path that O.J. supposedly took outside Rockingham after the murders. We walked down the back alley until we reached the fence the police said O.J. scaled.

The fence was taller than I was — a good six feet — and thick with brush. There was no way I could make that climb. How could a man with two arthritic knees possibly get over? Besides, O.J. had a secret path to the Watts' house, behind his tennis courts, that he always used.

On another occasion, I stood outside Rockingham's front gate, by the intercom where the limousine driver, Allan Park, would have been calling inside for O.J. on the night of June 12. Meanwhile, one of the defense team's investigators coasted my Bronco to a stop on Rockingham, to where O.J.'s Bronco had been found the next morning. The night was so quiet in that neighborhood that I could hear a pin drop. I could certainly hear a two-ton truck pulling in around the corner.

(During the trial, when Allan Park described seeing a man dressed in black cross the front yard, and everyone went wild speculating who that man might have been, O.J. turned to me in disgust. "This is ridiculous," he said. "That was me — I was getting my stuff together; getting my golf clubs." The problem was, he said, he couldn't admit to being that man. Bob Shapiro in his opening statement had said that O.J. was asleep at the time. "Why'd he have to go and say that?" O.J. said. "I didn't tell him that.")

Back inside the house, I went through O.J.'s closet to check for a dark cotton sweatsuit that might match the fibers found at the murder scene. I wasn't surprised not to find one, as the only sweatsuits I'd seen O.J. wear were cashmere. I also found several pairs of Bruno Magli loafers in the closet, but I considered them irrelevant. The sole print outside Nicole's condo was left by a Bruno Magli *lace-up* model, and no such shoes were in O.J.'s house.

Before the trial started, the defense did its best to chase down leads pointing away from O.J. Bill Pavelic, the detective hired by Bob Shapiro, came up with one scenario after the next. The possibilities were endless. Cathy Randa, Don Ohlmeyer — everyone had his or her own ideas and angles.

From the start, O.J. was saying that the murders were connected to Nicole's friend Faye Resnick and a drug deal gone bad. That seemed reasonable to me. I remembered when my brother Michael had a drug debt and a guy threatened to leave blood all over our front lawn if we didn't pay up.

That summer, while still in Panama City, I hired two local investigators to see what they could come up with. They flew out to Los Angeles and nosed around. "Some strange things" were going on out there, they reported. They found a lot of drug use at one of the nightclubs that Ron Goldman had been promoting, as a sideline to his waiter's job.

Then came the punch line: The guy who took over the promotion job from Ron had been found murdered in his front yard.

With his throat cut.

We wouldn't be able to bring that chilling story into evidence, however. And once the trial began, O.J.'s team had to focus on the issues raised by the prosecution. From that point on, we were literally on the defensive.

The true story of what had happened on South Bundy Drive, it appeared, would remain a mystery.

Whenever O.J. got upset by some development in court or report in the press, he'd tearfully profess his innocence — to me or anyone else in earshot. He always sounded spontaneous, never calculated. Nobody could be this good an actor, I thought.

Once O.J. asked me where *I'd* been on the night of June 12, as if he were checking my alibi. That floored me yet confirmed my faith in him.

And that's exactly what I had, a faith in O.J. that was nearly spiritual. I wouldn't ask him hard questions about the night of the murders. I couldn't bear the thought of hurting him, not when he was under attack from every side. My job was to be supportive. To keep O.J.'s head up, and mine as well.

But it was more than caution or concern that held my tongue. Except for a few rare weak moments early on, those hard questions did not occur to me. I simply could not imagine O.J. committing this crime.

Or to be more precise: I couldn't *allow* myself to imagine it.

If O.J. was guilty, my past would be a hall of horrors. He'd been my best friend and my sweetheart — if O.J. was a murderer, what would that say about me? How could I live with myself after giving body and soul to him?

Even more petrifying, what would I do now, this very day, and in the days to come? I'd be chained to a killer, with no easy way to break free.

No, I had to keep the faith. I had to hold that O.J. was innocent and that any fair jury would agree. I couldn't afford to falter, not for a minute. I couldn't even think the word *guilty*, much less say it aloud. Once I let it creep into my mind, O.J. would be sure to lose in court — hadn't Nicole died after I'd wished she'd disappear?

God is testing me, I thought. It was all on my shoulders. I could no more doubt O.J.'s innocence than I could sleep with another guy. I had to be the perfect woman and stand by my man.

Anything less would destroy us both.

As the preliminaries ground on, O.J. became more insistent about taking the stand. "Who knows my life better than me?" he'd say.

"You don't know what lawyers do," Bob Shapiro told him one day in the visiting room.

"But I know what *I* did, and I know what I'm talking about," O.J. insisted.

Appreciating how hard it was to argue with O.J., Bob took a different tack. "All right," he said. "Let me give you a little taste of what it's like."

As I watched, both fascinated and horrified, Bob tore O.J. apart in two minutes. He started with harmless-sounding questions like "Did you ever raise your voice with Nicole?" Then he subtly stepped up his attack, maneuvering O.J. into corners he couldn't just skate his way out of. And if O.J. tried to explain, there would be four more questions waiting to knock him back again.

At the end, O.J. was in checkmate. Bob had made him look like the most terrible guy in the world.

"You don't belong on the stand," I told O.J. "Please, please don't do this."

"I get the point," he said. But O.J. being O.J., he wasn't deflated for long. The next day he told Bob, "Let's get somebody to work with me."

O.J. practiced over the next several weeks. When his visitors asked, "Are you really going to testify?" he had a ready reply: "Let me give you an example of what it's like."

He'd proceed to grill them on what they'd done the previous Saturday night. O.J. beat them all; he did it to me, too. You couldn't be honest without hesitating, but if you hesitated it sounded incriminating.

How could O.J. possibly reconstruct a day back in June?

None of the attorneys was eager for O.J. to testify. But neither did they rule it out. As Johnnie Cochran said, "We'll see what cards are dealt us, and take it day by day."

Around this time I got a surprise visitor: my father. I was happy to go get him at the truck stop and put him up for a couple of days.

While I knew I wouldn't be opening my heart to him, it was just nice to see someone from home.

Installed in a guest house at Rockingham, Dad got a strong whiff of what my life was like. He heard the tabloids' helicopters buzzing overhead, saw me hide from passing cars and their cameras. He even got on the phone with O.J., his old drinking buddy from that tumultuous dinner at La Dôme. "This too will end," my father told him.

Dad was crazy about Abba in those days, so I took him to a Brentwood video store to buy a tape. While my father hunted it down, one of the store's employees asked me if I wanted to hear a Michael Jackson joke.

Right away my guard was up; I sensed the guy had recognized me. "I don't think so, thank you very much," I said.

"Well, how about an O.J. Simpson joke?"

"No, really, I'd rather not." I walked away, but the guy wasn't through, and he followed me down the aisle.

"When they get him in the electric chair," he said, "I hope his skin just crisps up and sizzles, and his eyes pop out . . ." He went on in that vein, and it took everything I had to hold back my tears and hustle Dad out of the store. I couldn't let him see how upset I was. It would get back to Mom, and she'd be harping on me to come home right away.

I had a really bad dream that night. When I told one of O.J.'s guards what had happened, he complained to the manager, and the worker was fired.

At the time, most people in Brentwood still seemed to keep an open mind: *We have a wonderful, healthy neighborhood here, so let's hear all the evidence and wait for the verdict . . .*

Like so many things over the next year, that outlook would drastically change.

For the most part, O.J.'s grown children and I got along well at Rockingham, though it bothered me that they visited their father so rarely. Jason and I would hang together out by the pool and

Jacuzzi and play catch with his pit bull in the water. We were also partners in mischief. When we got sick of people leaving their cars and pointing big lenses over the fence, we'd get a dozen eggs and bombard them.

But as time went on, I could feel the tension rise between us. Jason and Arnelle had lost someone they loved, and now here I was in his place. It didn't help when O.J. called and one of his kids answered. "Hey, how are you?" O.J. would say. "Put Peola on the phone." Then we'd talk until the guards shut us down — it had to hurt Jason and Arnelle.

When I confided to O.J. that I felt uncomfortable around Nicole's photographs, he told me to take them down. Arnelle, who'd been close to Nicole, had a real attitude toward me after that. The bad feelings spread to Marguerite, who called one night and told me, very abruptly, "Get the housekeeper on the phone."

Wanting to heal the rift, I wrote to Arnelle: *"I'm not asking for pity, just understanding. I'm here for your father."*

Not long after that, Debbie and Terri Whitehurst flew out to L.A. to check how I was doing. After a day at Disneyland, we stopped at Rockingham for a cup of tea before heading back to the airport. I just wanted my friends to see where I was staying, and that it was fine.

We spent fifteen minutes out by the tennis court. "See, it's peaceful and quiet here," I said. As we were leaving, Arnelle stepped out the door and coolly stared at us.

We'd just pulled out of the drive when my cell phone rang. "Who *were* those people?" It was Jason, screeching at the top of his lungs. "How could you bring anyone here? This isn't your house. It's my father's, and you have to show him some respect!"

I understood that Jason was marking territory and that he'd been stressed-out himself, but I was steaming. Debbie and Terri heard Jason's every word, and I could see the concern in their eyes.

"I'm not going to talk about this with you," I said. "You talk to your father about it, and you talk to him about your attitude, because I'm not going to deal with you."

After I hung up, Terri looked at me and said, "Just leave, Paula. You don't deserve this. Come back home with us."

I couldn't desert O.J. because of Jason's snit. But I was ready to pick up my stuff and stay in my apartment for the duration.

"No, that's not right," O.J. told me. "I want you at the house." As he saw it, to be in his house was to stay part of his life. So I continued to split time between the two addresses, but it was never quite the same between Jason and me.

On November 15, the *National Enquirer* ran the following story: "*O.J.'s Girlfriend Kicked Out Of His Mansion — After His Son Finds Her With 2 Men!*"

I can't be sure who told them this lie, but I know it wasn't me, and it sure wasn't Terri or Debbie.

Whenever things looked really bleak or O.J. seemed about to break, I'd call Jack Reece and we'd pray together over the phone. On the few occasions that I made it home to Panama City for a weekend, I'd go to see Jack in his office. Each meeting dug my faith a little deeper. With Jack as my guide, I found that the Bible never failed me. It had an answer for every question, a solution for every crisis.

I soaked up new scripture. I knew so little, and there was so much to learn. I learned verses by the dozen, but my favorite was out of Psalms: "The sacrifices of God are of a broken spirit; a broken and contrite heart."

Broken and contrite — that was me, head to toe.

The Bible was primary in my development, but Jack knew I needed more. I was so lonely in Los Angeles. It hit me every night when the clock struck ten and O.J. had to leave the phone, and the only company I had was the television or my glum and weepy thoughts.

Without my saying the words, Jack could hear me crying out for family, for people to come home to and rely upon. He suggested that I attend a Sunday service at the Church of Christ.

I hesitated at first. I felt like a thorn, an outcast, someone no-body decent would want to know. When I finally walked into the church's modern new building in a wooded area of Panama City, my eyes studied the carpeting. I was so afraid that someone would recognize me and say something about O.J. or the case. I tried to blend in unnoticed.

It didn't work. A hand reached out to shake mine, then a second, then a third. I got caught up in a sea of smiling faces and friendly eyes. I was taken aback by all the attention — it was only later that I'd realize that the "greeters" did the same for anyone walking through that door.

The church, I'd learn, was one place I'd never get stared at or whispered about. The members didn't care about my tabloid no-toriety. They cared about me for the person I was, and the better person I was trying to become.

I saw O.J. drawing closer to God as well. His talks with Mr. Whitehurst had made their mark, and he was moved by the letters and Bibles sent by Christians through the mail. To get the Bibles through to O.J. without red tape, I'd cut off their binding, punch holes through the pages, and tie yarn through the holes. Though I must have sent him a dozen or more, O.J. preferred a worn leather New International Version; he got put off by the *thees* and *thous* in the King James.

His Bible was especially dog-eared around the Book of Job. Cut off from Sydney and Justin, still mourning the death of Nicole, O.J. identified with Job's loss of his family. He also liked Psalm 97, which tells how the faithful will be delivered "from the hand of the wicked." O.J. thought of himself and Marcia Clark whenever he read that verse.

For a while the sheriff's department sent in their jailhouse psy-chiatrist to check on him, but O.J. didn't see the point. "He comes in to make sure I'm not suicidal, and I'm *not* suicidal," O.J. said impatiently one day after the doctor had left. "You don't see me trying to find shoelaces to hang myself, do you?"

As we went on to discuss the Bible together, I could see that O.J. found more solace there than in any psychiatric analysis. When one or both of us were having a terrible day, O.J. couldn't fall back on his old dodge: that some things didn't have answers. Now we'd look up a pertinent verse and hash it out instead. Now we had a whole book of answers just waiting to be received.

We got a big lift when Rosey Grier, the ordained minister and former football star, began praying and studying with us on the weekends, when visits were held in the jail infirmary. As big and tough as Rosey looks, the strongest part of him is his spirit. Rosey prayed like no one else I'd ever met. He'd start his closing prayer, and O.J. and I would bow our heads. Twenty minutes later we'd steal a glance at each other — Rosey was still going strong.

In *I Want to Tell You*, O.J. wrote that his troubles were God's way of "getting my attention." Before the murders, O.J. had everything his way. Riding high on material things, he thought he could conquer the world. Then came the rude awakening — and a chance to discover what really mattered in life.

During O.J.'s year and more in jail, I believe he was walking in the right direction. His faith was growing, but he had yet to get that *hunger* for God, that urgency to be baptized. Like a lot of people, he was using God as a crutch in a hard time.

Every now and again, O.J. would backslide. One time in the jail, I casually remarked that I'd seen Steven Spielberg in his light green Mercedes convertible, my favorite color.

Sometime later, O.J. told me, "I'd love to get you that little green Mercedes convertible." He was trying to be nice, but it sparked a big fight between us. I was running through my savings, just getting by on residual checks from old commercials, and here was O.J. talking about a $120,000 car.

I might have seen then that O.J. had kept one foot in the material world, and that he'd swing back into it if given half a chance.

*   *   *

On November 29, *Star* ran a hot exclusive: a transcript of O.J.'s interrogation by Detectives Lange and Vannatter back on June 13, when they first brought him to Parker Center.

Someone got me a copy of the tabloid. I was skimming through it when I was caught short by the following exchange, about a bracelet that O.J. had given Nicole for her birthday in May:

LANGE: And did she return [the bracelet] the same day?

SIMPSON: . . . I get into a funny place here on this, all right? She returned it . . . three weeks ago or so, because when I say I'm in a funny place on this it was because I gave it to my girl-friend and told her it was for her, and that was three weeks ago. Told her I bought it for her. You know? What am I going to do with it?

So much for a gift from the heart.

O.J. had given me a sapphire-and-diamond art-deco bracelet around that time, such a stunning piece of jewelry that I felt nervous wearing it out. I recalled Chris Darden asking me about a bracelet in the grand-jury room. I'd had no idea what he was talking about.

Now I was getting the picture. Feeling insulted, I confronted O.J. in the visiting room. "What's the truth about this?" I demanded, showing him the transcript through the glass. "What else is there that I don't know about?"

"No, I bought that bracelet for you — that's your bracelet," O.J. said earnestly. "Go and see so-and-so" — he rattled off a name — "at the jewelry store, and he'll confirm it."

I was unconvinced: "Look, don't make me look like an idiot when I get on the stand. Go ahead and tell me now if you bought it for Nicole first."

It wasn't true, O.J. insisted — "That's tabloid journalism, they just made it up. That whole thing was fabricated."

I had to decide: Would I believe O.J. or *Star*? Ever since the

Enquirer's "alphabet soup" story I trusted nothing in the tabloids.
I simmered down. I even apologized to O.J. for doubting him.

Once again, it was a case of sink or swim. However gullible I'd
been at the start with Dolph Lundgren or Dean Hamilton, I became openly skeptical after they betrayed me. But I couldn't pick
and choose what I wanted to believe from O.J. Because if he could
lie about the bracelet, he could lie about larger things. . . .

I was in such huge denial in those days. I altered reality like a
pair of slacks, till it fit my hopes and needs.

If I thought O.J.'s story might die down some that fall, I couldn't
have been more wrong. There might be news about mass graves
in Bosnia, and yet there would be O.J. on every magazine cover. It
never let up.

The tabloids were the most ferocious, of course. I had to be so
careful about whom I talked to. When a few old friends sold stories about me — while others turned down offers that could have
bought them a new car — I got more paranoid still. Every time I
opened my mouth, I worried that I'd be reading it in *Star*.

For my brother Michael, it didn't matter how little I spoke to
him. Squeezed for money, he simply made things up. Later he
signed a broad agreement allowing the tabloids to attribute anything they pleased to him, which made the magazines just about
libel-proof. I had to hand it to my brother — he was selling out on
a high level.

I remember coming home for a visit one time and changing
planes in Memphis, where I ran into a tabloid TV crew getting off
at the same gate. A call to my mother revealed what they'd been
doing in Panama City: They'd just left my brother's house.

I was so furious that I drove straight to Michael's apartment to
have it out. My brother was totally shameless. "You shouldn't have
gotten yourself into this mess," he told me. "It's your own fault."

The more I challenged Michael, the more spiteful and destruc-
tive he got. In one typical "world-exclusive interview," he supposedly told *Star* how O.J. once begged me to visit him "dressed

like Nicole"; asked me to have breast-enhancement surgery "just like Nicole"; ordered me to place flowers at Nicole's graveside and candles in her "honor" at Rockingham.

When *People* asked Michael to talk to them for free, he was offended. "I'm not going to stab my sister in the back for nothing," he said.

Michael's behavior really hurt me, but I could rationalize that he was an addict and therefore out of control.

With my father, the betrayal stung deeper. When Dad visited me in Brentwood, he saw the huge strain I was under. But rather than give me a shoulder to lean on, he sold a televised interview in late November to *Current Affair*.

My father said ridiculous, hateful things on that program. He voiced concern that I hadn't been able to concentrate on work because of my involvement with O.J. He went on to beat his old, tired drum — that it just went to show that mixed couples shouldn't be together.

The interview was heavily promoted, and I couldn't stop myself from tuning in. Watching it was one of the biggest disappointments of my life. I felt like I'd been stood up at homecoming weekend all over again.

What Dad had done was inexcusable. He hadn't helped my sputtering career by telling a national TV audience what a basket case I'd become. Worse, he'd taken money for blood. Ever since I was a child, I'd believed that family was more important than anything. That you stood by your family, no matter what.

Now I saw I'd been kidding myself.

When I hooked Bobby Bender into one of our three-way calls, he tried to lighten me up a little: "Boy, your father, he's a piece of work."

"You don't know how much this girl's done for her family," O.J. told him. "This is so unfair."

And to me O.J. could only say, "I'm sorry."

The lawyers discouraged me from fighting back against the tabloids. "The best response is no response," they maintained. "They'll just take what you say and turn it around."

This is my "almost marriage" to Dean Hamilton. I was looking for a quick fix.

George Hamilton and I at a party given by Lord and Lady White. We danced until my feet hurt.

O. J. and I on our first trip to Laguna.

12/92
O. J.'s first trip to meet my
family in Panama City.

Elite Christmas party, 1992.

This is our 1993 Valentine's trip to
Miami, for the Dan Marino
Tournament for the Quarterbacks at the
Doral Country Club. That's Donald
Trump next to us.

Believe it or not, I was pretty steamed at him in this photo, taken during a party at the Doral Country Club.

O. J.'s "surprise" birthday party. Sherman White posing with us.

In Las Vegas, goofing off. I loved that O. J. would dress like that just to see the kids smile.

In Palm Springs with Sydney and Justin.

*Diane Sawyer and I at Big Bend
Ranch in Tennessee, just days after
the Bronco chase.*

Terri Whitehurst visiting me at the Rockingham house. On the drive to the airport, Terri and Debbie Whitehurst urged me to "just leave this place."

Diane Sawyer arranged for me to meet Tony Robbins. This is his infamous "pole of adversity," and my partner (of all things a lawyer) and I made climbing the pole many things, and left much stronger.

Bobby and Robin Bender, who not only took care of me when I was in New York, but also telephonically kept both O. J.'s and my spirits up. This was right under the goal at a Knicks game.

Tom Hunt, my longtime friend, and Michael Nasatir, criminal attorney, escorting me to testify before the grand jury.

During the DNA portion of the trial, O. J. was on the computer and got creative. He gave me this during my jail visit that afternoon.

This marked one year after the murders. Tom Hahn, who was working for Jon Peters, got me to leave Los Angeles. We hiked to the Seven Sacred Pools in Hawaii.

On my left is Albert Watson and on my right, Richard Pollman, a publicist to whom I was introduced by Mickey Rourke. They got me back to work with a shoot for Details *magazine.*

APLA Fashion Show by Ferre. Walking down the runway and looking not at my feet but at the audience, as well as the wall of cameras and the media at the end of the walk, was quite a feat, considering that I had stepped out of one shoe, in a "toe in front of toe dress," and kept on going, with a prayer in my mind the whole way.

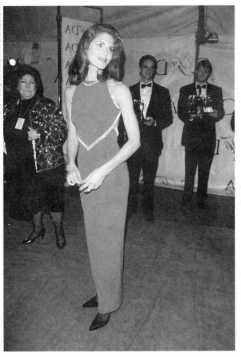

Post-trial and alone in a room full of people. Katherine Saxon (next to me) tried to keep me working. I wasn't eating, my dad was very, very sick, and it was Valentine's Day too.

Mother and I at a wedding reception in September 1996.

Post-trial, tired, trying to put on a smile for the camera.

So I let my actions speak for themselves. If the *Enquirer* ran a story that I'd bailed out — *"Paula Drops O.J., Runs Off With Another Man"* — I'd just show up at the jail on schedule that Monday afternoon, and people would see the truth.

When I went to Jack Reece to discuss Michael and my father, we spent a lot of time on the subject of forgiveness. I considered that a Christian returns good for evil. I heard the message of Matthew 18: "Then Peter came to Jesus and asked, 'Lord, how many times shall I forgive my brother when he sins against me? Up to seven times?' Jesus answered, 'I tell you, not seven times, but seventy-seven times.' "

But I wasn't yet up to infinite forgiveness. The best I could do was accept that Dad and Michael wouldn't change. There was no use in putting my effort out there. I just stopped talking to them, froze them out of my life.

More and more I stayed within O.J.'s orbit: Cathy Randa, A.C. and Bobby Chandler, the Benders, O.J.'s lawyers and detectives, his mother and sisters. These people *understood*. We didn't have to explain ourselves.

My own family was broken into pieces. Only my mother was left for me, and she and I had been distanced by the trial. But I'd found another family to embrace. Emotions were intense there and the energy always high. We shared more than affection and respect. We had this huge cause — O.J.'s acquittal — to unite us.

I never considered what would happen when the cause was no longer there.

O.J. spoke with Sydney and Justin twice a week on the phone, unless Nicole's parents were out — or, O.J. suspected, refusing to pick up the phone. I could tell when he'd just gotten off with the children; he'd be really down.

O.J. missed the hugs from "little Justila" and really worried about Sydney. He knew that she was old enough to be hearing terrible things about him, maybe even from the Browns. "Sydney needs her daddy," he said. "You can tell she's unhappy where she's at."

When O.J. felt guiltiest about being gone, I'd tell him, "No matter what, Daddy can't do any wrong. Whatever your father does, you still love him. You put him on a pedestal so high, and you know that he loves you."

I was speaking from my own experience. I still loved my own father, despite my chronic hurt and anger, just because he was my dad. "Your kids are okay — you'll see them soon enough," I'd tell O.J., the way Mom had once soothed me.

Holidays were especially difficult. Though O.J. encouraged me to go home to Florida for Thanksgiving, I knew it would be rough for him on his own. As I left the jail for the long weekend, I walked extra slowly, watching his eyes watch me till the last possible moment.

When O.J. called me in Panama City that night, it was worse than I'd feared. I used all my tools, set up calls with Bobby Bender and Rosey Grier. We talked for hours, but O.J. couldn't rise out of his gloom.

"I've been a good guy all my life," he kept saying. "I don't understand why I'm here."

Finally I handed off the phone to my mother and said, "Here, please, you try to talk to him."

Mom is a great storyteller, and she put her all into it — "I thought we were going to lose him," she'd say about that night. She went to the Book of Ruth and read it to O.J., elaborating as she went. It was a good story for O.J., the tale of a woman who'd persevered against adversity. It helped him blot out his pain and get to the next day.

My father had gotten my dander up. I wanted to prove him wrong. I wanted to show him I could work when I wanted to, and that O.J. hadn't been my downfall.

I had basically stopped modeling in June. At first it was by my own choice. During the summer I just couldn't deal with people.

Then, in L.A., each day revolved around O.J. There simply wasn't time or energy left over.

By late autumn, my job offers were drying up. The agencies saw me as weak, unreliable. I tried to stay positive, to the point of fooling myself: *If just one person gave me a chance, they would see I could do it.*

The great photographer Albert Watson gave me that chance. He invited me to his studio in New York to shoot a poster as a "teaser" for an all-Barbieri calendar. It was a big opportunity and a huge compliment. An Albert Watson calendar sells itself. Any girl involved gains the best kind of notice.

Albert's brownstone studio is a marvel in itself. When you walk onto the set, it's all black around you — except for a beam of sun from a skylight three floors above, like a natural spotlight. It illuminates an Italian sculpture of an angel, with a broken wing lying at its side.

Albert's idea of background music is the sound track for *The Last Temptation of Christ*. There's amazing vibrancy in that studio. Albert is very calm, but when he looks at you, you can see his mind working — you can tell that he sees more beauty than anyone else.

It was a big morale boost just to work in that kind of environment. Albert and his wife, Elizabeth, were really there for me; they were fronting the project out of their own pocket. Albert wrapped me in a fabulous silk leopard print, and he shot some beautiful pictures that day.

And when it was over, I had to admit that Dad was right. I was in no shape to work.

I was sick as a dog, emotionally. My focus was spotty and my turmoil showed in my face.

I was also way too thin for a calendar. Albert must have seen it the instant I came through his door, but he was too kind to call the shoot off.

My appetite had been missing in action for months now. My collarbones and pelvis were lethal weapons. I kept dwelling on O.J.'s jailhouse cuisine, but it was more than that. I just couldn't digest what was going on around me. I couldn't swallow or absorb it. Life was too big and toxic for me to take in.

When I visited the jail, I'd dress big and heavy to hide my bones. But O.J. wasn't fooled. He was going through the same thing and could see what I'd lost in my face and my jeans.

"You gotta eat, girl, you gotta eat," he'd urge me. He'd tell Cathy Randa to take me to lunch, "and not that sushi stuff, either. Go get a hamburger — get some serious red meat."

But it was hopeless. I'd stare at that burger but I couldn't touch it. I couldn't even get a cookie down.

At Rockingham, O.J.'s Philippine housekeeper, Gigi, would cook up an egg for me or some rice and spicy sausage or her famous chicken adobo. Those were the only meals I could enjoy. But Gigi was pregnant, and it wasn't her job to cook for me, so I didn't make it a regular thing.

At night I'd get back to Rockingham after dinner was done. Or I'd go home to my apartment, where the fridge was pretty well empty — I wasn't doing much grocery shopping. With no one watching me there, I could get away without eating. Some days I'd have a cup of dehydrated noodle soup, and that would be it.

Mirrors disoriented me. Who was that haggard person? I could barely recognize her. At times she seemed barely to exist.

I wasn't anorectic. I could *see* myself dwindling down to nothing, and it scared me. How could I survive getting nothing into my system? After Dr. Huizenga did my blood work and found some mineral deficiencies, he put me on one of those special canned milkshakes. They had 120 calories per can, and it was so hard to get even one of those down.

I was the incredible shrinking woman and had no idea when it would stop.

Grammy B. had a special wisdom. She was my grandmother on my father's side, and in my modeling days I'd stop to see her in Connecticut whenever I could. No matter what my problem, she always knew what to say in a few well-chosen words.

Now she was dying. On December 4, the day after my shoot with Albert Watson, a car took me to Grammy B.'s hospital. The night before she left us, I stayed up with my cousin Melissa and fed Grammy B. her beloved chocolate ice cream — it was all she could eat.

When I saw my father at the funeral, I hugged him and said, "I'm sorry that you've lost your mother." Then I walked away from him; we had nothing more to say. I knew that our rift made Dad's whole family uncomfortable, but I wasn't ready to give in.

I thought it was ironic that the priest who offered the eulogy was from India. Over the last eighteen months, when Grammy B. had been too ill to attend church, this man had gone to her home every Saturday afternoon to give her Communion.

It should have been a lesson to my father, I thought — that people's hearts mattered more than their color.

Back in Los Angeles, I stayed by O.J. through Christmas; I didn't dare leave him. By my birthday on New Year's Eve, I was missing family and friends and feeling pretty rotten. Then I got a call from Terri Whitehurst. I assumed she was wishing me a happy birthday, and I made some joke about getting older. But it wasn't that. It wasn't that at all.

Billy Whitehurst had just died of a sudden heart attack.

"We're going to get through this," he'd said. Mr. Whitehurst was the strong arm that kept me going when I was sure I'd collapse. But he didn't get through it — and what would I do without him?

At the wake, I held on to the Whitehursts so tightly that people thought I was another daughter. A pilot recited the poem "High Flight": "Oh, I have slipped the surly bonds of earth and danced the skies on laughter-silvered wings . . ." Then they played that sweet song "The Wind Beneath My Wings."

Through it all, I kept wondering how this could possibly happen to such a good man — it just wasn't fair. Then a sour thought took to drumming through my head, till finally I blurted it out to my friends:

"Why him? Why couldn't it have been my daddy instead?"

12

On Trial

O.J. knew just what he wanted in the jury box: older black women who'd known their share of racism and had seen how it damaged their sons. "A jury of my Mammas," O.J. called it. His defense team got it for him — a majority of the twelve initial jurors were black women.

Now he had to choose the attorney to lay out his case. Bob Shapiro and Johnnie Cochran both hoped to deliver the opening statement. Given the stakes, O.J. gave each of them a shot at the prize.

Bob came into the visiting room first. I was about to leave when O.J. said, "No, I want you to stay here for this."

I settled back and listened to Bob make his case. He was positive throughout; he wasn't out to put Johnnie down.

"I've carried us through the whole preliminary, and I think I've done a very good job," he said. "I think the jury will have more respect for us if I do the opening. They'll see that we're consistent in having one person lead the team."

Johnnie came in a few hours later. His message was simple

and direct: "I'm the best person to connect you with this jury. I can really *talk* to them. They're going to hear you through me."

Both men were impressive, but it was obvious to O.J. that Johnnie was right for the job. It was a tough setback for Bob. He was already going through a difficult time — getting booed at Lakers games, finding himself and his wife ostracized from their old social circles. After Bob lost out on the opening statement, he seemed more detached from the case, more marginal to the defense.

Johnnie, meanwhile, kept zipping along. He had astounding energy and was such a fast talker that I could barely keep up with him. But Johnnie was also methodical and organized, and he listened patiently to his clients, even one as repetitive as O.J. Whenever the prosecution threw us a curve, the two of them would talk it out. Johnnie would say, "I am so sure of what you're telling me, Juice, because you've told me this a thousand times before, and your story never changes."

Once Johnnie won out, everyone knew he was top dog among the lawyers. But it would be wrong to call Johnnie the captain of the team. The captain was the man who paid the bills, the man whose life was on the line. And he never let anyone forget it.

In *The Run of His Life,* Jeffrey Toobin would call O.J. "an uneducated, semi-literate ex-athlete who could barely understand what was going on around him."

That's not the man I observed in Central Jail. No question, there were parts of the proceedings — the DNA evidence, for example — that befuddled everyone, including most of the attorneys. But O.J. stayed on top of the case. I think he had to, for sanity's sake. If he'd just sat there and brooded while his lawyers carried the ball, it might have made him crazy.

O.J. was too assertive — and too bright — to let that happen.

(For that matter, I thought he was too smart to bumble his way through a crime, as someone had done in Brentwood. To leave one bloody glove at Nicole's place and carry the other one home — that was a blunder, it seemed to me, that O.J. would never make.)

Earlier that month, when Bob Shapiro and F. Lee Bailey were picking at each other in the press, O.J. called them in and said, "Look, you guys have got to put this kid stuff aside. This is my life on the line. We don't have time for this penny-ante bullshit. We've got to stay focused."

It was part plea, part reprimand, part pep rally — and it worked. O.J. was really skillful in juggling the egos on the Dream Team. He knew each person's strengths and weaknesses, with maybe one exception: his own.

After my bad time at A.C.'s grand jury hearing I really disliked Chris Darden. But when I watched him work on television, I saw that his hostility toward me hadn't been personal. He was just an unhappy person. He was twitchy and hypersensitive, and aggressive in a weird way with everyone.

Darden kept telling Johnnie that he wished he hadn't been assigned to this case — not out of any feeling for O.J., but because of his predicament as a black assistant D.A. The defense wasn't sympathetic. If anything, Johnnie delighted in pushing Darden's buttons. He knew that Darden was never too far from a meltdown that might hurt the prosecution.

A master needler himself, O.J. got a big kick out of the byplay. He'd call me at the lunch break and say, "Hey, make sure you watch this afternoon. Johnnie's going to do something." Then, when I'd come back to visit him, O.J. would crow, "Boy, Johnnie just *got* Darden, did you see that?"

After the famous "N-word" debate on January 13, where Darden tried to shield Mark Fuhrman by calling his language too "inflammatory" for black jurors to hear, I almost felt for the poor guy. "He's not going to be able to walk in South Central L.A. after this," Johnnie said.

O.J. described Darden in two words: Uncle Tom.

⋆   ⋆   ⋆

The previous summer, when I chose to stand by O.J., I was step-
ping lightly. I was saying, "I love you, I care for you," as I would
to any dear friend — I don't hold back from telling people how I
feel about them.

Then, ever so gradually, the meaning of the words began to
change. How did it happen? I can't point to any one incident or
date. But as the case dragged on, my world kept paring down.
My family, my career, my bank account, even my health and
looks — all were slipping away from me.

What identity I had left was tied up in a man behind bars. Every
visit and phone call with O.J. reminded me how much he needed
me. All the rest was down time and waiting, and that was scary.
Because I'd be left alone with Paula, and I didn't know who she
was anymore.

Then I'd see O.J. or hear his voice, and I'd feel like myself again.
Because it was all about *him* — he was my whole life now, my sole
purpose. O.J. pulled me to him like gravity. I was engulfed by his
world, until one day I realized that he was calling me his girl again.

And I was calling him my guy.

In a way, you could say that we'd revived our earliest bond,
when we'd talked by phone for weeks before our first kiss. Except
this was more intense, because now we had nothing else to distract us — no jobs, no travel, no golf. We just had this amazing
closeness, though we couldn't so much as shake hands.

Conversation, after all, had always been the shortest route to
my heart.

Make no mistake — I yearned to touch and hold O.J. My day-
dreams were definitely R-rated. But it was also a relief to leave
sex as an issue for a while. I could feel safe again in opening up to
him. I didn't have to wonder where a good-night kiss might lead.
I didn't have to deal with O.J.'s ritualized lovemaking and the way
he'd turn himself off to me when he was through.

"I love you," we'd say for hello. "I love you," we'd say for good-bye, and many times in between. And I *did* love O.J., without conditions or limits. How could I draw the line between friendship and romance? Who was I kidding? O.J. was the most important person in my life, and both of us knew it.

This was not your normal love affair. When I walked into that glass cubicle at Central Jail, the energy between O.J. and me was like a fire in there, a combustible mix of sympathy and sexual tension. Cathy or A.C. might be in the room with us, chatting away, but it wouldn't matter. No one else existed. More than once, the neglected third party just got up and left, unnoticed.

On the weekends, when a young attorney named Nicole Pulvers would schedule other people around my visits, O.J. made no big effort to be polite. "When's Peola getting here?" he'd mutter over and over. "When's Peola coming?"

I think he might have hurt some people's feelings. "Boy, am I glad *you* got here," one of his friends told me as I arrived one Saturday. O.J. had barely responded to a single thing the guy had said. All he wanted was to see my face.

Though he saw that face every day, it wasn't enough, not for either one of us. My love overflowed into letters. I'd get them delivered to him before court in the morning; I wanted him to go in there feeling positive. An example:

> *Dearest Orenthal James,*
>
> *It's a beautiful Saturday afternoon in sunny Los Angeles. The day started with a ring . . . from you on the phone, of course. A kiss, a hug and a smile in your eyes, so near and yet so far. . . .*

Let's just say that it only got mushier from there.

The Trial of the Century finally began on January 24, 1995 — seven months after the Bronco chase, five months after I'd returned to L.A. and watched my life stop like an unwound watch.

Like much of the country, I was already exhausted by the case, and it was only beginning.

Chris Darden's opening made no sense to me. I couldn't fathom that O.J. would have killed Nicole "out of jealousy. . . because he couldn't have her." I remembered how Nicole had asked O.J. for advice about her love life, and how pleased and relaxed he'd been about giving it to her.

I drove down to the jail at five o'clock, as usual. When O.J. joined us inside our glass room, he'd forgotten his pencil. Under the rules, attorneys were the only ones allowed to reach over the partition and make physical contact with an inmate. Nicole Pulvers was available at my side, but something came over me that day. Without thinking, I reached up over the glass partition and extended a pencil.

The guard at the back had turned away from us to watch the inmates in the open area.

O.J. stretched to take the pencil, and our fingers touched.

I hadn't been hugged or kissed or touched for so long — it was as if I'd never been touched before. First a shock to steal my breath away, then a warmth that flowed down my arm.

We held the touch for seconds, for an eternity. Not a word passed between us; not a word was needed. They could lock me up and bury the key, I thought, and it would have been worth it.

In those delirious, life-changing seconds, I knew that O.J. was mine, and he was innocent, and I loved him, loved him, *loved* him.

He was all I had; he was more than enough.

It was, I honestly thought, the happiest time of my entire life.

The next day it was Johnnie's turn at bat. Aside from challenging the prosecution's outline of events, the core of his argument was that O.J. had no motive to murder Nicole. "Stalkers," he declared, "don't go all across the United States working, doing commercials, shooting movies, *having a new girlfriend,* going on with their lives."

As I watched on TV, I squirmed in my chair. Johnnie knew

all about my "Dear John" message to O.J. on the morning of the crime. He knew that our relationship had been less than peachy-keen at the time. Now he was twisting the truth to sway the jurors.

There was nothing to do about it. There wasn't anyplace I could go. Who was I going to tell — Chris Darden? Besides, if I peered too closely at my past with O.J. and the guilt that I still felt from it, the present would be absolutely unlivable.

If I didn't stay positive, every minute of the day, I might wind up in the back of a truck with a gun to *my* head.

Once, in the fall, I tried to talk to O.J. about my June 12 message and the feelings behind it. He'd just discovered that I'd been with Michael Bolton that day. I was distressed about it; I wanted to clear the air.

"There was so much that was wrong with us," I began. "Remember how I said our schedules weren't working —" I could see O.J. rolling his eyes at Nicole Pulvers, as if to say, *What's wrong with this girl now?*

"— and how I couldn't get the answers I had to have, and the pain was too much —"

I was breaking down. I got even more upset to see O.J. mouthing silently to Nicole, *I have no idea what she's talking about.*

I never brought the message up again. Over time, I stopped dwelling on it. Maybe O.J. had never received it. Maybe he'd heard it but taken it lightly.

Maybe I never really *meant* what I'd said. How could I have ever wanted to leave O.J., after all? What could my life have been without him? It was like trying to fathom a life without water, or oxygen, or love.

Even before the jury was in place, Marcia Clark was trying to paint O.J. as a wife-beater. In early January, while the lawyers argued over the admissibility of domestic abuse evidence, I was taken to lunch by Bert Kitay, O.J.'s longtime therapist.

It was one of my many low points. I couldn't help thinking

about the ugly night in Laguna, when O.J. had told me about his "wrestling" with Nicole on New Year's Eve 1989. Now I began to wonder: Had there been more to it than that?

When I asked Bert about it, he assured me that nothing in O.J.'s makeup fit the profile of a habitual batterer. "You're keeping O.J. together, you know," he added. "The two of you seem so different, but you make a really good team."

Feeling pressured, I clammed up.

On January 31, when Darden played the tape of Nicole's 911 call, I heard a familiar O.J., loud and animated. I'd been on the receiving end of that voice — the night when O.J. pounded on my door in Laguna, for starters. Was it physically threatening? I couldn't be sure.

I'd grown up in a house where I'd seen big fights, with lots of hitting. Nothing I heard on the tape put me in that place. I listened for the sound of a slap; I just couldn't hear one. Nicole might have called the cops, I decided, because she got sick of being talked to that way.

As I see it now, I had two ways of dealing with negative developments in the trial. I either gave up trying to understand them (the blood evidence, the time lines) or I pretended that they didn't exist.

Trust doesn't work halfway. I couldn't say this was right about O.J. but that was wrong; the puzzle was too complex for that. O.J. had to be innocent, and he was sure to be acquitted — those were the beliefs I lived by. Those were my articles of faith, and they kept me from falling off the edge of the earth.

Of all O.J.'s old friends and teammates, none had been stauncher than Bobby Chandler. During the hysterics at Bob Kardashian's house, Bobby had been a mountain of calm reassurance. He never seemed to shake, even when the lawyers got rubber-legged.

Then, without warning, Bobby was dying. One week he came in to visit O.J. and told us about some tests. The next week he was in surgery for cancer.

The week after that, we found out that Bobby had made his last visit.

He never lost his strength or optimism. "You're gonna beat this, Juice," he'd say over the phone, "and I'm gonna beat my problem, and we're gonna be down in Mexico playing golf together."

Bobby's sudden illness tore O.J. up. It brought him to his biggest fear: that something would happen to his mother while he was still in jail and he wouldn't get to be there for her.

On January 27, Bobby was gone.

I believe that O.J. never felt so confined as on the day Bobby was buried. I drove straight from the funeral to the jail: more bad news. O.J. was racked with chest pains. I summoned Dr. Huizenga, who examined O.J. and made his diagnosis.

"It's just anxiety," he said.

As I knew too well, we didn't have a cure for that.

By February, I was soaring off the stress charts.

Over the past two months, I'd lost three people I loved. *Current Affair* brought Dad on for an encore. He told America that he hoped I wouldn't come to his funeral — and, by the way, that O.J. was guilty.

The trial — *showtime!* — was finally here, and it felt like a huge, grinding machine, beyond fighting or belief.

I spent less time at Rockingham and more at my apartment. It was a relief to walk around without having to be personable to anyone. I was closing in really tight now. I had the phone, the jail, the Catholic church around the corner for emergency prayers. I'd have Chin Chin deliver its tasty chicken salad to my door. Then I'd throw the food out, untouched.

I thought I was safe at home, until Marcia Clark put a document with my unlisted number up on the screen in court. I was watching it on TV when my phone rang.

"Is Paula there?" The voice was male, adolescent, excited.

"This is Paula."

"It's true!" the boy screamed. "It's the number, it's the number!"

I had the number changed. No one could know where I was, who I was.

When it was time to go see O.J., I'd have the doorman bring my car out front to minimize my exposure. I found it harder and harder to leave the apartment — it took a tremendous effort just to get on the elevator, much less the freeway.

I was always grateful to get back inside and turn the bolt. After O.J. signed off at ten o'clock, I channeled my nervous energy into cleaning every inch of my living space. There was no dust in my closet; my bathroom gleamed like something out of *Martha Stewart Living*.

When my tiles could bear no more scrubbing, I sat down and wrote myself a heart-to-heart:

"You are never alone if you walk with Jesus. You have at least two angels looking out for you. Mr. W. and Grammy B. Listen to your instincts. . . .

"So what do you do? Cry? No. There have been enough tears. . . . So what do you do now? Define exactly what you do want to ensure your happiness."

I knew what I wanted, or at least I knew the words. A genuine Christian life. A sense of integrity and sureness. A trusting relationship with a man who would be a good father.

But I also wanted O.J., first and last. Everything else would wait.

"Juice," Bobby Bender said one night, "you better not screw up. You better marry this girl when this trial gets over. After all the crap she's been through, man, I'm going to have the preacher ready at my house."

Bobby was teasing, but marriage no longer sounded like such a crazy idea. Everything was fitting together for O.J. and me: the compassion, the closeness, that thousand-volt energy we had in the visiting room.

"We've been through so much, and we're still talking," O.J. would tell me. "It's meant to be — we're supposed to be together."

I couldn't argue with him. Our history felt like a Himalayan climb, so immense and overwhelming that I couldn't dream of starting at the bottom again with someone else. Our relationship had cost me such work and pain — how could I possibly abandon it?

Once the trial got under way, O.J. would tell me, half-kidding, that I'd have to wed him in jail if the verdict went the other way: "Girl, you *better* marry me — I'm going to need that conjugal visit."

I thought it was just another O.J. fantasy, like the way he'd play the seventh hole at Hombre in his head, or close his eyes when I described the gazelles and wildebeests in Africa.

But as time passed and we stayed in perfect tune, O.J.'s tone changed. He started talking about moving Sydney and Justin to a new life in New York, where mixed-race children could easily blend in. He particularly liked the Benders' town on Long Island.

"Bobby, is that vacant lot down the street from you still there?" he asked.

"It's waiting for you, Juice," Bobby replied.

"When I get out," O.J. would sigh, "I just want to get my Peola and my kiddos, and go far, far away."

That sounded good to me.

One Sunday in February we were really clicking over the phone. It was one of those soft, sweet times when we could laugh together and life seemed almost normal.

Then O.J. lowered his voice and said, "Peola, will you marry me? I mean it this time — will you marry me?"

He didn't go down on one knee, as one of the tabloids reported after his jailhouse proposal leaked out. His arthritis wouldn't allow it. But I knew that O.J. meant business this time. This was for real.

"Now listen to me, Peola," he said. "I'll take as many children as you give me."

I almost dropped my receiver. I was both flattered and

flustered — if pauses can be pregnant, we were expecting twins. How could I push O.J. away? I knew I'd give up my life for him. In a sense, I already had.

If things turned out as we expected, and O.J. was acquitted, what could stop us?

And if things turned out badly, and I was the bride of an inmate for a long, long time — well, that would be a sad life, but at least we'd be together. . . .

Then I had to quit thinking that way, and fast, because bad thoughts could make themselves come true.

I found my breath and smiled a lover's smile at O.J. "I love you," I said, "but it really isn't the right time to talk about this."

So I didn't say yes.

But I didn't say no.

They say that money can't buy you love, and a good thing, too, as I was stone broke. I had next to nothing coming in and a total overhead — including my apartment in Los Angeles and the house in Bay Point — of $10,000 a month.

I'd sold my stocks and pension plan and exhausted my savings, but the debts kept mounting. Chronically late on my mortgage payments, I found the bank's letters less and less friendly.

To stave off bankruptcy, I'd borrowed money from O.J. and some dear friends. It killed me to ask them. I'd been supporting myself since I was seventeen years old. When I'd first lived in New York and I'd run out of money for food, I wouldn't ask even Mom for help. I'd just have some more cheese and bread and wait for the next check to arrive.

I remembered how O.J. had once described me to a Boston newspaper, with loving exaggeration: "She's the second-highest-paid model in America — and she can cook. She is the first woman I've been involved with who has a career of her own, and is a success."

And now *look at me*: I was taking money from a man, the one thing that I thought I'd never do.

I told Richard Pollman, a publicist who graciously volunteered his services, that I wanted to strap my boots on and go to work. Richard drummed up a couple of European magazine shoots. Albert Watson hired me for a job for *Details*. But they were all editorial jobs, paid at $90 a day. Any advertiser who looked at me — at my emaciated body, my sad, drawn face — would have gone screaming into the night.

We did get one lucrative magazine offer: a *Playboy* cover and inside photo spread, for $750,000. I'd had no problem working with *Playboy* in 1993, but this was different: an out-and-out exploitation of the murder case.

I needed the money, but I also needed to be able to look in the mirror. I turned the deal down.

Both Tom Hahn and Jack Gilardi, O.J.'s agent at ICM, found a chilly reception for me on the acting front. I couldn't even read for the good parts; I was too controversial for any producers with aspirations for their films.

That left the less desirable regions of show business: the cheesy, the tasteless, the exploitive. I could have been a murderer in *The Cinderella Killer* or the girlfriend of an inmate in some other silly movie — thanks, but no thanks.

One deal I signed for would have used my voice and likeness as a cyber-guide in a computer game called *Heidi's House*. The script was too provocative for my taste, but I thought I could somehow make it work. The money was really tempting — as much as half a million dollars, with royalties.

But when I found out I'd be guiding the players into peeping on a girl as she soaped herself in the shower, I pulled the plug. It cost me $5,000 in lawyers' fees to get out of the contract.

Then a real opportunity, for a change: an audition for a part in *Baywatch Nights,* a TV spinoff of *Baywatch*. My first appointment with the casting directors went great. I loved doing the reading, and they clearly liked me.

But when I returned for a second look, they'd been joined by David Hasselhoff, the hunky lead. O.J. and I had spent time with David on our plane back from the '92 Olympics. Just seeing him pulled me right back to Barcelona and the good days. David simply unhinged me. I was fighting back tears all afternoon long. I lost my focus, and any chance for the part.

I'd just about given up hope when *The Watcher* came around. The Paramount Network TV show wanted me to play a modern-day vampire. I auditioned and was thrilled when they called back to hire me. I was finally going back to work.

No one could say I was cashing in on my notoriety. I'd be working for scale, about a thousand dollars. And I made sure the contract prohibited any linking of my name with O.J.'s. We dotted every *i* and crossed every *t* in that document — it was critical that we not stoop to the tabloids' level.

When we came to shoot the program in Las Vegas on February 2, I found a swarm of media on the set: ABC, NBC, CBS, *Entertainment Tonight,* and *Hard Copy,* Paramount's own tabloid show. I knew why they were there, and I put my foot down. Either they left the set or I would.

The director came down on my side — he didn't need the distractions — and the set was cleared.

I woke up very early on Valentine's Day after a restless sleep. I turned on the TV and got the shock of my life. Over some raw, uncut footage of my *Watcher* episode, an oily voice-over was promoting that night's *Hard Copy:*

"Paula does Vegas! Watch O.J. Simpson's girlfriend cash in on their relationship in her hottest role ever!"

I grasped immediately what had happened. The *Watcher* people had forked over the tape of my work, straight out of the camera — the sound wasn't even mixed in — to their Paramount tabloid buddies.

To promote a silly little TV show, Paramount had taken so many jabs at me as a person. I wasn't sure which was worse — to be likened to *Debbie Does Dallas* or portrayed as a grubbing opportunist. I was nuts that whole day, working with my lawyers to stop the *Hard Copy* segment from airing. We failed.

I hardly noticed when holiday flowers arrived from O.J., with a cryptic card: *"From the guy who loves you and appreciates you — Me."*

O.J. couldn't use his name; he feared that the florist might leak it to the tabloids.

After I sued Paramount, an arbitrator found that the company "violated both the letter and the spirit" of our agreement and awarded me $50,000. The money was a joke. *Hard Copy* would have paid twice that to get on the set.

I went into a big tailspin after *The Watcher*. I knew my acting career was as good as done. Life just kept caving in on me.

I was still shrinking.

When I'd first met with Jack Reece, the previous summer, I was totally bewildered. Now it was different. Now I was frustrated — I knew where I wanted to go, but it was taking forever to get there.

As 1 Peter 5 points out, "God opposes the proud but gives grace to the humble." The trial had humbled me, all right, but grace seemed a long way off. I was still reaping the bad seeds I'd planted years before; I seemed to be harvesting a bumper crop, in fact.

Jack would remind me that conversion was a slow and gradual growth, more like an oak than a mushroom. I knew he was right, but it takes some powerful faith to wait for an oak tree.

When the frustration grew too much to bear, I'd retreat to a Catholic church around the corner from my apartment. As a children's choir sang like angels, my first prayer would be for O.J.: "Lord in Heaven, my Heavenly Father, please take O.J.'s pain away. Please lift him up and give him strength to see this through. Thy will be done."

Then I'd pray for Sydney and Justin, that they'd somehow be shielded from the Browns' anger toward their father. I'd pray for Mrs. Simpson to get through the trial and for the Whitehursts to bear up under their grief.

Finally, I'd pray for patience. At the time it seemed that I was taking one step forward then two or three back. There were nights I felt so unbearably lost that I couldn't sleep without a Bible on the pillow next to me, like a buoy in a storm.

Jack took the long view. He'd quote Oliver Wendell Holmes — that it wasn't where I was now that mattered, but the direction in which I was headed. If anything, Jack believed, my faith was growing in the face of adversity. The detour I'd taken was a rocky road, but it had also brought me closer to the Lord.

One thing was for sure: The events of the past year had stripped away my old illusions. I'd had money and a man and a thriving career, but none of it made me whole.

Something was missing, and I'd found it in the book that lay upon my pillow.

"What is it you want in life?" Jack asked me one day.

"I always thought I wanted to win the Academy Award," I said.

"Well, isn't it a good thing," Jack said, "that we don't need an Academy Award to get into heaven?"

That threw a bright new light on my concept of success.

"How are you?" said Diane Sawyer. She'd called me at home to see if I wanted to go back on her show. I told her the time wasn't right for me, but that I was doing just fine.

"What are you doing today?" she asked.

"Well, I'm going down to the jail in a little while," I said.

Diane was a good enough reporter to sense how depressed I was behind my facade. She called Tony Robbins, the world-renowned expert in helping people realize what they want in life. Tony called me and said, "What can I do for you?"

That was a switch: someone asking about *me*. It opened up my whole wound. "Where do I start?" I said. "My life's so screwed up here — where do I start?"

Tony invited me for a private session, for which he'd ordinarily get $20,000 an hour. "I have no way of paying," I said. Tony assured me that was fine. Diane had told him that I wasn't working and that I hadn't sold any stories. He wanted to help.

At his beach house, Tony started by asking the same question: "What can I do for you?" He was a huge man who looked as if he could solve any problem in the world. He opened my floodgates; I was crying convulsively, stuck in the mire.

"The first thing we have to do is take you out of this state," Tony said. "If you're hysterical, I can't fix your problem. Why don't you get up and walk around the room a little bit?"

It was a minor miracle. As soon as I got up off the couch, I left the bad stuff behind me. I could actually take a calm breath. Tony kept asking me questions, and I found that I could think clearly as long as I kept moving. But as soon as I stopped, everything piled up on me again, and my mind stalled.

"Whenever the burden of commiserating catches up to you," Tony said, "get up and do something about it. Don't sit there and let it build into something worse.

"You can get up and walk, or you can do this" — and Tony snapped his fingers.

Oh, boy, I can't wait to tell O.J., I thought. *I can't wait for him to see me with a smile on my face.*

Tony spent four hours with me, then invited me to one of his seminars. "I wouldn't take any money from you," he said. "I think you have such integrity, and you've been such a lady through this."

Now *there* were some powerful words for my shriveled self-esteem.

With O.J.'s blessing (he knew that my spirits needed some heavy lifting), I flew out to Tony's goal-setting seminar in Phoenix. When I got my name tag, I scrawled "Paula Whitehurst" on it. I didn't want anyone treating me differently — or shunning me, as the case may be.

The seven hundred people were split into teams of sixteen and then into pairs. My partner, ironically enough, was a prosecutor from Texas. We proceeded to the highlight activity of the day: a cooperative climb up a sixty-foot telephone pole.

Naturally, my fear of heights kicked in. But I took courage from a paraplegic, who made it all the way up by sitting on another fellow's back. And I got some needed support from O.J., who called just as my team was about to start.

"I know that you can do it — just don't look down," he said. "Remember my teammate who sang out that play? You can always find a way to do something if you need to."

Partners were supposed to climb the pole together, but the prosecutor was very brave and skedaddled right up. I put one foot on the first metal peg, and then my legs went on strike. But I couldn't quit. That pole represented all the hardship of the trial. I had to prove to myself that I could get through, all the way to the top.

I started praying, and I prayed every step of the way. That pole wasn't going to beat me. It seemed to take forever, but I made it. My partner was plainly delighted for me.

Tony had told me to look around at the top — that it was important to appreciate how far you'd come in life. I opened my eyes wide and looked out into the distance, to the spare and beautiful desert landscape.

With our hands locked overhead, my partner and I faced each other and stepped out on a pair of cables. As we moved along toward a second pole a good fifty feet away, the two cables drew farther and farther apart. We had to lean out more and more horizontally to keep our balance.

My partner and I made the far pole our goal, something no one had yet achieved. Our eyes were locked as tightly as our hands. It was a lesson in total trust. At the farthest point, my body was fully extended, completely flat.

Two steps from the end, farther than anyone else had gone, we decided to jump down in our safety harnesses for the fun of it.

At the closing session in the hotel auditorium, Tony pulled names out of a drum for prizes. "Paula Whitehurst!" he called out.

I laughed my way up to the stage. This wouldn't do much for my anonymity, I thought ruefully. I spun a wheel and won three days at a race-car driving school, which I gave to my partner.

After retaking my seat, I listened to a woman talk about how important it was to be proud of yourself, no matter what you do. Some impulse possessed me. I thrust up my hand and Tony recognized me.

"I don't know who I've been fooling," I said, "but my name is not Paula Whitehurst. It's Paula Barbieri, and I'm darn proud of who I am."

And Tony said, "In case any of you don't know, Paula Barbieri is O.J. Simpson's girlfriend."

Without any hesitation, I corrected him: "Excuse me, I am O.J. Simpson's *friend*." I'd gone back to my old distinction — if anything, I thought I meant *more* to O.J. than a traditional "girlfriend."

If O.J. had been there, he would have rolled his eyes to beat the band.

Everyone just laughed and laughed, and gave me such applause and affirmation.

In using my real name that day, I reclaimed a small part of myself.

13

Self-Preservation

On March 4, 1995, I did a shoot with Annie Leibovitz for a photo essay on the trial, to be published in the *New Yorker*.

I was thrilled to be working with Annie — to be working, period. We started on a cliff over Malibu, overlooking the ocean. I sat in a lawn chair, wearing shorts, a big shirt, and sunglasses. The result was very intense. I thought it told a real story about longing and isolation.

We moved on to the Château Marmont for some interior shots. I declined to be shot in bed or in the back of my Bronco. But I wanted to please my Hall of Fame photographer, and Annie can be very persuasive. When she asked me to lie on a couch in an open man's shirt (one of O.J.'s shirts, for the record), I complied.

As we explored different poses, I was just doing what I did, which was to model. It was natural for me to move into the position that ultimately appeared in the magazine. I wasn't thinking about how suggestive it might look.

I was just wanting to get my life back. To get back to the person I was.

As the photograph turned out, I appeared to be naked under O.J.'s shirt. I actually had on my underwear, but I'd been around long enough to know that perception beats reality, every time. Packaged among the attorneys in their power suits, I stood out as an object of titillation, just what I'd hoped to avoid. If I'd had it to do over again, I would have turned Annie down from the start.

"I can't believe you did this," O.J. said after seeing the magazine. He was really upset with me. "You should have been in pants or a skirt and a jacket — this is just so explosive."

He was right. I felt stupid. If I were just a model, that photograph would have been a great career step. It would have won me recognition and new clients.

But I wasn't just a model, not anymore.

I wasn't the only woman in the Simpson trial to be taken down a peg through overexposure. One day Marcia Clark broke down sobbing at the counsel table after the *National Enquirer* found some old topless photographs of her and shared them with the world.

O.J. thought Marcia had great legs and appreciated her short skirts. He also marveled at her vile language. By all accounts, Marcia had a mouth like a truck driver.

I remember one visit when O.J. walked in with a smug grin on his face. What was so funny, I asked.

"Marcia said the 'C-word' today," he replied.

O.J. had an uncanny way of gauging a woman's menstrual cycle. Cathy Randa, Nicole Pulvers, myself — he could always tell when we were two days from our period, or "in that zone," as he put it. I thought it was an obnoxious little game, but I had to hand it to him: He was never wrong.

During the trial, Marcia got under O.J.'s skin about every other hour. But once a month he would get his revenge. When he determined that Marcia was premenstrual, he would pass it on to Johnnie Cochran and tell him to work her over.

"Johnnie's gonna push her buttons today," O.J. would confide to me at lunchtime. "I told him that Marcia was in the zone."

That afternoon, as often as not, Marcia would lose it, and I knew that O.J. was hard-pressed to keep from laughing out loud.

Among the many time bombs in my life, one ticked especially loudly: When would I be asked to take the stand?

The prosecution might call me at any time, and I was also a potential trump card for the defense. I told O.J., "If it helps you in any way, then you know I'm there for you."

Brave words. I knew that testifying would be torture. I'd be asked to reconstruct a two-year relationship. I'd have to air all my dirty laundry, and do it for days and days and days.

I'd already had my fill of Chris Darden, and I knew that Marcia Clark wouldn't be all sweetness and smiles, as she'd been for Mark Fuhrman.

In the end, I think the district attorney's office saw me as a loose cannon. Lacking knowledge of my "Dear John" message, they couldn't be sure of what I'd say about my relationship with O.J. If I agreed with the pretty domestic picture that Johnnie was painting, it could backfire on them.

The prosecution was probably right. I wouldn't have lied to them, but I was carrying some vivid wishful thinking and a whole lot of denial. That was just the way my mind worked then.

During one of my brief escapes to New York, the Benders took me to a Knicks game, where they had seats right under the basket. I can vouch that it is real awakening to see Patrick Ewing coming at you full-speed to dunk the ball.

But what struck me most was how the cameras would converge on front-row celebrities at time-outs. Spike Lee and Billy Baldwin were there that night, but I was the hot item; I dreaded what might show up in the papers the next morning.

I was never allowed to forget what a huge thing I'd fallen into, even for jaded, seen-it-all New Yorkers.

One day I went to visit my agent at ICM. While I waited out by the receptionist, the elevator opened — and in walked Michael Bolton, with his manager by his side. Seeing them brought back that high-spirited, carefree time we'd had in Las Vegas, the night before everything changed.

After a glance around the ICM lobby, Michael pulled me out onto a fire escape for a big hug. He asked me if I needed anything. I said I was doing all right, that I had big shoulders and I'd be okay.

I felt that hug for hours. It was just what I'd needed — to feel a man's arms around me, holding me close, holding me up. It made me wonder what a different turn my life might have taken.

On another night, the Benders took me to *Kiss of the Spider Woman* on Broadway. I thought I was going to a light musical romance. When the curtain went up and I faced a set full of prison bars, I wanted to peel out of there. It took all my courage just to stick in my seat and not run crying up the aisle.

The best thing I could do for myself, according to Tony Robbins, would be to overcome my greatest fear. In the spring of 1995, that meant working a runway show. If I could stand tall in front of hundreds of people, it might help me get out into the world without staring at my feet.

Though I hadn't done much runway work before, it seemed like an excellent idea. A model could earn $10,000 a show on the European circuit, and people might be less obsessed about the trial over there.

Monique Pillard, the Elite vice president, put out feelers to all the top designers — and got back to me more frustrated than I'd ever heard her. The designers didn't want to get involved, she said. They were afraid that people would look at me instead of their clothes.

I told myself it was just another rejection in a business that was full of them. But deep down I suspected that I would never model again. O.J.'s case had taken on a life of its own. I couldn't begin to understand its worldwide repercussions, much less control them.

In one last-ditch attempt, I went to Gianfranco Ferré, the great Italian designer, who was staging a gala fundraiser for AIDS in Los Angeles that spring.

"I'll even do it for free," I told him. "I just want to walk down that runway and be able to hold my head up and look in people's eyes, and let them know that I'm going to be okay."

Mr. Ferré was on my side. "If she wants to do this for a good cause," he told the press, "that's great."

At the afternoon rehearsal I got to see all my old friends: hair stylists, makeup artists, other models. They treated me a little gingerly; I could tell they were concerned. Jennifer Flavin, a model who was married to Sylvester Stallone and who'd had her share of ups and downs, was especially supportive. Bernard Baski, an actor from my former class in Los Angeles, told me how beautiful I looked — I'm not sure I believed him, but I appreciated the sentiment.

When it came time for the show, I felt nervous but ready. I walked out on the runway straight as a string, just like Mary Lou had taught me back in Pensacola. I looked at the men in their tuxedos and smiles, and I smiled back. I didn't have to imagine them in their underwear anymore.

Then, a crisis. Swathed in one of Gianfranco's long couture dresses, I walked entirely out of one shoe. If ever disaster beckoned, this was the time.

But I didn't stop and melt. Without breaking stride, I smoothly reached down with my hand and slipped the shoe back on my foot.

Backstage I felt shook up, until a veteran runway girl named Janice Dickinson took me in hand and said, "Let me tell you about the time I fell in Sophia Loren's lap in Rome!"

Then Janice repeated to me what the great Loren had told her that day: "Honey, you'll do a great job. Just get up there and you finish your walk."

She was right. The show went on, and so did I.

* * *

I was on one of my rare outings, to Rodeo Drive for a haircut. My friend Laurent, the owner of Privé, had done my hair gratis since I was eighteen and still never charged me a penny.

All of a sudden a car horn beeped behind me — it was Dolph Lundgren. We had a cup of coffee and a relaxed hour together. I felt barely a pang for the past.

That night, around twelve, I got buzzed by my doorman. Dolph was downstairs, asking to come up. I didn't have to think twice; I told the doorman to send him away.

The next day I was so proud of myself. If anyone could have tempted me to stray, it was my old Swedish boyfriend. "That's how much I love you," I told O.J. "I'm finally over my thing with Dolph."

I saw Dolph just one more time, in one of my blockbuster, technicolor dreams. I was lying on a bed with my arms spread out and my head slumped over the edge. My eyes were wide open. They were looking up at Dolph.

He had a huge knife in his hand.

He'd already used it on my throat.

In May, Gretchen Stockdale joined the circus. A model and former Los Angeles Raiders cheerleader, she surfaced with a tape-recorded voice mail that O.J. left her at 7:35 P.M. June 12, or about three hours before the murders.

Inevitably, the text of O.J.'s message leaked out to the press:

"Hey, Gretchen, sweetheart, it's Orenthal James, who is finally at a place in his life where he's like, totally, totally, unattached with everybody. Ha haaaah! . . .

"I'm catching a red-eye at midnight or something to Chicago, but I'll be back Monday night. If you leave me a message, leave it on —"

The media's slant was that O.J. and I had squabbled the night before. According to the *Daily News* in New York, I wanted to attend Sydney's dance recital the next day, but O.J. didn't want me there, "saying the event was for 'family.' "

According to Kato Kaelin, the famous Rockingham houseguest, O.J. had talked to another model, a *Playboy* centerfold named Tracy Adele, shortly before Sydney's five o'clock recital. "I've got everything in the world, but I'm not a happy man," O.J. supposedly told her. "How can you make me happy, Tracy?"

If the reports could be believed, O.J.'s coarse and casual overtures were less than appealing. And I couldn't deny feeling jealous when I read about them. But I also couldn't say O.J. was cheating on me. I'd broken up with him that morning, after all, and I was with someone else myself that day.

If anything, the messages suggested that O.J. *could* be a one-woman man — that he'd waited until we split before casting his line.

This is what I told myself: O.J. would step outside a relationship when it was troubled and when he needed affirmation from another woman. That wasn't right, but I didn't think it was so unusual for a man, either.

But when times were good between O.J. and me, I *knew* he'd never cheated. He'd never hurt me that way. He loved me too much, I could see that now.

Such was the power of my denial in those days. I'd blocked out O.J.'s elaborate hoax in Palm Beach, when he needed to cover his tracks to carry on with the models at Donald Trump's party. I'd expunged his mysterious disappearance in San Francisco, when I suspected he'd gone back to Nicole. I'd hit the delete key on those awkward memories. I could no longer call them up.

Trust was my lifeline. Doubt was the enemy. I couldn't keep going unless I was sure that O.J. would be true to me. Unless I had faith that he'd return my loyalty, with or without shackles to keep his hands from roving.

Besides, I had other, more serious concerns. When I heard about Gretchen, I was facing a crisis that was truly undeniable.

I was losing my home.

I'd bought the condominium for $250,000. I paid $1,700 a month for the mortgage and another $600 to the homeowners association for upkeep. That was $2,300 a month, at a time when I couldn't afford the maintenance on a birdbath.

If I'd been smarter, I would have cut the fat and sold the apartment in the fall. Now my options were few. I was three months behind to the bank. I couldn't ask O.J. for more help; he had too much money going out for his defense.

It was one of those things that couldn't be fixed.

I'd had the apartment shown discreetly earlier in the spring, in hopes of making a quick sale, but I'd waited too long. Faced with foreclosure, I settled on a "short pay" arrangement. I turned the condo over to a third party for a price well below the market, with all proceeds going to the bank.

When the deal went through, it wrenched my heart out. The apartment was a symbol of my success and self-sufficiency. My whole identity was caught up in it. To lose it was final proof that the life I'd known was finished.

The incredible shrinking woman was about to disappear.

To add insult to injury, the press kept pumping out this image of me as a shallow, greedy woman who'd do anything for money. Even as I gave up my home, a Philadelphia paper reported that I was condo-hunting in Florida and would look at nothing under $2.5 million.

The media never came close to seeing who I was: a scared, lonely person who was losing everything in her life.

There was no way I could stick around while the vultures swooped down on my apartment. I needed time and space to heal. I hated the idea of abandoning O.J., even for a while, but self-preservation kicked in.

I had a very strong suspicion that I was about to break down.

On April 7, I went down to the jail to tell O.J. I was leaving. I didn't even sit — I wanted to say good-bye and gun the Bronco to the airport, without looking back.

"I just can't stay anymore," I told O.J., holding my hand to the glass, tears streaming down my cheeks. "I need to go home." I began moving toward the visitors' door.

"You can't just walk away now," he said. "Come back here and *talk* to me."

"I love you, but I can't talk right now."

"I can't follow you — I can't get up, I've got these chains on me," O.J. pleaded. Now he was crying too. "Don't do this, *please*."

But I was gone, oblivious to guards and Menendezes and reporters, just beelining to my truck.

I stayed with my mother in Bay Point for nearly a month, a real turning point. It was a time when I began to pull back — not so much from O.J., who still called every night, but from the waterspout that had sucked me so far down.

I sent the apartment's keys to Cathy Randa, who took care of the cleaning and packing. Soon no one would know that I'd ever lived in the place with the marble entryway and the whitewashed cabinets and the walls the color of a stormy Gulf sky.

Soon it would seem like a dream even to me.

I returned to Los Angeles on May 3 and camped out at Rockingham. Life resumed as if I'd never been away, with the same daily cycle of visits and phone calls. Grateful that I'd returned, O.J. was, if anything, more loving and appreciative than before.

But as the year marker of the murders approached, we both felt the weight of O.J.'s time in jail. To be inside a whole year and still not know when the end would come — it made you crazy to think about it.

I knew I couldn't stand to be in L.A. on June 12. That day would be all about Nicole for O.J., and it still hurt me to talk about her. When O.J. started venting in that direction — *Why would anyone want to hurt her?* — I kept changing the subject.

What could I possibly say about Nicole not being there? What could I do to make a difference?

When Tom Hahn invited me to Maui, my idea of paradise,

I jumped at the chance for a little jailbreak. It would be nice to see Tom again. We'd recently severed our business ties — I hadn't exactly been generating much revenue for him — and Tom had taken a job with Jon Peters, the movie producer. Earlier that spring, Jon and Tom had surprised me in Panama City while I was living there, to encourage me to go back to work. There was nothing going on between Jon and me, though he liked to imply otherwise. When a tabloid TV crew asked about rumors that we were an item, Jon boasted, "What can I say — she's Italian, I'm Italian."

Tom and I arrived in Hawaii on June 10 for a four-night stay at the Ritz Carlton. Jon joined us for the first night, then left to tend to business.

Maui was the sweet haven I remembered. When Tom and I went to a luau, no one recognized me, or at least they were good enough to avoid mentioning the trial.

Back at the hotel, I waited for O.J.'s call. I was thinking — hoping — that he'd be glad that I wasn't spending another Saturday in the Central Jail infirmary. But when the call came, O.J.'s voice was hard and abrupt. "Why didn't you tell me that Jon was going to be there?" he demanded.

I knew exactly why I hadn't told O.J. I hadn't wanted him stewing in his cell when there was nothing to be jealous about. But he'd somehow gotten wind of Jon's trip to Panama City, and now there was trouble.

"I called and asked for Jon Peters's room," O.J. went on, all in a huff, "and the girl told me, 'They're not in.' I got so mad I threw my Bible across the cell."

Taken by surprise, I said, "I don't know why she would say that, because we've all got our own rooms."

O.J. wasn't satisfied. He had a good argument going, and he didn't want to let it drop. If there was nothing going on, he must have reasoned, why had I concealed Jon's being there? I just swallowed the attack, and we traded cool good-byes. I reminded myself how desperately alone O.J. must feel, with the terrible anniversary looming. I felt a new wave of guilt over leaving him.

I made every excuse I could think of, because I couldn't handle the idea that O.J. thought so little of me.

Over the next two days, the acid of his doubting ate into my skin. *So O.J. had been checking up on me.* This was ridiculous; he knew Jon had a girlfriend. More to the point, he knew he could trust me. If he didn't, we had big problems.

Hadn't I, after all, trusted O.J.'s innocence throughout the trial — no questions asked, no doubts expressed?

Monday, June 12, was a horror show. Wherever I went, the murders were there. They lurked around each palm tree, hovered over every mountain view. I thought about the message I'd left O.J. one year before and the questions that had triggered it. I'd pushed those questions down for so long, but now they bubbled to the surface. How could O.J. doubt me? Wasn't *he* the one who had strayed in the past? Was his anger a projection — an admission of his cheating? Would he change after he got out of jail?

Could he change?

Too soon I'd have to get back to ground zero, to my locked-up life. For so long I'd wished it was I who'd been jailed, rather than O.J. Now I saw that I *had* been jailed, ever since the Bronco chase. I'd placed myself under house arrest, with no parole. My spirit was shackled to every tiny fluctuation in the trial, not to mention O.J.'s mood.

And the better I behaved, the more time they added to my sentence.

For much of that day I sat glumly in my hotel room, answering my phone. O.J. called at least half a dozen times. He was still going round and round about Jon Peters, who'd already checked out. He didn't ask me if I was having an affair, not in so many words. But the question hung in the air nonetheless.

Each call brought me closer to a boil. What had I done to deserve this? Hadn't I gone the distance for O.J.? I'd been celibate for nearly a year. I'd talked with O.J. for hours about my Christian values. I'd walked away from Dolph Lundgren, the first love of my life — and this idiot *still* didn't get it.

Finally I got exasperated and said, "Look, I'll be here two more

days. Why don't you have Bill Pavelic come out here — he's welcome to stay in my room to keep an eye on me. But right now I'm
getting away from everybody. I don't want to see a soul."

I hung up the phone and drove up to the Seven Sacred Pools
with Tom. The ride made me dizzy, but the walk up into the
mountain was so quiet and idyllic that I almost forgot what day it
was.

Then Tom broke into my reverie and said, "You need to get
on with your life, Paula. You've already given up so much." I'd
heard the same song for months from my mother. It was quite a
dilemma — should I move back outside, into the light, with people who supported me emotionally? Or should I stay inside, in jail,
with a man who couldn't trust me?

I was sorely tantalized in Maui to leave all the garbage behind
me. To just get up and walk off. What was it that Dolph had written? *Always keep a part of you to yourself.* . . . Now I understood. I'd
given everything to O.J., until there was nothing left. And what
good was I now? Thin as a rail, apparently unemployable, and perpetually on the verge of tears — what free man would want me?

But I couldn't give up. God was tempting me with an easy way
out; it was a big giant test for me. If I gave up, O.J. would lose the
trial. Superstition? I would rather call it faith. No matter what, I
had to believe that my commitment to O.J. had meant something.

If I left now, I wouldn't just be deserting O.J.

I'd be admitting that I'd thrown my life away, and for nothing.

Instead, I chose to hope that O.J. and I might find each other
again. That our past wouldn't ruin our future. And that after the
trial we might start fresh and new.

At Rockingham I still slept in O.J.'s bed — the bed I'd made, some
might say. But I was also blinking out into the sun a little bit. I began going out to lunch with Denice Halicki, Bob Kardashian's girlfriend. I worked out at Santa Monica Body Building with George,
the owner, who'd trained Dolph and Sly Stallone for the *Rocky*
movies.

After defense attorney Barry Scheck cross-examined Dennis Fung, the LAPD criminalist, and basically took the man apart, the blood evidence seemed pretty well discredited. The trial was swinging O.J.'s way. On June 15, I sat spellbound in front of the big-screen TV as O.J. struggled to put on the brown leather gloves — the left one found at the murder scene, the right at Rockingham. As O.J. said, "The gloves are too small," I exhaled. He'd just taken a giant stride toward acquittal.

But then I watched with concern as O.J. removed the gloves — had anyone else noticed how easily he'd pulled them off?

As the defense gained momentum, O.J.'s old sense of humor resurfaced, as devilish as ever. One night I put us through to Johnnie Cochran without saying hello, per O.J.'s instructions.

When his lawyer picked up the phone, O.J. said, "Johnnie, I just got Cathy to put us through. You're not going to believe this — are you sitting down?"

Johnnie sounded real solemn as he said, "No, man, but I'll sit down. Now go on, tell me what it is."

"I can't believe Paula," O.J. said. "She's down there with Marcia Clark and Chris Darden. I don't know how they got her or who they got her from, but they're sitting with her right now." He was really playing it up; I had to bite my lip to keep from laughing.

Johnnie was normally Mr. Unflappable, but now he sounded seriously concerned. "Wha-wha-what happened?" he stuttered. "What'd you *say?* What'd you do that got her upset?"

"Got you!" O.J. and I said together.

We were still talking every day, still exchanging our I-love-you's, but it wasn't quite the same. I'd lost a little bit of my heart in Maui. My old questions had seeped out like a genie from a bottle. Now they gave me no peace.

"You know," I told O.J. one night, "I was moving on when all this started."

"I'm sorry that you're pulled into this," he said. "I'm just a big trouble for everybody."

I wished I could take my cruel words back — how could I say such a horrible thing?

I bounced back and forth, from resentment to guilt and back. Rockingham was a minefield of memories for me, not the place to get well. I got away every weekend I could, cashing in my frequent flier miles from my modeling days. Most often I'd go to New York or to Panama City, where my Bible studies were gaining momentum.

I never stopped caring about O.J., and I never stopped supporting him, but we weren't doing each other much good of late. As his fortunes in court improved, he seemed stronger and less dependent on me. Toward the end of June, I decided to go home to Florida indefinitely.

This time O.J.'s pleas didn't move me or make me cry. He'd taken my blood and then some. I'd done my civil duty, my friendship duty, my loving duty, my human duty — I'd done it all.

O.J. was going to be okay, I thought. It was time to get myself straight.

In Panama City I stuck close to home — a little gardening and dog walking, a lot of Bible reading, all the sleep I could get. On my bad days, my mother gave me a wide berth. There remained considerable strain between us. Mom knew too much about my ordeal, and yet not enough.

I watched the trial less consistently; it just didn't seem like a healthy thing to do. But I was always by the phone when O.J. called in at 10 P.M. Central Time, after visiting hours at the jail. One month my phone bill topped $1,400 (O.J. had to call collect); one phone call alone cost almost $100 (it lasted two and a half hours).

While I missed him severely, physical distance seemed to take the edge off our problems. And O.J. wasn't a fool — he knew he had to step back for a while and let me sort things out. Rather than dissect the past, we'd ponder what we'd do after he was freed. How we'd move to some quiet, healthy place, where the children would feel safe and all of us could start healing.

O.J. seemed to understand that his old life was over, and to welcome the change. He wanted out of the Hollywood fast lane, he said — he wanted to live among people who'd stood by him, and who shared his faith in God.

I liked to muse about where we'd be twenty years down the road. O.J.'s legs were so bad that I might be pushing him in a wheelchair, but that didn't seem so bleak to me. I loved him so much that nothing else would matter. I'd take however many years God gave us, and be content.

In July I moved back into Rockingham one last time. While in Hawaii Tom tried, in a last-ditch attempt, to get me interested in my old life. I agreed to work on a low-budget, made-for-HBO show called *Night Eyes*. I was sick with the flu, and I knew the plot was tacky; I'd be playing a psychiatrist at a time when I needed one instead. But they were offering $30,000 for three weeks' work, and I had bills to pay, so I swallowed my medicine and took the job.

O.J. had always encouraged me to be the best actress I could be. "It doesn't matter how small the part is," he'd tell me. "As long as you're working, you're an actor. It's the experience that counts."

But when I told O.J. about *Night Eyes,* he thought it was bad news. Having seen previous episodes, he considered it soft-core pornography.

"But I'm not doing any of the nudity," I protested. "They're using body doubles, and they won't look anything like me."

O.J. laughed derisively. "Don't fool yourself," he said. "Do you think the guy in Middle America knows whose body it is?"

The finished product was as bad as O.J. had warned. They'd plugged in a love scene every few minutes, and the body doubles did all sorts of obscene things.

Worse yet was the rental-video version, which the producers had thoughtfully sent me. The cover of the box had three main elements: my name; a nude still of a body double, and a crude illustration of a knife-wielding man in a ski mask.

The masked man was an especially inspired touch, since there was no such character in the movie.

Burned again, I went back to Panama City. I'd finally learned my lesson. If my future had ever been in Hollywood, it wasn't anymore.

When I'd watched Mark Fuhrman testify in March, he seemed to be one of the prosecution's most effective witnesses: clean-cut, competent, believable.

That was before a set of audiotapes revealed Fuhrman to be a racist and a perjurer, a man who apparently took delight in beating up helpless black people. When Fuhrman returned to the stand in August, O.J. could hardly contain himself. He was furious when Judge Ito barred the jury from knowing that Fuhrman had pleaded the Fifth Amendment. The judge, O.J. said, "might as well be part of the prosecution."

Once the jury heard excerpts from the tapes, the Dream Team knew that O.J. had a strong chance of acquittal. But while our conference calls were upbeat, the Fuhrman affair left me uneasy. I'd been reading about the Ku Klux Klan and how it was spreading. I worried what it would be like for O.J. after he got out.

As a girl from the Deep South, I knew that a lot of people thought like Mark Fuhrman. Would O.J. have to watch his back for the rest of his life?

One thing seemed certain: This trial wouldn't end when the verdict came in.

14

Freedom

By mid-August, Cathy Randa was packing the remainder of my belongings at my Los Angeles condo — the movers would be there soon. Gigi called to say, "If the Bronco's not being used it needs to be moved out of here." I have to say, it hurt my feelings. A lot. The truck had been there since the beginning of the trial. I had left it behind for Carmelita or Shirley to take Mrs. Simpson to court each day. When Jason's pit bull bit Chachi, O.J.'s chow, I used the Bronco to rush the dog to the vet. I ran over a reporter's foot with it (at least, I think I did), and someone actually jumped the Rockingham fence and stole its license plates. When Jason borrowed it (without asking) to drive some buddies up to San Francisco, O.J. blew his top. I mean, this Bronco had seen a lot of history. But now it was being sent away. Or, to look at it another way: It was coming home.

At our house in Bay Point I was nesting with a vengeance. With some of the money from *Night Eyes* I hired a painter and bought flowers for the garden. I put up a fence by the pond behind our backyard, to keep our Yorkies safe from stray alligators when the dogs went out to play.

By September I was broke again, juggling my credit cards as best I could. As the days grew shorter, I found myself daydreaming about O.J.'s goofy smile . . . or the way I'd catch him looking at me when he was proud of something I'd said or done. I craved the clasp of his arms around my back, the brush of those pillow lips. I'd look at my right hand, at the index finger that had touched his hand over the glass. I still felt a faint warmth.

O.J. was imprinted on me. He would never wash away.

A hundred times I wished I were in Los Angeles. I even felt nostalgia for my old, draining routine: the drive downtown, the media gauntlet, the chats with the guards. But I couldn't go back into the black hole; I knew I'd barely escaped with my life.

As the end of the trial loomed and the future became less abstract, pressure built. O.J. and I never talked about the coming verdict, but our turmoil was there, just under the surface. What would happen when the trial was over? Where would we go? What would we do?

The questions bore down on me like a pack of snapping wolves. It was hard to imagine a life outside Judge Ito's courtroom and Central Jail. I felt like so many things had passed me by since O.J.'s arrest — I thought of poor Billy, O.J.'s friend just out of prison, jumping at his first jolt of Surround Sound.

O.J. was beginning to waffle about moving out of Los Angeles. "I need to get my life together first," he said. "I've got a lot of things to deal with."

I knew O.J. was worried about a custody battle with the Browns, but the conversation unsettled me. *What did that mean?* I wondered. *Where do I fit into the picture?*

Late on Friday, September 29, the case went to the jury. After eighteen minutes of deliberation, the jurors stopped for the weekend — giving O.J. and his lawyers more than sixty hours to rehash the entire case, with me listening in.

The lawyers' consensus was that we were looking at a hung

jury, in the worst case. O.J. was ready for that, though I couldn't imagine how I'd get through another year or more of this ordeal.

"No, you're going home," I told O.J. "Next week this time, you'll be home."

I assumed that after the acquittal, O.J. would gather his kids and go out to the Benders' for a while, if only to get away from the media. I thought that I'd probably join them there, but we made no set plan. We figured that the jury would be out at least a week, maybe as long as three, and we didn't want to jinx ourselves.

"Let's just wait and see," O.J. said.

On Monday, October 2, my mother and I went for an early dinner at Captain Anderson's. Midway through, our waitress came over all excited and said, "Paula, they reached a verdict!" I thought she was joking, and that it was so cruel; my eyes swam. I forced myself to stay calm, picked at my grilled shrimp. I resisted the impulse to call Los Angeles.

But when I got home, I saw the news: It was true. The jury was finished, and the verdict would be read the next day. I felt ill. All the commentators were saying that a quick verdict was a bad sign for O.J.

I remembered a warning from F. Lee Bailey, when he'd recently stopped off in Florida and made me a gift of a laptop computer; he'd been so kind to me throughout the trial. "Be prepared for the worst," Lee had cautioned.

"Say your prayers," a subdued O.J. told me before we hung up for the night.

I was up by six the next morning, or four o'clock in Los Angeles. A long time to wait. I sat with CNN in the upstairs loft outside my bedroom. By dawn the media had our house staked out. A few of the bolder reporters breached security and knocked on our door before getting escorted off the property.

To give me extra protection, one of the guards, a sweet granddad named Joe, joined me on my white couch and held my hand.

The consensus was for conviction; all the legal experts seemed very sure of themselves. I was dying inside. I couldn't eat a crumb. A few sips of coffee made me sick.

At around ten, O.J. called before leaving for the courtroom. "I love you, girl," he said.

"I love you, Orenthal James." I tried to keep the tremor out of my voice, but by that time my hands were shaking, and I don't think I did a good job.

"Got to go," O.J. said. I listened to the dial tone for several seconds before I hung up.

It was nearly noon my time when the jurors filed into the courtroom. I squeezed Joe's hand as the foreman inspected the verdict forms. My mind whirled in prayer. Joe and I stood up as the clerk began reading:

" . . . *in the matter of the State of California versus Orenthal James Simpson, case number BA097211. We the jury, in the above-entitled action, find the defendant, Orenthal James Simpson, not guilty of the crime of murder. . . ."*

When I heard those two blessed words — *not guilty!* — I think I must have screamed. I know that I clutched Joe's neck and fell into his arms. So often I'd thought this trial would never end. Yet now, as it happened, the ending felt very real and right and fair.

O.J. had earned it; I was thrilled for him.

I looked at my mother — she'd come up unnoticed in my haze — and the first thing I said was, "Dad must be mad right now." I was right on the money. Soon Dad was up there on the TV, a bigot to the finish. "The son of a bitch walked," he grumbled.

I was delighted when CNN cut to a jubilant church gathering in L.A.'s black community. Then the angry white people around the courthouse brought me down again. I thought of the clerk in the Brentwood video store, and the bitterness that could grow in people's hearts.

But that didn't matter so much at the moment. O.J. was innocent. O.J. was free.

He wouldn't have to spend the rest of his life in jail — and, in a way, neither would I.

Less than half an hour after the verdict, Joe came back with a different sort of news break: We had to get out. A hurricane was coursing straight at Panama City, maybe ten hours away. There'd been a bunch of warnings on radio and local TV, but we'd been so caught up with O.J. that we'd missed them.

The phone rang. I knew it was him before I heard his voice, which was racing like my heart: "I can't believe it, I'm on the freeway, I never thought I would enjoy being on the freeway as much as I am now." O.J. started reeling off the interchange signs, every little landmark on the road, as if they were wonders of the world.

"I love you!" I shouted.

"I love *you*," O.J. said. "Listen, I'm going home, I'm going to get my kids, and then I'm coming to get you, girl."

I couldn't wait. We *would* be together — how could I doubt it? We just needed to hold each other and talk without a panel of glass between us, and everything would work out.

We talked and giggled until O.J. reached his exit, when I snapped to and told him about the storm. I had to get off and get ready; a mandatory evacuation was nothing to play with. "I'll give Cathy the number where you can reach me," I said.

Except for Casey, our next-door neighbor, the rest of the neighborhood had already left. I went to the men at Bay Point Maintenance and pleaded for them to help me nail plywood over our floor-to-ceiling windows. The phone rang again. It was O.J. They were having a welcome-home party that night at Rockingham, he told me. All his friends would be there. "I want my Peola here, too," he said. "Why aren't you here?"

"I can't come out right now," I said. "I told you — they're predicting a direct hit. We've got to get out of here."

O.J. was frustrated, but there was nothing I could do about that. We got the truck packed, and Mom and Casey and I piled in with our five dogs.

We drove north, toward higher ground and away from the Gulf, to a country home in the woods owned by a friend of my brother Vinnie's. What was normally an hour's drive took four in the bumper-to-bumper traffic. We roughed it that night, sleeping on the floor.

Meanwhile, all the power and phones were out, including the station that bounced calls to my cell phone. There was no way for O.J. to reach me. At eight the next morning, five hours after the storm's peak, I talked Mom and Casey into trying to get back to the beach.

They were turning back civilians until the following day. After getting stopped at one police checkpoint, we took a back road and got blocked again at Hathaway Bridge. That's where Casey had the brilliant idea of saying that she worked for her uncle's sanitation company. "Got to get the trucks on the road," she explained.

The officer looked into my Bronco, at the three women and five dogs inside, and said, "Guess the trash has got to be picked up sometime." We were through.

Panama City had been devastated. Along the waterfront, the storm surge had risen halfway up the houses' first floors, and a number of homes had been leveled. Mom and I were lucky. Because our house sat higher off the ground, it was the only one on the block that didn't wind up needing new carpeting. We lost three pine trees — one of which had fallen across the driveway, missing our roof by inches. The place was in shambles; our garage door had blown askew. There was no electricity, no water, and there were dead fish all over the golf course, beginning to rot under the poststorm sun.

"Don't you ever scare me like that again," O.J. hollered over the phone when he finally got through. Come on out, he said. The Benders had a prepaid ticket waiting for me at the airport; I could stay at the Beverly Hills Hotel.

"I can't come out just now," I said. "There are things I have to take care of around here."

Well, there *were,* I thought to myself. But that wasn't the only reason I turned down O.J.'s invitation. Buying water at the Winn Dixie, I'd spotted the latest issue of *Star* — the rag (though not the only one) that had plagued me throughout the trial. Their "un-named sources" (as well as my brother) had detailed one lie after another — from bogus tales of three-way sex between O.J., A.C., and me; to O.J. punching me in the stomach at Magic Johnson's birthday party; to my getting silicone-injected lips. So what exclusive story did they have this day? Why, O.J.'s homecoming! The party that I had missed. Thank heaven.

Here was O.J. waving his Bible in jubilation. Here he was, on his knees in front of the bed where we had made love so many times (and where the police had found a framed photo of Nicole tucked underneath). Here he was with his family, who had gone through such hell for so many months.

Here he was, taking money for blood. He had sold his story to the *Star*.

But it wasn't just a sense of disgust that was keeping me away from the circus. I knew I didn't want to settle into Rockingham with security guards watching out for my safety. To protect me from what — or whom? In the worst case, some angry person might try to retaliate against O.J. In the best, I'd be trapped in a place I needed to forget. And after the dismissal of my Bronco by his family, how would I fit into this picture? What kind of life was that?

I'd come home to Florida for stability, and I wasn't yet strong enough to leave. I needed O.J. to come see me in Panama City. I knew it might take a while — he'd have to get his sea legs, spend time with his kids. He needed to experience his freedom without my being there to cloud things.

My life wasn't a fairy tale, where all I required was a kiss to live happily ever after. In the real world, I'd discovered, love often has to wait.

I'd waited fifteen months to hold O.J. in my arms. I would wait a few more days and be patient and understanding, because that was right for O.J.

Again, I had no choice.

The few days stretched into two weeks. In the interim, O.J. called me and casually remarked, "You know, they'll pay lots of money for pictures of you and me together."

How could he do this? I remembered how upset O.J. had been when the Browns sold his wedding video to tabloid television, or when one of the sisters cashed in on some topless pictures of Nicole. I recalled, too, how incensed he'd been with my father and brother after they'd betrayed me.

Regardless of how broke he was, how could he go over to the other side?

I called Cathy again. "If O.J.'s coming here to take pictures of me and my family," I said, "he might as well not come."

Don't worry, don't worry, said Cathy.

Well, there's one thing more, I told her hesitantly. "Do you think he'll mind if we take it really slow? I mean, fooling around, that is. I just don't know how I feel right now."

Now *Cathy* got worried. Oh, Paula, she said, after all he's been through . . . don't upset him . . . you can't let him down . . .

O.J. called. Hurriedly, he assured me no photographs would be released without my approval. I accepted the arrangement, but it put a cloud over his visit. Was he really coming just for me?

When *Star*'s chartered jet touched down in Panama City, though, my misgivings were laid aside. I felt like an eager bride whose soldier was home from the war. I was hopping up and down on the runway. My wait was almost over.

But as focused as I was on O.J. as he came off the plane, I couldn't help noticing Larry Schiller, the designated photographer. O.J. was dressed in chinos and a white golf shirt, and he looked wonderful, like a dream I'd almost forgotten. We flowed into our hug and kiss, my first real kiss since Michael Bolton, lifetimes ago. I smelled vanilla, and breathed deep. *He's so skinny,* I thought, feeling O.J.'s ribs. I'd idealized this moment for so long, and now it was as perfect as I'd dreamed it.

But then reality began to intrude. I felt inhibited with so many people around, almost as if I were onstage. Everyone was staring at O.J. It didn't help that O.J. kept looking around for Larry, who appeared ready to whip out his camera at any moment.

I took O.J.'s bag and bent over to put it in my friend Casey's Jeep Cherokee. O.J. cupped his hands wide, outlining my bottom. "I can't wait to get ahold of you, girl," he told my buttocks, with a sly smile aimed at Casey.

I felt shy and embarrassed. The whole atmosphere smacked of a first date, no matter how well I thought I knew this man. O.J. had been simmering in jail for so long, and now I wasn't sure that I could live up to his fantasies of me — or, worse yet, whether I wanted to. Our relationship could no longer be sculpted in my mind. It was there, in the flesh, and I had no idea how to handle it.

O.J. the Cause had been a lot easier to deal with than O.J. the Man. The Cause had been clear and unchanging; of the Man I was not quite so sure.

We took off with Casey driving and O.J.'s bodyguards behind us in a rental car. We went directly to a condo I'd reserved on the beach, and Casey dropped us off.

Now we were alone. Just the two of us. No one listening in. No glass between us. It was late afternoon, and the autumn light was clear and warm. The Gulf sparkled through a floor-to-ceiling window and again in a mirror on the opposite wall. I felt like we'd boarded a boat and were adrift in the sea.

After fifteen months of virtually nonstop conversation, there was nothing more to say. We both knew why we were there and what had to happen next.

As we sat on a couch in the living room, O.J. told me how much he'd missed me, how much he loved me. But those lines sounded stale to me. They had no freshness, no conviction — or at least none that I wanted to feel.

If nothing else, my life of late had been simple. Now it was about to get a lot more complicated. *Only if I let it,* I reminded myself. That was a new and revolutionary thought, born just that summer, after O.J. had lost his trust in me.

Only if I let it. . . .

O.J. told me to stand up in front of him. He stayed seated and unbuttoned my blouse; I held his shoulders, trying somehow to relax. I was nervous about so many things. Would O.J. still find me attractive? Would I be able to make him happy after all this time?

And then there was the oldest question in my book: *What was I doing here?*

As O.J. undid my buttons, I saw that one thing hadn't changed: He still closed his eyes when aroused. Even now, as he talked about missing me, he felt no need to *see* me.

O.J. pulled down my jeans and panties. I grabbed him tight and leaned over to kiss him, hoping his lips would be the antidote for all my uncertainties.

He turned me around and kissed the middle of my back. He worked his way up to my neck, where his kiss became a bite. I winced; my knees buckled.

O.J. gently pushed me toward the bedroom, toward the inevitable. As I marched ahead, I kept thinking: *I'm not ready for this.* How many times had I put up road signs in my head — STOP, or SLOW, or SPEED LIMIT? Now I was recklessly running them all.

And I was definitely under the influence — of a man who still controlled me, of a pattern I couldn't quite yet break.

I sat on the bed, with the same gleaming view of the water. I watched O.J. undress, just as I had back in Laguna that first time. Three years had passed since then, three years of my life where O.J. held center stage, even when we were apart. I'd kept my word to the man and my bargain with God. I'd squelched any doubts and stood firm to the end, like a little soldier. I'd given O.J. a gift greater than any my body could offer up: my faith.

But what could O.J. give me in return? Nothing. I needed clarity in my life. I needed a sense of direction and the inner calm to use it. How could I get those things from a man whose every movement was a national circus, whose bodyguards had to be stationed in the next apartment?

O.J. pushed me down on the bed and clumsily climbed on. We'd apparently finished our foreplay in the living room. I saw him wince from his arthritis and felt a twinge of pity. I spread my legs and let him enter me.

Today it's hard to remember what went on after that, because I wasn't really there. I'm sure that O.J. kissed my neck just above my collarbone, because that's what he always did. I'm sure he tried to reacquaint himself with my shoulders and breasts. I'm sure he stroked my legs, because he liked to do that.

And I'm sure he got no reaction.

He was finished quickly — it didn't seem like anything special for him. He didn't act like a man who'd gone fifteen months without sex. I thought back to the stories about his coming-home party and the women who were on hand.

O.J. knew something was wrong, but he didn't ask. His lawyers had taught him well — that you don't ask a question when you might not like the answer.

Instead, he did what he did best in our afterglow: He fell straight to sleep.

I would lie there all evening long and into the night, memorizing every inch of the ceiling.

We never made love again.

In the morning O.J. left early for the first of two rounds at Hombre, the course he'd played a hundred times in his head while in jail. I'd set the schedule myself. I knew how much O.J. had missed the game, and I wanted him to relive his affection for Panama City.

I had good reason to keep O.J. busy. Too much quiet time might lead to questions — scary questions about where the two of us were going, and whether we could get there together.

Playing the perfect hostess, I made lunch for O.J. and his bodyguards, then joined him at Hombre. As we puttered along in O.J.'s golf cart, I heard Larry Schiller's camera going a mile a minute from a cart behind us. Each whir of his shutter was a sharp stick in my ribs. *How could O.J. do this? How could he bring the tabloids, which had ripped my family apart, into our reunion?*

About halfway through the round, we came to the part of the course that abuts a public road. The media had set up there, everyone from local press and TV to several national correspondents and a raft of tabloids. It was paparazzi city — you could feel their greedy curiosity a hundred yards away.

Not even here, I thought grimly. Not even in Panama City could we get the privacy we'd need to straighten things out.

O.J. could see how uncomfortable I was and agreed that I should clear out. I hopped into a spare cart and made my getaway.

When I picked O.J. up at game's end, Larry Schiller tried to run interference for us by backing up his car in the parking lot. But the *New York Post* broke through, and soon we had a chase scene down Front Beach Road. There was hardly any traffic there off-season; we were running red lights, but so were they.

Finally I pulled up to a local police car for assistance. O.J. rolled down the passenger window and smiled, showing that famous face that had worked for him for so many years.

The officer peered into the car and said, "Oh, hey, Paula." It was a boy I'd grown up with, and he was happy to help. He went back to the *Post*'s car and took their video camera. Like a lot of people, they were trying to make a quick sale to *Hard Copy* or *A Current Affair.*

I drove on to a house in Bay Point that I'd rented for the month, just in case the press discovered the beachfront condo. O.J. was tired. He said he wanted me to rest with him, but first he had to make a call — to his *publicist.* I could overhear them talking about *Star* and the media at the golf course, among other things. There was obviously a lot going on.

To me, the whole concept of publicity for O.J. was stark, raving insane. The conversation he was having was dumb and disgusting. It didn't sound like the person I'd loved in jail.

Or maybe he just wasn't the person I'd wanted him to be.

I made some excuse about needing to do something for Mom and rushed out of the house before O.J. could see me cry.

It was the next day, his third in Panama City, that we truly fell apart. Back in the condo after the morning's golf, O.J. was lying down in the bedroom. I was in the living room, where I saw photos of the welcome-home party in an open suitcase. As I leafed through them, I came across a copy of *Star*'s article about the party.

"It looks like a nice time," I said absently. I skimmed past a mention of Gretchen Stockdale, whom I'd known had been there.

But when I turned the page, I found something I couldn't skip over — an article speculating that O.J. and I would get married.

Of itself, the article was nothing new. The tabloids had us engaged half a dozen times while O.J. was in jail, attributing their reports either to phantom "friends" or eavesdropping deputies.

But this story was different. It quoted O.J. as saying that yes, he thought we would tie the knot.

I flushed scarlet. I knew the rules as well as anyone. The tabloids wouldn't quote people unless they'd actually talked to them — generally with a fee attached. (After getting back to Los Angeles, O.J. would eventually admit that he'd done exactly that.)

Like my father and my brother, O.J. had *sold me out*. He'd betrayed and deceived me — how could I ever trust him after this?

I shouted into the bedroom, "I can't *believe* you made money off of me with this crap!"

O.J. got up, full of righteous indignation. "At my house," he growled, "we have a rule — we don't talk about gossip."

"Wait a minute," I said. "You sell a story, and I'm not allowed to bring it up?"

"I never sold a story about you."

He was playing me for a fool again. "You're lying to me, and you know how I feel about lies," I said.

"Besides," O.J. said, digging in for the debate, "my Mamma read that story, and she thought it was a very complimentary story."

"Then why don't you go marry your Mamma!" I screamed. I knew I shouldn't have said that; you don't disrespect a guy's mother.

The sore subject — our future — was out. We hadn't talked about it since O.J. had arrived, but I could read between the lines. He'd kept referring to the upcoming civil trial and the custody battle with the Browns, and how he needed money from *Star* to pay some pressing bills.

Throw in Larry Schiller and the publicist, and I could see that there wasn't much room for that quiet, Christian life I'd pined for.

And there wasn't any room for me. (As O.J. would exclaim to my mother, some weeks later: "What did she expect me to do — *marry* her?")

O.J. had pushed my biggest button, and we escalated from there. Though seated in his chair, he could barely contain himself. His hands windmilled the air as he yelled at me through clenched teeth.

"What's *wrong* with you?" he barked. I thought he looked ready to lunge at me, to pick me up and shake me. He seemed to be fighting with himself, as if there were some other person struggling inside. A person who was wild and violent, a person who scared even O.J.

Then O.J. outdid himself: "I waited *two whole weeks* to make love to you, and now you lay this crap on me!" Snatching the tabloid from my hands, he screamed, "I am not going to argue with you about this shit!" He threw the magazine at an end table. It hit a lamp, which fell to the floor without breaking.

But though O.J. stopped short of trashing the room, and though he didn't lay an angry hand on me, I felt a rush of fear nonetheless. In Palm Beach he'd lost his temper; here he had lost his mind.

Then the storm subsided, and O.J. went back to lie down. I felt sapped and pathetic, and faced with two terrible choices. I could believe O.J. and stay with him and lie to myself. Or I could challenge him for the liar I knew he was and topple the first fateful domino. Because if O.J. was lying to me now, how many times had he lied during the trial? Where did the falsehoods end? If held up to the light, would they form a trail, like the blood, all the way to Rockingham?

As I said, two terrible choices. So I lapsed into an old, bad habit — for the moment, at least, I'd table my decision. I slid back to my house of guilt, like a turtle pulling head into shell. *Poor O.J.,* I thought. *I've spoiled our reunion.* I followed him into the bedroom and lay my head on his shoulder.

"I'm sorry for not believing you," I said.

"That's all right," O.J. said. "I'm sorry I lost it with you."

I closed my eyes — I felt old and bone-tired. Then I felt a hand on my breast, his lips at my ear: "I love you, girl."

"No," I said. And for once he knew that I was serious.

That night I counted the hours till O.J. would be gone — till the man I loved was out of my life for good.

The next morning we went out to do the photo shoot, with Larry reassuring me that I'd have total approval. As we walked around the golf course, I played with the ducks and took dutiful poses, but I never looked in O.J.'s eyes and he never looked in mine. "You know," he said, "if you agree, they'll probably pay you a hundred thousand dollars for the photos."

I let O.J.'s comment pass. It was academic, since the photographs would never see the light of day. In truth, when I saw them later, I thought they were technically good but emotionally empty. My face couldn't lie to the camera. We were as distant as two people could be.

We moved on to St. Andrew's State Park, where Larry needed to shoot O.J. by himself for another project. I folded O.J.'s pants up so he could walk to the water's edge. At one point I saw him looking really dejected as he leaned over a fence — he just looked down and out.

Feeling guilty again that I'd spoiled his stay, I said, "O.J., smile! For heaven's sake, you're not in jail anymore. You have a lot to be happy about."

Then he turned to me and said, "Stop it — this is the way I'm *supposed* to look."

O.J.'s sorrow was just a photo opportunity, a publicity scam. Nothing was real anymore, not even his emotions.

A part of me died on that fence that day.

Looking back, O.J.'s phony display was his final lie to me. It led me to believe that the only true feeling he'd expressed here was his anger, and I wanted no part of that. I didn't deserve that kind of abuse, verbal or otherwise.

I didn't want to start taking Nicole's place.

Larry kept shooting all the way to the runway, where O.J.'s jet was waiting. We had a hug and a light kiss. "You need to start eating more, Peola," O.J. said. He knew I was mad; he just didn't know what I'd decided.

"Take care of yourself," I told him. As I walked him onto the plane, I touched his sleeve — for luck? I still feared for O.J.'s safety in Los Angeles, and I had a weird feeling that this was the last time I'd ever see him. The last good-bye in a relationship of good-byes.

But by the time O.J.'s entourage had joined him aboard, I could no longer hide my disgust. Casey eyed me and said, "You sure don't look like the same girl as on the day we picked him up."

When the plane took off, I felt so let down . . . yet at the same time airy and free, as though an anvil had been hoisted from my back. I floated back to Bay Point, where I fell into bed and slept a dreamless sleep.

The next day, Larry Schiller's photos arrived by FedEx, along with a bizarre paperback that O.J. had found in a supermarket and wanted me to read. It was the story of a woman who'd had an affair and whose husband imprisoned her — I hated it from start to end.

O.J. called me the day after that. "They're beautiful pictures, aren't they?"

After a while, O.J. and Larry realized that I wasn't going to approve the pictures — beautiful or not. It was one deal they wouldn't be able to make.

If O.J. "wants Paula back, he'll probably get her," Liz Smith wrote in her column around this time. "After all, he has now been declared 'not guilty.' And then, of course, there's all that power, money, celebrity — and redemption. It would be hard for any woman to resist such a package of aphrodisiacs."

Not so hard as you might think, I thought. *Maybe not so hard at all.*

"I know you're disappointed, Paula," Bert Kitay told me over the phone. "All of O.J.'s friends are surprised that he's not doing the things he said he'd do."

That included Rosey Grier and his church, who'd done so much to support O.J. during the jail time, and now were left out in the cold. O.J. wasn't talking much about God lately. He'd used the Bible as a crutch, and now he'd cast it off. He thought he could walk straight and tall without it.

He didn't realize he was limping worse than ever, and his arthritis was the least of it.

To me, it seemed that O.J. had gotten intoxicated with his freedom. I can't entirely blame him. It must have been mind-altering to step out of his cell and jump back into the luxury of Rockingham.

What did O.J. in, I think, was his desperate need to be liked. It wasn't enough to be acquitted; he had to win back his public's affection. I think that's what he was trying to "fix" with his publicist and his video, which made him a good sum of money up front. But he went about it too fast and all wrong. Rather than gain back people's love, he inflamed them all the more.

At the same time, he got caught up in pleasing the opportunists who came creeping around him. A lot of people were whispering sweet nothings to O.J. about deals with big numbers attached. O.J. wanted to believe them; he thought they could help him retrieve his old life. He thought they could restore the glamour of being O.J. Simpson.

He was denying the obvious: that there wasn't any glamour anymore.

"So what are you going to do," said Tony Robbins, "when these people come up and ask you, 'What about O.J.?' "

"Don't ask. I don't know," I shot back.

That's how I developed my little slogan: "If you want to know about O.J. Simpson, don't ask me." It felt good every time I said it. My life was no longer sewn up with a man who was bad for me, and I wanted everyone to know it.

Which brought me back to Diane Sawyer.

If I'd simply told O.J. it was over on the phone or written him a letter, he might have shown up at my door the next week. He was so persuasive, and I was so weak and lonely. Who's to say he wouldn't have lured me back, one more time?

I felt I still loved him, after all. You don't erase that, not after what we'd been through.

No, there was just one way for me to break up with O.J. and make it stick. I'd have to do it in public, with maximum visibility. *PrimeTime Live* fit the ticket.

It was a drastic step — humiliating for O.J., terrifying for me. But it would definitely put him in check and keep him from pursuing me. With his civil trial coming up, O.J. couldn't risk behaving like the man Marcia Clark had described, the one who "couldn't let go."

He'd have to respect my decision. My interview would protect and shelter me — from my dark impulses, from O.J.'s charm and O.J.'s rage. I had to make sure that we wouldn't start in all over again. The cycle had to be broken, at any cost.

But I wasn't quite so certain of things when I watched the program on November 1. It was such a big step I'd taken, to confirm that I had no relationship "of any kind" with O.J.

Would he believe me? Would the calls keep on coming? Is this really the end?

Was I truly *ready* for it to end?

I wasn't seeking revenge through Diane Sawyer. "I just want to put a closure to this," I told Diane at the end of our segment. "I just want to work. I want to have children. I want to love. I want to fall in love!"

"The way you loved him?" Diane asked.

Could I ever love a man the way I'd loved O.J., through thick and thin — and thinner? Could I ever find such passion and intensity in a man who was worthy of my trust?

I looked at Diane and summed up my dream with one word: "Better."

With all the people O.J. and I knew in common, the drums were always beating. I wasn't surprised when he called me shortly after Diane left Panama City, just before I was on TV.

"So how was your interview?" O.J. said, trying his best to sound nonchalant.

"Fine," I said.

"I hope you feel better now that you've done it," he said.

"I do, thank you."

O.J. could restrain himself no longer. "So what did you say?" he said, a little too eagerly.

"You'll see," I said. It felt good to have some control on my side for a change.

After the show was aired, O.J.'s therapist called me. "You've said your piece now, Paula," Bert Kitay told me. "Now it's time to quiet down and go away. Remember — whoever's the right man for you will be watching what you do now."

Bert knew just how to couch his message, to hit me where I was most vulnerable. He made me think about how O.J. and his "team" had manipulated me into silence from the start. How Bert had dismissed the stories of domestic abuse. How Johnnie Cochran had concocted a fiction of our romance for the jurors' benefit, one I couldn't dare contradict.

And they were still doing it. Still playing me as a pawn in O.J.'s game of chess.

But Bert didn't have to worry. I had resigned from the match.

I was through playing games, I hoped. I was ready for something real and true. But the waiting — the transition — would be one of the hardest things I'd ever done.

In the days and weeks that followed *PrimeTime Live* I faced a huge void in my life. I couldn't live with O.J., that much was for sure. We'd had three chances and struck out each time.

But could I live without him?

Or to put it another way: I knew all about the person I wasn't. I wasn't O.J.'s "girlfriend" anymore or even a special "friend." That was all fine and good, but it begged one very serious question:

Who *was* I?

Viewers of *A Current Affair* might have formed their own opinion, based on an eight-year-old home video which resurfaced in October: that I was an incorrigible, racist redneck.

The video was shot in 1987, when I was twenty years old and

on a catalogue assignment in North Miami Beach. As I joked around with a second model, our conversation turned to a delivery man who'd recently raped an eighty-year-old woman in New York.

The delivery man was black, and I flippantly let loose with a string of primitive remarks that could have come straight from my father's mouth.

That humiliating tape played all weekend on tabloid TV. The worst slurs were also transcribed in the *National Enquirer,* which quoted one civil rights leader as saying, "This is as bad as, or worse than, anything Mark Fuhrman said."

My past had come back to bite me, in the most wounding way imaginable. I wondered what O.J.'s sister Carmelita must think of me now. I liked her so much, and we'd spent so much time together — we'd been almost like sisters.

I couldn't blame her if she never spoke to me again.

The video forced me to think about the course my life had taken. I'd been raised in a poor white family with more than its share of problems. Racial epithets rolled off our tongues; we were just ignorant that way. It was like we needed someone else to look down upon — which was kind of silly, when you think about it, because who was I to look down on anyone?

The first time I went to Paris, I remember seeing a white woman strolling arm in arm with a black man down the Champs-Elysées. They were obviously in love, and I was so stunned that I had to sit down. I'd never seen anything like it in the socially segregated town I'd grown up in.

I didn't really begin to change until after I started working in Los Angeles and met Stevie Ray Vaughn. We were hanging out with some friends of his when I lapsed into talking "southern," making careless racial comments the way we did back home.

Stevie picked up on it and said to me, "Be ready to go out tomorrow night."

That's when I joined Stevie and his girlfriend to see an all-black musical called *Mamma, I Want to Sing.* The performers were so beautiful and stirring; I admired them so much.

From there we went to Stevie Wonder's studio. Suddenly I found myself sitting at a piano between the two Stevies as they sang to me. There was more talent per square inch of piano bench than I'd likely ever see again.

I was getting the message, without any lecture attached.

My outlook on race began to change after that evening. I looked at black people with less suspicion and more respect. But I still went through life with my eyes half-shut. I was like the good German in Nazi Germany — when confronted with racism, I put my blinders on and thought, *It's not my fault.* When I heard someone talk about "those people," I'd get angry, sure. But I wouldn't respond, even after O.J. and I started dating. I told myself that the fact that I was with a black man should be statement enough.

I was intimidated, I guess. And besides, *I* would never say such a thing — not any longer, at least.

But after being shamed on national television, I started looking for small ways to make a difference. One day I visited Coach Whitehouse's preschool — my old "Dad" from St. Andrews had found a second calling — just to play with the children and forget my troubles.

When I asked the kids to hold hands for "Ring Around the Rosy," a little girl with blond curls said, "I'm not holding his hand, because he's black."

"Let's all sit down," I said — and I put the little boy who'd been rejected on my lap. "Have you ever heard 'Jesus Loves the Little Children of the World'?"

I'd learned the song many years ago, on the JOY bus, but I hadn't really known what it meant. Now the words seemed especially meaningful:

> *Jesus loves the little children,*
> *All the children of the world.*
> *Red and yellow, black and white,*
> *They are precious in his sight;*
> *Jesus loves the little children of the world.*

I thought it was so important for the little girl to see me treasure the boy on my lap. I didn't know what sort of impact it would have, but I wanted to plant a seed, as Jack Reece would say.

Before we all stood up again, the blond girl took the black boy's hand.

15

A New Person

After my second appearance with Diane Sawyer, O.J.'s world pulled away from me. Jason, Arnelle, Carmelita, Cathy Randa — none of them called from that day on.

I'd hoped that someone would thank me for my support, or just say it was all right, the way things ended. But I guess that was wishful thinking. I couldn't be a part of O.J.'s circle anymore, despite what we'd all been through together.

I was a nonperson, and by my own choice.

When I was subpoenaed to give the first deposition for O.J.'s civil trial, on December 14, 1995, I assumed that Michael Nasatir would continue to represent me. But Skip Taft, who'd hired Michael to help me with A.C.'s grand jury, wouldn't even take his calls.

I had no money to pay Michael — I was two months behind on my Bay Point mortgage and staring at bankruptcy. During the trial I'd come to rely on my little web of friendship and compassion. Now price tags were popping up all over the place. I felt confused and abandoned all over.

Then Susan Keenberg, a lawyer I'd known for years, stepped into the breach. She led me to Larry Stein, an attorney who would represent me while deferring his fee.

Best of all, Larry would be looking out for my interests first. He had no other boss or agenda.

The attorneys for the plaintiffs wanted to depose me in Panama City, but I said no — I didn't want them invading my one sanctuary. Instead, I agreed to come to Los Angeles, though I had no idea how I'd pay off the charges on my American Express bill.

I went back to California a few days early, to unwind and stay with friends. One night I gave in to Tom's urging — "You need to get out" — and went along to a *Vanity Fair* party at the Beverly Hills Hotel.

As soon as we walked in, my legs started shaking so badly that I had to lean on one of the hosts. It seemed like every major character from the Simpson case was there: Bob Shapiro, Chris Darden, even Faye Resnick.

I sat down at a table and asked for a glass of water. "I can't believe Faye Resnick is here," I said, half-aloud, half to the man sitting next to me. To my horror, he turned out to be a friend of Faye's — I watched him walk over to her and tell her what I'd said. They had the biggest laugh about it, just ten feet away from me.

I was grateful to see Bob Shapiro, but he was leery about speaking to me with so many reporters around. "It's better that we talk later," he said.

I felt overwhelmed. My past rushed back at me; I could almost smell the jail's stale air. I downed three glasses of champagne in fifteen minutes, just to steady myself enough to get up a flight of stairs. Then Tom took me home.

On the ride back, I thought about the famous faces I'd seen, and how their lives had progressed. Now they were on to their next case, or their next party.

But the case went a little deeper for me, I guess. My pain and guilt remained unresolved. Whereas O.J. had been released when the verdict was read, my own jury was still out.

★   ★   ★

The evening before my deposition, Susan Keenberg and Larry Stein came out to my hotel room to talk about what might lie in store. For several hours we went over the case to clarify what I knew, and what I didn't.

The most important thing, they stressed, was to be honest. I had no problem with that; I'd reached the point where I had nothing to hide.

As our discussion proceeded, the room began to spin, until I had to lie down on the couch while we talked. I'd been feeling sick for a while; I was bedridden the week before and had just gotten off antibiotics. But I'd never felt this dizzy, not even during the trial.

I put it off to stress. I knew I'd be contending with two sides the next day — not just the plaintiffs' lawyers, but the defendant's as well. I was pretty sure I'd be saying things that O.J. wouldn't want to hear, especially about the phone messages we'd traded on the day of the murders. What would happen then? Would they lash back at me in the deposition room? Attack my character in public?

After Susan and Larry left, Tom Hahn showed up. When he asked me why I was lying down, I showed him a lump behind my right ear, about two inches in diameter. I'd discovered it that morning, when brushing my hair. Tom called a doctor he knew and talked me into going to the doctor's house — for a B_{12} shot, Tom said.

I think he was trying his best not to scare me.

After Tom's friend, Dr. Brian Novac, examined me, he got very serious. He called Dr. Uyeda, the head of surgery at Cedars-Sinai, who came over right away. The two of them urged me to come in for a biopsy in the morning. I said it would have to wait. I had my deposition to deal with first.

I awoke feeling pretty terrible the next day but steeled myself to make it through. The media was out in force in the lobby of Daniel Petrocelli's office building, and the flashbulbs were popping. But when I went upstairs and emerged from the elevator, I found a greeting party of just one: Fred Goldman.

I gave him a hug, and he hugged me back. I felt so much for that man; I wished I could take some pain away from him.

"I hope you can help us," Mr. Goldman said.

"I can just tell the truth," I told him. But I knew there was nothing I could say or swear to that would fix his hurt.

We stood in the corridor, waiting for the inevitable: waiting for O.J. When he stepped out of the elevator, trailing a bodyguard, I wasn't surprised. O.J. was too diligent to miss anything connected to his case.

Plus I'd had this feeling that he wouldn't skip a chance to see me. I was anxious about the encounter, but I wanted to see him, too.

I couldn't help myself; I missed him.

Just as O.J. came up to me, the dizziness got worse, till I was ready to fall over. I excused myself and rushed to the bathroom, splashed some cold water on my face. When I came back out I felt O.J.'s eyes on me, hot as spotlights. We didn't dare come close to touching as we passed, but I never stopped feeling his heat.

As we moved into the conference room, O.J. was trying to keep things light. He'd stay business-as-usual the whole day, so at ease that I assumed he was on some antidepressant.

I took my place at the end of a small conference table. O.J. sat on one side, just an arm's length away, to my left. Fred Goldman sat opposite him, to my right, with their attorneys at their respective sides.

Everyone's attention converged on me. Over the next nine hours, I would lock my eyes on Mr. Goldman or Daniel Petrocelli, the lead attorney for the plaintiffs. I could feel O.J. seeking eye contact, trying to smile at me, but I refused to turn my head. To look at him might lead me to hazardous places.

If I'd anticipated another inquisition, à la Chris Darden, Mr. Petrocelli quickly put my fears to rest. While a thorough questioner, he seemed gentle, even friendly — I would have served him tea had he asked.

As the morning wore on and I felt more and more lightheaded, I lost concentration and fell into a passive rhythm: "Yes; no; yes;

no." Or the lawyers might get me on a roll of "Yes, yes, yes, yes." My head was hurting so bad that I didn't care; I probably lost a number of questions altogether.

I snapped out of it when I heard a frustrated sigh on my left. I glanced over to see O.J. rolling his eyes, and then I realized what I'd done. Mr. Petrocelli had asked me if I'd ever heard O.J. deny committing the murders. I'd answered in the negative, when of course he had — how many times had I heard O.J. wail, "I didn't do it, I never killed *anyone*"?

After a break I corrected my mistake. But I didn't stop there — I came clean. I pushed a weight off my chest that had lain there like a rock for a year and a half: the "Dear John" message I'd left for O.J. before taking off for Vegas.

When Mr. Petrocelli asked me if I believed that O.J. had received my message, I affirmed that I thought he had, based on the messages I'd gotten back from him.

I rigidly faced Mr. Goldman's side of the table as I related all this. I was afraid to so much as peek at O.J. from the corner of my eye. But then it was *out*. There was no taking it back, and I felt such tremendous relief; I even forgot about my headache for a moment.

I wasn't looking to "get" O.J. in my deposition, or even to help poor Mr. Goldman. I was only trying to rid myself of some guilt that I'd shouldered for too long.

It helped, of course, that O.J.'s freedom was no longer at stake, as it had been during the criminal trial. But the fact remained that I'd told the whole truth, as I'd sworn I would. Whatever happened from here on out was up to someone else.

Mr. Goldman had to leave for work after lunch, and the process got tougher for me. The pain started spiking down my neck, to my shoulders and my back. The dizziness was the worst — there were times when I thought I might topple from my chair.

All this stress is catching up to me, I thought.

Every so often I'd excuse myself and stagger out to the bathroom. I ran cold water on my hands; I'd read that you could calm your mind that way.

After one such excursion, as I walked back to the table, I caught O.J.'s eyes roaming up and down my legs, then settling on my bottom, with that little flirtatious smile of his playing at his lips.

There wasn't much skin for him to see — I was wearing a pantsuit — but it made me madder than hell nonetheless.

And yet, and yet . . . Toward the end of the day, Mr. Petrocelli asked about a talk I'd had with O.J. just before leaving Kardashian's house, on the day of the Bronco chase.

> Q. And did you reiterate to Mr. Simpson how much you loved him?
> A. Yes, sir.
> Q. And you did love him.
> A. Yes, sir.
> Q. And you still love him, don't you?
> A. Yes, sir.

The truth, the whole truth, and nothing but the truth . . .

When it was over, I quickly shook hands with Mr. Petrocelli, then with the other attorneys — I couldn't wait to get out of there. Yet I also felt oddly relaxed, despite the drum and bugle corps inside my head.

There was nothing more I could say or do about what happened in Brentwood on June 12, 1994.

But before I could escape, O.J. came up to me and said, "I'm sorry that you had to go through this."

Then he gave me a hug.

For a moment I froze. The plaintiffs' lawyers were coolly gauging my reaction. Susan Keenberg was so incensed, she was ready to snatch the white out of O.J.'s eyes.

But I didn't recoil; I didn't push O.J. away. Maybe it was a gesture of forgiveness on my part. Maybe it was something more. I felt like I'd just run a marathon on a broken ankle, and here was this strong pair of arms, this pillar of a chest to lean on and make the rest of the world go away.

Whatever else was wrong with us, we still fit together awfully well.

★   ★   ★

Dr. Huizenga gave me a magic potion called Darvocet to sleep on, and the next morning I went in for my biopsy. I've got a phobia about needles; they actually make me pass out. But I was so grateful to shed my pain that I didn't mind this one.

Rather than wait for the results, I decided to go home and check in by phone. At LAX I was sure that the lump was nothing and everything would be fine. Wasn't it time for things to start going my way?

When I changed planes in Atlanta, I called Dr. Uyeda from the gate. At first I made no sense of what I was hearing. My brain had rehearsed a happier script.

"Your results are back," my surgeon said. "It's a tumor — it's not cancerous, but it has to come out right away or there could be major complications."

As things turned out, my operation got postponed to mid-January, due to an illness in the surgeon's family. There is no good time for major surgery, but I welcomed the hiatus. Those few weeks would be precious and eventful for me.

Since settling back home in Panama City, I'd become more consistent in my studies with Jack Reece, more regular in my church attendance. I spent more time with the church elders, wise people like Brother Gil Wilson. "It's not what man tells you the Bible is saying that matters," said Brother Wilson, who since has left us. "It's your own study of the words that lets you decide what the answers are." I began to see what he meant — that I had to reach out directly to the word of God, because that was where I'd find my truth.

Once he saw I was up to the challenge, Jack got more direct. His questions became more pointed. Now he was asking, "Do you consider yourself a Christian?"

That question lit a fire under me, because I knew I didn't measure up to what a Christian should be.

And I knew I really wanted to.

The stronger my faith, the more I felt driven to confess my

sins. Toward the end of 1995, I'd repented and Jack would say I was "dead to sin." I was far from perfect, don't get me wrong. But I was eager to start my new life. I thought I might be ready for the next, crucial step: to be baptized in the blood of Christ and leave that Paula-Barbieri-goodtime-girl behind.

To be buried in water and born again.

No less than marriage, baptism was serious business. I didn't want to walk that aisle until I understood the commitment I'd be making. I held off for months. But as we approached the new year, I wanted to enter it as a Christian. I didn't tell Jack or anyone else. It would be my own brimming secret, until it was time.

The first Sunday of 1996 dawned cold and rainy — the devil's last shot at me, I thought. But I jumped out of bed and two hours later was sitting in church. I purposely lodged myself in the second row.

Still shy about my voice, I usually sang softly during services. But this Sunday I felt so proud and happy that I gave forth at the top of my lungs. I couldn't be loud enough.

Jack's lesson that day might have been written for me. He told us how Christians are *new* in every respect: in their life, their attitude, their mission, their destiny. At the end of his lesson, my minister made his appeal:

"The new year means very little if you're not in Christ. It means another year of delay, of waste, of placing your soul in jeopardy. Why do you wait? Won't you allow Jesus to cleanse you with his blood, and start this new year as a new you?"

As the congregation stood to sing an invitation song, "Nothing but the Blood," I knew I could wait no longer. I walked forward and sat in the center of the front row; I didn't waver. My friend Melanie, who'd started me down this path when I visited her beauty shop months before, came to sit with me. "You don't know how hard we've been praying for you," she said.

When the song was over, Jack had me stand for my public confession. My knees were shaking as he talked about my hunger for knowledge, and how hard we'd studied. Then he asked, "Do you believe Jesus Christ is the son of God?"

"Yes," I answered. Had I ever felt so confident of anything in my life?

I went back to a dressing room to take off my shoes and change into a navy nylon robe, zippered up the front like a jumpsuit. I stepped down to the baptistry, a small, circular pool above and behind the pulpit. Jack met me there in his own baptismal clothes and hip boots.

As we stood in the pool of water, drawn from a well three hundred feet deep, Jack reminded me of what we were about — that the water, through faith, represented the blood of Christ. Then he placed one hand over my nose and the other behind my head.

And submerged me, completely.

It was a moment I shall never forget. I truly believed that I was in Jesus' blood, dying with him. I felt the sins of my past wash away behind me, and it was such a relief. From now on, I thought, I would be putting God first. It was just as I had read in 2 Corinthians: *Therefore, if anyone is in Christ, he is a new creation; the old has gone, the new has come!*

I came up out of that water as a new, free person. I hugged Jack and got him all wet from my hair. As the congregation sang, "God bless Paula, my Lord," I faced them, smiling from ear to ear. I tried to look into each person's eyes. I was so happy to be their sister.

Back in the dressing room, I embraced Melanie and Mrs. Wilson and all the other women who'd clustered around. It was like being in a hospital when a baby is born. I wasn't nearly an oak yet — a sprig was more like it.

After so many things had ended for me, this was only a beginning.

The day before my surgery, I splurged at Neiman Marcus: five sets of their silk pajamas (on sale), all charged on my belabored AmEx card. Even if the surgery went well I'd be in the hospital for a while, and I wanted to feel pretty.

And if something went wrong — well, I wouldn't have to worry about the bill.

After my admittance into Cedars-Sinai, Dr. Uyeda went over the procedure with me. The original plan would have left a scar down the side of my face. But they'd brought in a plastic surgeon, who'd devised an alternative: an incision circling behind my ear.

It would be a delicate operation, the doctor said, because a tangle of nerves had wrapped around the tumor. Once they got inside, they'd attach wires to the nerves, to avoid cutting them.

Even with every precaution, Dr. Uyeda went on, there were still heavy risks: loss of sight, loss of hearing, facial paralysis.

I thought about how I'd smiled for a living for so many years. What would it be like to go through life without being able to smile again?

Would that be my penance for the trial — my sentence?

A year before, even a month before, I might have been terrified. But now I'd been baptized and I felt very safe. I had the power of prayer to see me through.

The next morning, as they wheeled me toward the prep room for anesthesia, I used the same prayer that had pushed me up the pole at Tony Robbins's seminar:

Lord, please lift me up. Please carry me through this. Thank you for all of my blessings, and please watch over Mom.

They told me the surgery took five hours. I awoke to the friendly face of a resident on the floor — a beautiful young man, just the prettiest thing I'd ever seen. Either my eyes were fine or I'd gone to a better place.

As if on cue, the phone rang. I gingerly brought the receiver to my ear. "Is this Paula Barbieri?" the reporter asked. "How are you feeling?"

Now *there* was a stupid question, but at least I knew that I still had my hearing.

Then I gingerly felt around my head. The bandages covered my face like a mummy's, to within an inch of my mouth. I touched that small patch of skin and took my shot.

"Am I smiling?" I asked the nurse standing nearby.

"You are definitely smiling," she replied.

Everything was in its place. "I'm so grateful to God," I exclaimed.

Then the young resident smiled back at me and said, "Oh, are you a Christian?"

It turned out that "Dr. Brad," as I'd call him, was not only a talented resident physician but a Christian as well. So was the private nurse we'd hired, to help make sure the media was kept at bay. She always had her Bible with her. Once I felt more up to it, we did quite a bit of studying in that room.

As I regained my strength, I began to feel more optimistic. I saw my tumor as a symbol of all the poison that had built up inside me. Once it was removed, I told myself, I wouldn't even remember the trial and what it had done to me.

And then they *did* remove the tumor, and I thought: *Wasn't it perfect that they took out a piece of me and threw it away?*

Back in November, when Mom told me that my father had been diagnosed with lung cancer, I reacted with dismay and disbelief. I refused to believe it was true; I brushed it off.

By Christmastime, Dad had gone to live with Michael in Pensacola. But when the family got together at my house in Bay Point to share a cake — my father's sixty-second birthday fell on December 26 and my twenty-ninth on December 31 — he looked healthy and strong.

I'd been deceived so often by my father that I no longer trusted him on anything. I still couldn't accept the idea that he might be terminally ill. If anything, I resented it. I'd just gotten my own shocking diagnosis, and it was all I could handle.

Was Dad's cancer just a ploy to get me to forgive him?

I know that sounds harsh and irrational. But I'd pushed both Dad and Michael so far away from me, and I didn't want to bring them back. I loved them, but I didn't want to be hurt again.

And despite my work on forgiveness with Jack, I begrudged their betrayals. Michael was still at it. In November, he took money for two more outrageous stories. The first was a *Globe* account that I'd "called off the wedding" after finding that O.J. was two-timing me with Gretchen Stockdale. The second, in the *Star*, claimed that O.J. had faxed me a roster of men I was forbidden to date.

The "list" included Michael Bolton and Jon Peters, but also Mike Tyson, John F. Kennedy Jr., George Clooney, and Sylvester Stallone.

(In fact, O.J. was keeping a civil distance. I hadn't heard from him since my deposition, except for this birthday card, typed in capital letters: *"Wish I were with you today to help eat your birthday cake. I'm with you in spirit, Your friend from the West."*)

I thought it was appropriate for Michael to take care of Dad. In many ways, they were two peas in a pod. They were staying in a small two-bedroom house with a dock on the waterfront, where they could drink their vodka and eat their venison. I saw one picture of Dad in an inner tube being pulled by Michael in his little speedboat. They seemed to be having a genuinely nice life.

After my surgery, I heard that Dad was getting radiation treatments, and we talked on the phone a few times. By February the doctors added chemotherapy, until Dad got so sick that he couldn't eat and began shuttling in and out of the hospital. He didn't want the chemo — he said it killed everyone he knew who'd gotten it. But the doctors said it would give him another six months.

One day, after I came by his room and read the Bible to him, my father said, "I need you here for this."

That's when we connected, and I began visiting Dad more often. That's when I started to let my bitterness go.

My father always had the thickest hair. One day I teased him, "You're just an exception to everything, Dad — you're not losing your hair at all."

As the chemo advanced, of course, he'd lose all of it.

By early spring I was making the four-hour round trip to Pensacola two or three times a week, often staying in Dad's hospital room overnight. Still recuperating from my operation, I got bronchitis and had to be checked in myself on a different floor, in quarantine from my father. His immune system was so weak that a cold could kill him.

On the round trip to Panama City, I'd listen to the soundtrack from *Les Misérables,* which I'd seen several times. I'd remember how a light shone down from above whenever a character died, to show that God was taking them.

Now, more than anything, I prayed that God would take Dad. My father's soul was surely in jeopardy. He'd talk about "the big J.C." and he'd become open to talking about the Bible. But he hadn't lived a Christian life.

Dad really wanted to come down and thank our congregation for praying so hard for him. I picked him up on a Friday in June, and we both knew that this would be his last trip to Panama City. He was fine that night, but on Saturday he started choking, and I had to rush him back straight to the hospital.

Dad was so upset that he hadn't made it to church on Sunday. I shared his regret — he probably would have been baptized.

By July, Dad was failing fast. Vinnie and Michael and I gathered around his bed as he struggled for his life. There is no better argument against cigarettes than the final stage of lung cancer. It's like drowning, except that it goes on forever — for about twenty hours, in my father's case. He kept fighting for his next breath, but his lungs were shutting down on him.

Dad was too far gone to talk. When a doctor came by, he motioned toward him with his eyes. I knew just what he was asking me to do: *Tell him that I can't breathe.*

I'd never felt quite so helpless. I felt like I'd let my dad down.

There came a point where he had just a few hours left, and he lapsed into a coma. Michael had to leave the room for a while, he just couldn't take it. I got into the bed and lay back against my father, praying hard for his salvation.

There was no room for our twisted history in Dad's semi-private room, just as Central Jail was too cramped to hold my complaints against O.J. I released my anger as I lay against my dying, comatose father. And I whispered, "I forgive you, Daddy."

By late that night, I could tell it wouldn't be much longer. I turned to my brothers and said, "You guys, we've got to pray. He doesn't know where to go — he's scared right now, he's lost."

"Aw, be quiet about that," Michael said, really angry with me. Of the three of us, he was having the hardest time. He glared at our father and pleaded, "Come *on*, Dad, let's go home."

"Listen," Vinnie said. "Let's just pray for Paula, let's make her feel better."

I was thankful when a minister came by to lead us in prayer. Then Chinese food arrived, our first meal of the day. But I didn't eat, because my eyes were fixed on Dad's face. My brothers were arguing over the hot mustard when I thought it happened: "You guys, he just stopped breathing."

"No he didn't, no he didn't!" Michael yelled, and it was like we were kids again, hollering at each other.

Vinnie told us to knock it off, and we all got real close to Dad to watch. I was praying for him with all my might, and a few seconds later it happened for real. Dad took his last breath. Even as I embraced his lifeless body and cried out for him to come back, I could tell by the look on his face that he'd seen something.

Something that didn't frighten him, because he smiled. Something leading him, I hoped, to a better place.

Vinnie turned around and said, "That prayer worked."

I learned a powerful lesson that day. My father hadn't given me much in life. But to forgive him was the greatest gift I could receive. It just took me a while to realize that I had to give it to myself.

16

Moving On

It's taken a lot of patience to sort out my life. By the summer of 1996, my financial crisis reached the point where I bounced a check for $5.38 for a watch battery I'd purchased at the Panama City Mall. (Predictably, a photo of the check showed up in the tabloids.) That fall, I nearly closed a deal with the Home Shopping Network on a skin-care line I'd developed, only to be torpedoed by the ever-visible Bob Kardashian. While taping a segment for *20/20*, Kardashian escorted Barbara Walters on a tour of his house in Encino. When they got to O.J.'s bedroom, he said, "And Paula slept here . . ."

The shopping-network people pulled out. With O.J.'s civil trial still in progress, they wanted to avoid any association with the case. Viewers might be offended.

I might be through with O.J., but much of the world still linked us together. Gossip and innuendo chased me at every turn. The fact was that I hadn't gone out with a man for ten months. I felt like a leper, a total outcast — who could possibly want to be with me?

It took a lot of courage for me to start dating a young man from my church that summer, to risk more rejection and hurt. Coincidentally, on the night of our first date, David Letterman kicked off his show by asking something along the lines of, "Do you know who Paula Barbieri's new boyfriend is?" His answer: "Mike Tyson." To make it worse, Letterman didn't bother to say he was joking.

Calls came to me from all over, including my extended family in Connecticut, about that nasty little rumor. It made me feel ridiculous to have to deny it.

I did my best to ignore the civil trial on television. Every now and then someone would tell me, "They're talking about you again." I wouldn't prod for details. I told myself I didn't care.

But one day around Thanksgiving, I happened to turn on the news, and there it was: a clip of Daniel Petrocelli questioning O.J. about his attempts to reach me on June 12, 1994. I sat riveted to the screen, queasily fascinated.

> Q. Now, the truth of the matter, sir, is that you were desperate to get in touch with Paula because she had left you, true?
> A. False.
> Q. And you were trying all day to get in touch with her, call after call after call, as these records show, true?
> A. That's not necessarily true, no.

And a bit later:

> Q. And the reason you were trying to get in touch with her is because you were feeling alone on that evening, weren't you, sir?
> A. That's not true.

Then Mr. Petrocelli homed in on the message O.J. left for me at 10:03 P.M. — that somber-sounding, "I understand what you mean." The plaintiffs' theory was that O.J. had used his cell phone to make the call from his Bronco, en route to South Bundy. O.J. insisted that he'd called from Rockingham, a scenario that reinforced his alibi.

(O.J.'s version of events had always been credible to me, since I knew he had no portable phones at home. He often used his cell phone when he was moving around the house or out in the yard.)

Now I couldn't help wondering: Had O.J. detoured to South Bundy that night after getting no answer at my apartment?

Would it have made a difference if I'd been there — if I hadn't gone off to see Michael Bolton that day?

Mr. Petrocelli wasn't done with his line of questioning. There was more — and much, much worse — to come.

Q. You blamed Nicole because your relationship with Paula was over?

A. No, I didn't believe that.

Q. You blamed Nicole for your problems with Paula?

A. Nicole was a problem with Paula.

This led me to the worst thing I could imagine — that my "Dear John" message could have triggered two murders. I knew it wasn't logical, given how casually O.J. had responded to our many breakups in the past. But it floored me, nonetheless, to hear Mr. Petrocelli saying it out loud in the courtroom. He was a prominent attorney, respected by everyone. I couldn't just shrug him off.

Could he possibly be right?

Did I secretly *want* him to be right?

In a dark and twisted way, Mr. Petrocelli's theory fit my emotional needs. Clark's premise had made Nicole the center of O.J.'s emotional universe in June of 1994. Mr. Petrocelli restored me to my pride of place, though it was a place no sane woman would want to inhabit.

Here is what I wanted to believe about that time: O.J. cared about *me*, loved *me*, feared losing *me*. He was done with Nicole — or how else could I have gone back to him that spring?

How else could I have stood by him for all the time that followed?

So my bruised ego bought into the Petrocelli theory, at an awful cost. I felt transported back to another flickering television screen, in a hotel room in Las Vegas, when I'd knelt and prayed to a dead woman for forgiveness.

When I might have been content to join her.

Back then, my biggest fear was contained within my private hysteria. But now this impeccable lawyer had seen through me. He'd settled upon a motive for the murders in Brentwood, right there on national television.

And the motive was me.

He's thinking what I'm thinking, I thought, squirming like a suspect under the lights. *My worst nightmare. . . .*

In my more rational moments, I didn't think that O.J. blamed Nicole for our problems. We had plenty of issues on our own, after all. Nicole hadn't made O.J. lie to me in Palm Beach about Donald Trump's party. She certainly hadn't made him hire a publicist after his acquittal, or sell me out to *Star* magazine or fly into a fury after I challenged him about it.

But guilt is more emotional than rational; that is where it gets its power. Just the idea that I could somehow be responsible for what happened to Nicole and Ron Goldman — it was unthinkable, definitely unspeakable.

Yet here was Mr. Petrocelli speaking it aloud, with the matter-of-fact sureness of someone reciting a times table. His theory *couldn't* be true, I kept telling myself.

Because O.J. was innocent, remember?

But what *was* the truth? For so many years, I'd believed the best about the men in my life, only to be confronted with the worst. I'd been proven wrong, time after time.

If I were wrong this time, the implications would be too much to bear.

I took a big step backward that evening. Guilt washed over me like a flood tide, sweeping me back to when O.J. was in jail and my delirious mind drummed that I should be there instead. I'd hoped the case was behind me. I'd done everything I thought was right — I'd held firm through the criminal trial and told the truth in my deposition.

I'd prayed to God for forgiveness, and I believed that by His mercy He would grant it.

But then I'd flicked on the network news, and months of healing were wiped away. Those few minutes stole back the permission I'd given myself to move on. *Maybe I haven't suffered enough,* I thought.

Maybe my penance was only beginning.

Over the next several weeks my mind raced like Forrest Gump. I didn't know where I was going or when I'd reach the end of my road. I only knew that I had to keep running, keep busy, stay occupied. If I stopped, I'd lose my balance.

If I stopped, the bad feelings would catch up to me.

I hadn't spoken to O.J. for more than a year, going back to my deposition. After my surgery, the Benders told me how concerned he'd been; when my father died, O.J. sent a card.

But it wasn't until the day in December 1996 when he won custody of Sydney and Justin that O.J. called my house and I returned his call.

We talked for a good hour, mostly about the children. We were friendly, engaged, lighthearted, just like we used to be. I told O.J. how important it was for him to raise his kids in a good Christian lifestyle — how he needed to set the example himself, by joining a church family and bringing the kids into it.

Every so often I could feel O.J. drifting, and then he'd sigh and say something like, "I wish it could be the way it was."

Or: "Couldn't we just have one of those jailhouse phone conversations for a minute?"

I skirted his digressions, steered us back to the topic of faith.

But I couldn't help thinking how remarkable it was for O.J. to feel nostalgia for Central Jail.

Then again, I missed our old talks, too.

On February 4, 1997, I watched the final day of the civil trial.

When I heard the reading of the verdict, I felt like someone close to me had died.

Only recently, in preparation for this book, could I bring myself to read O.J.'s civil trial testimony — to see if it might edge me closer to the truth.

What I found, to be blunt, was a pack of lies, the final nail in the coffin of our dead relationship.

Some of the falsehoods were old news — the recycled art deco bracelet, for example, that O.J. gave to Nicole before passing it on to me.

But I also made a number of fresh discoveries in O.J.'s deposition, and each one made me madder than the last:

- Back on Christmas of 1992, far from being surprised when Nicole showed up in New York, O.J. conceded that he "got her a first-class ticket . . . even though it was sort of a problem with me, 'cause I had a girlfriend back in New York."

- O.J. had repeatedly denied calling Tracy Adele on June 12, 1994. "Oh, no," he'd told me, "Kato put her on the phone with me." But in his deposition, O.J. acknowledged ringing the model at her hotel and talking for twenty minutes.

- O.J. had led me to assume that he'd never taken a lie detector test. "It's not admissible in court anyway," he told me, "so why should I do one?" But now I found O.J.

had not only submitted to a polygraph test two days
after the murders but had failed it badly.

It was all there in black and white: O.J. had played me for
a chump whenever he'd felt the need. But of all the lies now
confirmed to me, none cut so deep as the ones about Nicole. I
knew that O.J. hadn't stopped loving his ex-wife in the spring of
'94, even as he told me they were finished. His suicide note had
reflected that much. Still, it pained me to read:

*"I have always loved her, when we were apart we always said we
loved each other even when we weren't married. . . . I could never cut off
my emotional attachment to Nicole."*

But the worst thing I found in O.J.'s deposition had nothing
directly to do with me. The most sickening material of all, the stuff
that turned me inside out, concerned an incident long before we
met.

As I read the transcript, word by repulsive word, I finally put
together what really must have happened at Rockingham on New
Year's Eve 1989, when Nicole called 911.

I flashed back to a lunch with Bert Kitay early in the criminal
trial, when Denise Brown was on the stand to charge that O.J. had
abused her sister. In the supermarket I'd recently stumbled onto
some tabloid cover photos of a battered Nicole, and they'd made
me cringe.

But according to Bert, the photographs weren't what they
seemed. O.J. had gotten Nicole a part in a movie, Bert explained,
and they'd made her up to look bruised. Nicole had saved some
Polaroids as souvenirs, and now the tabloids were using them for
a cheap shot at O.J.

Bert's theory seemed dubious to me. As the person who'd
counseled both O.J. and Nicole for many years, he had to be
reaching for some answer he could live with.

On the other hand, I knew from the *Time* cover that computers
could do funny things with pictures. So I filed the photos of Nicole
in that triple-locked safe, along with everything else that I could
not explain.

But O.J.'s testimony told a different story. I found out that Nicole had come out of their New Year's Eve confrontation with a split lip and a welt over her right eye. Those were facts that no one was challenging.

And while O.J. denied striking Nicole, he admitted "wrestling her" and putting her "in a headlock . . . in trying to get her out of the door, so I would assume that my hand was somewhere around her face."

Later on, O.J. conceded that he "was being wrongly physical with her. . . . I physically tried to impose my will on Nicole, and I shouldn't have done it."

Now *there* was an understatement, I thought. O.J. outweighed Nicole by eighty pounds. No matter what kind of athletic shape she'd been in, this couldn't have been a fair fight.

It's hard to explain how mad that transcript made me. All I knew was that I wanted to hit O.J. back, to hurt him as he'd hurt Nicole.

My anger opened a door. As I kept reading, I began to see Nicole in a new light — no longer as a rival, but as a woman much like me.

Yes, I had entered a relationship of three, but the triangle was shaped differently than I'd thought. O.J. had sat at the top of it all that time, using and abusing Nicole and myself, playing one against the other.

"*I could never cut off my emotional attachment to Nicole,*" he'd said. I didn't doubt it, but O.J.'s "attachment" had little to do with loyalty or respect. He was just another guy who took what he could get, wherever he could get it.

At one point in his testimony, O.J. talked about how Nicole reacted when she discovered a picture of me in one of their old wedding-photo frames. And I wondered: Did Nicole feel about me what I felt about her? Did she too feel threatened and insecure — that she was getting pushed out of O.J.'s life?

As O.J. traced the history of his marriage with Nicole, I found other familiar details. In Nicole I saw a woman who'd get fed up and walk away — for good, she'd think. But time after time, she'd get pulled back by O.J.'s charm. She was helpless to resist. Something inside her — insecurity or blind passion or a streak of self-destructiveness — kept her tied to a man who was obviously bad for her.

What *was* it with Nicole, I wondered. And what was it with me?

I was especially struck by O.J.'s account of the night before Mother's Day 1994, when he'd already decided to leave Nicole, once again, and get back together with me.

They were at the beach house in Laguna, preparing to go out for dinner. But when Nicole reached the front door, O.J. testified, "she started shaking and just — I can't even describe it. Just started saying, I can't do this, and shaking and — she couldn't explain what she was feeling, she couldn't explain what was going on. . . ."

When Mr. Petrocelli returned to this part of the chronology later on, O.J. quoted Nicole as saying: "Look at me, I'm having a nervous breakdown."

O.J. seemed to be implying that Nicole was on drugs at the time, but I wasn't so sure. I recognized the symptoms of Nicole's "breakdown": the shaking and crying, the lethargy and turmoil, the aimless sense of loss.

I'd experienced just the same feelings myself, you see, when this man was abandoning *me*.

O.J. was never lonely for long. He'd met Nicole while still married to Marguerite. After splitting from Nicole, he was soon finding comfort from other women — the infamous Robin, for one, whom I'd met that first day in O.J.'s kitchen — and then he was primed to meet me. He always had backup.

When you were O.J. Simpson, there was always a woman ready to share your life, or at least a night of it.

I remember times at Rockingham when I'd awake in the dark to find O.J.'s side of the bed empty. He'd be taking one of his late-night ambles around the house, pausing now and then to gaze out a window over his grounds. He was simply in awe of how wonderfully his life had turned out. This was *his* beautiful house, his stunning estate.

To have a desirable woman upstairs, in his bed, was just another piece to the puzzle that made him complete.

Did O.J. fear being alone? Did he need a woman's constant affirmation because he was hollow at his core? At the end, it didn't really matter — not for the lover waiting upstairs, nor for the ones locked outside the gate.

At the end, those women were interchangeable.

Had O.J. loved me? Of course he had. He'd loved plenty of women over the years. But a hard look at his track record tells me that all but one of those women were replaceable.

And she's the one he can never have again.

Q. Do you still believe he's innocent?
A. Yes.
Q. Completely?
A. Yes.
Q. Never one night, lying awake, during this entire year, thinking?
A. Uh-uh. Faith. Faith. He didn't do this.
— My second interview with Diane Sawyer, November 1, 1995

I left my relationship with O.J. when I finally grasped what a life with him would be like. I left because of his lies and betrayals, and from the tastes of his rage in Palm Beach and Panama City.

I did *not* leave the relationship because I thought O.J. committed murder.

Some people might think that my history with O.J. gives me a unique insight into the question of his guilt or innocence. They're forgetting that love is blind, and that I was very much in love.

Over the three years O.J. and I were together, on and off, I lived in a world of my own imagining. To put it another way: I have been many things in my life, but a great judge of human behavior isn't one of them.

To be honest, I've grown tired of Diane Sawyer's question — it seems pointless to me, and unfair. The justice system has run its course; the killer, whoever he is, will have to answer to God. As for me, I somehow managed to survive my time with O.J., though not without damage. How could it help me — or anyone else — to pronounce my own verdict, now that O.J. belongs to my past?

I'm led back to my slogan from Tony Robbins: *"If you want to know about O.J, don't ask me. . . ."*

In the period just after the murders, real doubt crept in only once. That was when I spouted my concern — my intuition? — about O.J.'s possible guilt to Tom Hahn as we left Kardashian's house. My brief wobble was so hard on me, so annihilating, that I made sure it never happened again as long as O.J. was in jail.

Then came my moment of revelation, after the acquittal, when I confronted O.J. with having sold me out to *Star* magazine. It wasn't so much his display of anger that day. It's a long stretch from knocking over a lamp to stabbing two people to death.

But when O.J. denied my accusation to my face, he shook me to my foundations. I'd just lived through a murder trial with the man. To believe he was innocent, I'd had to trust that he was truthful. And now he was lying to me, way beyond a reasonable doubt.

Where had the lies begun? Where had they stopped? I lost my bearings that day in Panama City; I felt less certain about a lot of things.

As soon as the crisis passed, though, my armor of denial snapped back into place, and there it has stayed. If I were pushed to the wall this very minute and forced to answer Diane's question one more time, I would say again what I told her: I believe O.J. was innocent.

My response on *PrimeTime Live* wasn't just for public consumption. It was the emotional truth that I felt, and still feel.

Because I have no other choice.

Even now, I can barely say *guilty* — it sticks in my throat. Because it isn't just O.J. who'd be condemned by that word. It's also the woman who broke up with him by voice mail on the morning of June 12, 1994. The one he futilely sought out and kept calling all day long, right up to half an hour before the crime.

The one who might have changed his course that day, had she done things a little bit differently.

And consider: the one who might have stayed an angry man's hand.

When I was a girl, and my mother had her hard times with Bill, I'd wonder: *Why does she keep going back?*

When I was a young model, and I'd hear how old classmates had married abusive or philandering men, I'd think: *Why do they stay in bad relationships?*

I was sure that I'd never get trapped like Mom and so many others had. My mother's great mistake in life was to seek identity through a man. When the man turned out to be an alcoholic or an abuser, Mom went into free fall. She had nothing left inside to prop herself up.

But I was different. I'd been financially independent since high school, after all. I'd never have to depend on a man, I told myself — not for money, not for support of any kind.

Even in my most serious romances, I wasn't "Dolph's girl" or "O.J.'s girl." I'd never be anyone's "girl" again, because once upon a time I'd been Daddy's girl and the worst possible thing had happened: Daddy left me.

I'm not just talking about my father's abandonment when I was three years old. That event merely set the stage for a lifetime of desertions and betrayals. My homecoming halftime — when I stood there waiting, my pom-poms limp in my eleven-year-old's hands, my eyes trained anxiously on the parking lot — was our whole relationship, in miniature.

To the end, I kept wanting things that Dad could not deliver.

I don't blame my parents for what's gone wrong in my life; I don't see what good can come of blaming. But I do believe that what happened with my father left me with some pretty tough conflicts. I became allergic to dependence, yet scared of being unwanted and alone. There was a lot of tension in my dealings with men.

Above all, I had a great, yawning need to *connect* with someone. When I met a man I liked, I threw all my need and trust into the relationship, as a child does with a parent. My love was absolute, unconditional, almost uncritical.

To be worthy of that love, my man had to be just about perfect. I had endless debates with Dolph ("All European men cheat") and O.J. ("All men cheat"). I didn't hesitate to confront them when they fell short of my standards.

But I'd also deny the underlying problem: the simple fact that neither man was right for me. When they inevitably let me down, I'd fight and scratch to cling to them. I'd work even harder at being the most wonderful woman a man could ever have.

To my mind, there was no worse failure than a failed relationship. My father and mother were both married and divorced three times. My brother Michael is already up to four. I wanted to believe I was different, that the family pattern stopped with me. I *had* to be different, because the alternative — a life ultimately lived alone — was too painful to contemplate.

Good-bye was the ugliest word in the English language, and I just wouldn't hear it.

So I stuck things out long after they'd grown hopeless, to the dismay of my mother and the friends who loved me. I told them I was trying to "understand" my man's strange behavior. In truth, I was hoping against hope that he'd change, and that our problems would go away.

The reality, of course, is that you cannot change a man. I'd get burned to the third degree, not once but many times. To shield myself from further scalding, I denied more and more, till I was having a make-believe affair with a fantasy suitor.

That was where sex came in. Long after real intimacy had dissolved, sex was the counterfeit I could enjoy anytime. When I gave Dolph or O.J. what he wanted in bed, everything was okay again. I felt secure in those throbbing moments and wished they could last forever.

When O.J. shook his head at my insatiability, he wasn't quite getting it. I didn't push him to make love three or four times a night out of a need for dozens of orgasms. It was the closeness I craved, and the amnesia that only sex could bring. I needed to lose myself in physical desire, less for the desire than for the *losing,* the forgetting of our latest rift.

That was when I felt safe again — when I made myself most vulnerable to a man. But sex wasn't the drug that had hooked me. My addiction was to intimacy, in the broadest sense of the word.

There came a time, however, when my fantasy would crash beyond repair. I'd find Grace Jones in Dolph's bedroom. Or Dean would hit me up for cash before the ink had dried on our marriage license. When that happened, I'd run as swiftly as I could, without so much as a good-bye — as if I could leave the failure behind, with *him,* if I got away fast enough.

Enter O.J. Simpson, nearly twenty years older than I was, married twice already with two sets of children, and a well-known ladies' man to boot.

I didn't need hindsight to see that O.J. was a bad bet for me. A pinch of foresight would have done the trick.

Our relationship followed my pattern with Dolph: a giddy courtship, then a string of leaden letdowns. As time went on, O.J. lied so outrageously that even I had to call him on it. But once again, I stayed way too long after things turned sour. I had no business going back to O.J. a month before the murders. Deep down I knew nothing would be different.

I was stuck. While I had to trust this man to love him, it killed me to let go even after that trust was shattered.

My "Dear John" message was an overdue attempt to do the right thing for *me,* for a change. Even so, I have no regrets about going to O.J. in Encino, when the doctors feared what he might do next. It was a matter of life and death. Had I bailed out on O.J. then, and something bad had happened, I couldn't have lived with myself.

But the decision I made two months later — to stand by O.J. for the duration and virtually incarcerate myself by his side — was something else again. By the time I came back to Los Angeles, O.J. was no longer suicidal; he didn't require my intensive care. Had

I limited my involvement, who could have blamed me? No one faulted Bobby Bender or Don Ohlmeyer for continuing to work and lead a normal life.

But it wasn't enough for me to be a loyal supporter. I felt such guilt and responsibility that I had to go far beyond the call of duty.

From the day of the murders, I methodically chopped away every piece of my identity. I lost my career, my home, my social life, my healthy figure. By the time the actual trial began, all I had left was my loyalty to O.J. His plight defined me. His suffering framed my day.

"I'm so impressed with you," a reporter once told me as I arrived at the jail for my daily visit. "You're doing the best thing you could possibly do."

I was thrilled by the compliment. For once the press was right, I thought. My life wasn't easy, but no one could say it lacked purpose. O.J. needed me, and wasn't that enough?

When I look back, I think I subconsciously took O.J.'s imprisonment as my own reprieve, as a chance to draw him back to me and cancel my latest failure. For all the stress of those strange days, on one level I was worry-free. As long as he stayed in Central Jail, O.J. was in no position to abandon me.

I'd become O.J.'s whole world, as he'd become mine. Within the artificial environment of prison, it was easy to mold my fantasy of O.J. to order. In jail he became exactly the man I wanted: a sincere Christian who loved me with all his heart.

I was shaken when I lost my condo; I was deeply wounded by O.J.'s suspicions about me and Jon Peters. But there was something else working when I pulled back from O.J. in the summer of 1995. As the trial neared its end, and O.J.'s release loomed closer, I could feel him pulling away. He was heading toward a looser orbit, back to the L.A. lifestyle that no longer worked for me.

By withdrawing to Panama City, I might beat him to the punch. It was a move of self-protection as much as anything else.

Then O.J. got out, and he was free — free to be simply himself again. He wasn't chained to my imaginary world any longer. He was just another guy with a wandering eye and an appetite for easy sex. He was a man who'd grown up poor and had no intention of going back, even if it meant doing business with the devil — or *Star* and Larry Schiller.

I could shout that O.J. deceived and betrayed me, and he had, in ways large and small. But he couldn't have gotten away with it unless I'd turned my head in the first place. Even the smoothest con man needs a willing mark.

All my adult life, I see now, I've been looking for a man to fit my pedestal. I've been searching for someone to fix my life, and make me whole and happy, and keep me from feeling alone.

In other words, I've been using men to replace God. Was it the men's fault that they never measured up?

At first they were little black puffs, dancing on the horizon. But now the tornadoes are here, just a step away from me, leveling all in their path. One of them swallows a door and spits it out as kindling. If I don't keep moving, I'll be next. . . .

I'm in a room with a man named Chris, who was drum major at my high school. I put a gun to his neck, fire point blank, and I know that he's dead.

There is turmoil all around me. Everyone's trying to find the murderer. But there's no evidence against me — except for the bloodstain on the nape of my neck, hidden by my hair.

I see Sherry, who loved Chris so much in high school. It's my fault that she'll never see him again. My secret is too much for me; I must share it. I go up to Sherry, reach back for my hair, and begin lifting it up —

It comes to me every other month or so, this nightmare, and I wake up sweating and crying. Every time it's the same; every time I'm the guilty one. A good therapist could probably tell me what it means, but I haven't cared — or dared — to ask one.

The Simpson case isn't quite over for me. I'm still spooked when I go to a McDonald's, where O.J. got his last meal before the murders. I still have to "snap" myself out of bad thoughts from time to time.

But I think I'm improving. Mom and I are getting back to normal again in Bay Point. I know she always did the best she could for me. She's the greatest housemate a girl ever had — she still cooks up a mean plate of blue crabs and spaghetti.

Several months ago, when Bill's daughter was getting married, I stopped by his house. I went out to the garden and helped Bill pick some ivy for the wedding.

We hadn't exchanged more than a few words over the past dozen years; I'd held on to my anger that long. But as Bill and I worked side by side in our labor of love, I felt something thaw between us. When he invited me in for a cup of coffee, the strongest drink he takes now, I was wary at first. But we sat on stools in the kitchen and a remarkable thing happened: Bill and I actually talked to each other. And soon I was remembering the things I'd once liked about him — his wisdom and warmth and compassion — but it was even more than that. I was discovering what a truly wonderful man he had become. I was proud of him. And, it turned out, he was proud of me.

From that day on, I've been grateful to have Bill in my life again. *Not seven times, but seventy-seven times,* I thought. If nothing else, the trial had taught me to forgive, and to lay my bitterness down.

I know it's possible to live "inside the fence" in Los Angeles — I've met a lot of good Christians there.

But for me, it was definitely harder to follow the Bible in southern California. And the lifestyle I'd been leading with O.J. made it downright impossible.

Now I'm out of L.A.'s fast lane, and glad of it. I love feeling rooted in the place I grew up. At the supermarket the other day I ran into a woman I knew from the third grade, right there in baked goods. A simple thing, but it made me happy.

It's not easy to start over when you're thirty, geographically or spiritually. Lots of times I feel like Bambi on his first day in the world, all clumsy, spinning legs. I still bear scars from the mistakes I've made; I still find it hard to forgive myself. But if the Lord could forgive Paul, that "chief of sinners" and killer of Christians, I have to accept that He'll do the same for me.

Assuming, of course, that I accept how awful my past errors were, and offer God "a broken and contrite heart." I'm just coming to understand what true contrition means.

And assuming, not least, that I show how intent I am about changing my ways.

How do men fit into that change? I wasn't lying to Diane Sawyer. I yearn more than anything to fall in love and have a family. But I want to do it on my terms, for a change. I want to do it as a Christian, and as a woman who values herself.

In Proverbs 3 we're told: "Trust in the Lord with all your heart and lean not on your own understanding." A sound relationship, I now realize, must begin with faith. If both people love God first, they'll always be in love with each other. They'll be set on the same path, with the same goals.

By applying the Bible to my life, I'm starting to see more clearly who I am, without using O.J. or any man as a filter. And I like what I see; I think I can live with this person. I'm feeling a lot more powerful in my life — strong enough, maybe, to break my old patterns. I can't tell when the winds of romance might blow my way again, but the pressure is off. My old urgency has vaporized.

You might say that I've found a relationship for a lifetime — and now that I've found Him, I will not let Him go.

The Church of Christ's weekly routine now anchors my life: Bible study Tuesday morning, church on Wednesday and Sunday. I even play softball with the women's team two evenings a week.

Whenever I can, I try to go the extra mile. I'll load a bunch of children from an inner-city project into my truck and bring them to church. We'll trade work for fun; the kids paint a fence, and then we have a pizza party by the pool.

When I deal with members who are sick or dying, or kids who have their own problems, I snap back to feeling healthy again.

The JOY formula — Jesus first, Others second, Yourself last — still works.

Becoming a Christian has meant huge changes not only in my life, but in others' as well.

Part of a Christian's responsibility is sharing the word of God. At the depths of his troubles, I had about given up on my brother Michael. Then, a few months back, a remarkable chain of events happened. My old friends Sarah and Danny began studying and were baptized shortly after learning they were expecting a child. The baby was born three months premature and was rushed to the neonatal facility in Pensacola, where my friends kept vigil for many long and agonizing weeks. One weekend, a group of us from church journeyed to Pensacola to visit the baby. On Sunday, we all attended a local church. At the end of the service, I felt a light touch on my shoulder, turned around — and there was Michael. What an unexpected — and blessed — gift! Sarah and I had often wondered if Michael would ever, could ever, open his heart to God. Here was my answer. He's been studying with the young minister there ever since.

The Bible has taught me that Dolph and O.J. were definitely off base about one thing. I've decided that it's right to love completely, after all. As you sow, you will reap. I will always give my heart and soul when I love. That's the type of person I am.

But now I understand the "catch" — that my gifts can be valued only by the right man, in a healthy relationship.

I think it's worth the wait. I believe that it just might be possible to find joy and passion without lies and cheating, not to mention a murder trial thrown in for bad measure.

It took a while, but I feel no bitterness toward O.J. anymore. He seems to me a sad figure, a shadow of the man I met five years ago. Even if he puts his life back together financially, O.J. will never regain what he cared about most: the affection of his public.

The most outgoing man I've ever known is a pariah, cut off at every turn. That may not be enough for the people who think him guilty, but it is a hard, hard sentence, all the same.

While O.J. and I haven't talked for months, our channels stay open through friends. On a visit to New York this spring, I phoned the Benders to confirm a dinner date. When we got together the following evening, Bobby said, "It's just uncanny, the two of you."

"What are you talking about?" I said.

"Just ten minutes after we hung up the phone with you, O.J. called," Bobby related. "And we hadn't talked to him in four weeks."

Things like that have been going on for years with O.J. and me. Sometimes O.J. would joke with Cathy Randa that I had to be a witch.

"When we told him we were having dinner with you," Bobby continued, "he said, 'Well, tell her I love her.' "

And there was one more bit of news. O.J. was thinking about moving to Panama City, Bobby said. "How would you feel about that?"

My first thought was that I felt threatened — that O.J. was still pursuing me, against all odds and good sense. We both knew we had no future together. We were done for all sorts of reasons, from our tortured history to the rupture of our trust.

There was no turning back. I hadn't just closed the book, I'd burned it. O.J. didn't fit my new life, it was that simple.

I knew all of this as well as I knew my own name. It wasn't an issue or an argument. I was a self-respecting woman now, a God-fearing woman, a clear-sighted woman. To see O.J. again — even for so much as a friendly dinner — would make absolutely no sense.

But there is one thing more that I must confess. As soon as the Benders mentioned O.J.'s name, I started thinking about the good times, and how I missed those fabulous phone calls. I thought of how much I still cared for him. O.J. would always be part of me; there was no way around that.

And when I heard what O.J. said about loving me, I know that I blushed and — this sounds absolutely crazy — my sleeping heart stirred and lifted up, like a wild bird uncaged.

I heard my own voice then. It had the good sense to stay inside my head, but it startled me nonetheless.

I love you too, it said.